T0143767

BUILDING

INSPIRATIONAL TOOLS &

PERSONAL

TECHNIQUES FOR WORK & LIFE

LEADERSHIP

JOE FARCHT

GENESIS PUBLISHING

An Imprint of Morgan James Publishing • NEW YORK

BUILDING PERSONAL LEADERSHIP

Copyright ©2007 Leadership Advantage, Inc.

ISBN: 1-60037-165-5   (Paperback)

Published by:

GENESIS
PUBLISHING

An Imprint of
Morgan James Publishing

Morgan James Publishing, LLC
1225 Franklin Ave Ste 32
Garden City, NY 11530-1693
Toll Free 800-485-4943
www.MorganJamesPublishing.com

Interior Design by:

Rachel Campbell
rcampbell77@cox.net

■ DEDICATION ■

This book is dedicated to all my teachers and my life purpose. It is further dedicated to the men and women who defend our freedom and serve our country making personal sacrifices for preserving our way of life.

■ The Birth of a Book ■

The idea for this book was born after nearly six years of writing monthly newsletters and weekly e-mails to serve hundreds and now well over one thousand people that I have worked with, met, or have encountered. I sought to share what I learned, taught, and lived with those who might want to improve their own work and lives. I have received inspiring and motivating feedback from many recipients and I treasure each bit of feedback I receive. Listed here are a few excerpts taken from numerous responses to the hundreds of newsletters and e-mails that I have sent.

"Joe - Wanted to thank you for forwarding your leadership insights. I truly enjoy the new perspectives I receive from your email newsletter. I appreciate your depth of wisdom and expertise and have found much inspiration in your emails this year."

- Nancy T., HR & OD Manager,
Fortune 50 Technology & Manufacturing Co.

"Great information and so true. I always look forward to your newsletter each time, Joe, you have a wealth of knowledge and what you send is so educational. I'm always learning from you and thanks. I appreciate your input....."

- Connie J., Marketing Director, Retail Furniture Company

"Dr. Wayne W. Dyer, move over. Joe Farcht has a new twist on speaking to the absolute right moment of time, to the right situation at hand, with the absolute match of words causing forward movement. Joe, thank you once again today for the guidance. We always have everything we need when we need it. I went through the list you sent, I stopped dead in my tracks, became centered and focused honestly on each question. And some of the answers I was not please with but pleased to realize. Thank You."

– Mary D., Principle, Book Publishing Business

"Thank you so much for the weekly inspiration!"

– Penelope C., Community Relations Manager,
Medical Society

"I continue to enjoy your newsletter and wisdom. Thanks for your constant enthusiasm and professionalism."

– Barbara S., Director, Architect Firm

"You hit on many hot buttons this week. I completely agree with the notion of growing as a person is vital to success. I hope to continue growing my skills everyday and I consciously seek out new training as well as experienced people like you to learn from. Thanks for all you do."

– Todd B., President, Technology Association

■ ACKNOWLEDGMENTS ■

The creation of any book isn't normally completed without help. Building Personal Leadership is no exception. I'd like to thank my wife Cathey for her help in early editing of the E-Mails and Newsletters. Feedback is a wonderful help in any endeavor. I'd also like to thank Marc Reilly for his passionate editing of the material when it first took book form. There were many great improvements. Lastly, I'd like to thank the real power house project manager Martha Gold for her determination, perseverance, and hard detailed work to compile the articles and manage every detail of getting this book to the publisher. Without her wonderful help, I would have gone completely nuts! Thank you all.

■ CONTRIBUTING AUTHOR ACKNOWLEDGMENTS ■

I have promoted some very competent authors and books in Building Personal Leadership. I am grateful to you for your contribution to the growth of leaders everywhere. The authors and books I have promoted include:

Bourget, Lynne, Ph.D. - What You $ay Is What You Get

Carnegie, Dale - How to Win Friends & Influence People

Carter-Scott, Cherie, Ph.D. - If Life is a Game, These are the Rules

Colan, Lee J. - Passionate Performance

Conner, Daryl - Managing at the Speed of Change

Connors, Roger & Smith, Tom & Hickman, Craig - The OZ Principle

Connors, Roger & Smith, Tom - Journey to the Emerald City

Douglass, Merrill - Supervision, Vol. 59, ABC Time Tips

Ford, Debbie - The Right Questions

Frankl, Viktor - Man's Search for Meaning

Hargrove, Robert - Masterful Coaching

CONTRIBUTING AUTHOR ACKNOWLEDGMENTS

Hill, Napoleon – Think and Grow Rich

McNally, David – Even Eagles Need a Push

Morris, Tom, Ph.D. – The Seven Universal Conditions of Success

Kouzes, Jim & Posner, Barry – The Leadership Challenge

Myers, Paul J. – Attitude is Everything

Oakley, Ed & Krug, Doug – Enlightened Leadership

Rohn, Jim – Leading an Inspired Life

Shanahan, Mike – Think Like a Champion

Stack, Jack – The Great Game of Business

Tracy, Brian – Extract from His Material

Unknown Authors – Thank You

Waitley, Denis – Several Extracts from His Material & Empires of the Mind

Wardroom, James, Ph.D. – The 12 Bad Habits that Hold Good People Back

■ TABLE OF CONTENTS ■

▪ INTRODUCTION ▪

E ach person, including myself, can't begin to imagine the potential to create and achieve all that they possess. An authoritative book that I read states, ". . all things are possible." I've come to believe that this statement is true. Developing portions of that vast potential is quite a challenge. One thing is certain; our changing and evolving world requires us to acquire more knowledge and develop more of our talents and skills. The faster we can develop our knowledge, develop our talents and skills, the greater advantages we can enjoy from work and life. Those advantages come from developing the Leadership Advantage in yourself.

When I was "right sized" from a Fortune 50 company, my work and life had to change, and change it did. Leadership has been a passion from the earliest day that I can remember. But the experiences thereof were average, mediocre, and just okay. Those leadership experiences were not what they could have been. Why? I was not investing time and resources into developing more of my potential and personal leadership. I was just "winging it."

Like most young folks, life's demands consumed most of my energy and effort. Yes, there were some seminars, schools and other development opportunities, but the conscious deliberate daily effort was not there. Not until work and life require re-invention. Learning, developing skills, changing attitudes, and developing leadership became a priority development project. Change brought the necessity to study, learn, grow, develop new skills, and risk new initiatives. And that change has made all the difference.

Part of the change I made was supporting the people I was working with by writing and sending encouraging monthly Newsletters printed on paper. Next came weekly e-mails and Newsletters on subjects that supported the positive changes they were making in their work and life. Tens became hundreds. Hundreds became over one thousand. Before I knew it, I had articles on a large variety of subjects. Why not form the articles into a book? Then people could reference subjects and material that could help them in their life journey. And so it is!

My experience working with companies showed me that many leaders do not spend sufficient time developing productive and effective work skills and attitudes. The model of leadership that is often presented is much less than it could be. Being a model of a high performing, effective and efficient leader, manager and supervisor is critical to you and your company's success. The material contained in the articles of this book, if internalized and used in the work place and life will help you become that high performing model of leadership.

The articles are organized into a logical development progression. First, it's very important to develop and hone your own work skills and habits to ensure that you are as productive and effective as possible. Your time and how you spend it is the only resource you have. Spending it wisely is critical and foundational to your development journey. Secondly, Personal Leadership is about leading yourself through your work and life. If you are not effectively leading yourself, then you are like a ship without a rudder wandering aimlessly on the waters of life. Knowing your life's vision, purpose, mission and values are essential to a directed life that brings joy, happiness and peace. Your personal and work goals are essential to developing and modeling inspiring personal leadership. Lastly, every leader needs to invest some time in learning about the Barriers to Success, the behaviors and attitudes that can derail your career and life.

That is the essence of this book. It contains articles on Productivity, Personal Leadership, Business Leadership and Barriers to Success. You may enjoy reading each article in sequence. If you wish to explore certain article subjects or thought, an index is provided to guide you to the right material. Either way, your decision to read this book will be a choice that helps propel you into a bright and wonderful future.

The journey to developing more of your potential doesn't need to be triggered by a career wrenching change or emotional jolt. You can accelerate your progress by reading these articles, identifying insights that can be applied in your work and life to get new results and taking action to make changes. "If you do the things you have always done, you will get what you have always gotten." It is said that the Chinese definition of insanity is "doing the same things and expecting different results." My hope is that this book will talk to you in ways that can lead to lasting change and greater happiness and joy. I hope that you will be inspired by its contents, and that by applying what you learn, you will lift yourself to higher levels of performance, leadership and spiritual joy and happiness. In this way, you will create the Leadership Advantage in your life. Enjoy!

■ PART ONE ■
PERSONAL PRODUCTIVITY

"Everything in life is a progression of steps."
- Scott Reed

■ CHAPTER ONE ■
BACK TO THE BASICS

*"The expectations of life depend upon diligence;
the mechanic that would perfect his work must first
sharpen his tools." - Confucius*

SPORTS: Every year, before the regular playing season, athletes attend and participate in preseason training camps. In these camps, they practice the fundamental skills and moves of their sport. The complex plays come much later, after the sports team has shown a mastery of the basics. Without a mastery of the basics, the more complex plays and moves cannot be attempted or successfully completed.

WORK: We treat work as a different kind of game. People often labor eight, ten, or even twelve hours every day of every work year. Rarely does the worker take the time to brush up their basic work skills. Most people are not aware that they use basic work skills and that over time they need to "tune-up" those skills. They become conditioned to doing the same activities repeatedly despite flawed skills. Can that explain the limited productivity and effectiveness common to most work environments and executive teams? A common expression of degraded performance is the

1

person who at the end of the day states, ***"This day was just one big interruption (or meeting). I didn't get anything done."***

PEOPLE: We have shadowed managers and executives and found many small things that if changed, could significantly improve their work effectiveness and productivity. These things never fall into the category of complex behaviors or thinking. Instead, they involve very basic work skills and attitudes that include: work space arrangement, management of interruptions, use of e-mail or telephone, planning work, keeping commitments, delegation, and communication. As they tune-up these skills, work becomes more effective and they get more done. They work smarter, not harder.

TUNE-UP: If you have not had a performance tune-up in the past year, it's time to wake-up, look at how you do your work, and brush-up your basic work skills and attitudes. Because you are in the thick of the battle called work, conditioned by the past performance, and often unsure of improvement techniques, getting a performance coach who can observe and help you with the needed changes is almost essential. We have participant data to show that supervisors, managers, and executives who take the time to tune-up their work skills and attitudes achieve between ***15% and 30% improvements in their productivity***. If you are a business owner, operator, or decision maker, you recognize the benefit that this kind of system improvement can deliver. Few other business systems can show 15% to 30% improvements with such a small investment of time and resources.

ACTION: *Information and insight without action is only entertainment!* Take action now to tune-up your work skills and attitudes. While you're at it, tune-up your whole team.

2

Re-Master the Basics

Being highly effective and productive in your work is possible when you *"Re-Master the Basics."* The basics include most of the following:

    Goal setting & planning
    Organizing for productivity
    Managing your time & activities
    Keeping every commitment
    Delegating and follow-up
    Communicating effectively
    Task focus and self-discipline
    Handling interruptions
    Managing e-mail & telephone
    Developing yourself
    Maintaining a positive mental attitude

THE *Problem*: At one time you may have "Mastered the Basics" in all these areas. But today, are you still at the top of your work game or is there **some room for improvement**? It is common for almost everyone to inadvertently slip into unproductive habits that can rob them of precious work effectiveness and productivity. This can be caused by the current work culture, imperfect examples from superiors and peers, lack of feedback, inattention, or just trying to accomplish too much and thereby creating inefficient short cuts that develop ineffectual work habits. **It happens to us all!**

SOLUTION: Regularly - maybe once a year or every two years - stop and sharpen your saw (work habits). If your saw is dull, you will work harder and longer to get the same amount of work done. Taking just a little time now to sharpen your work habits will enable you to get your work done easily and in less time. It is quite common for a person to gain an hour and one-half each day if they just fine-tune their work habits to *"Re-Master the Basics."* Let us see. One and one-half hours a day translate into how many more hours available in a year? With about 240 work days in a year, that is 360 more hours available! You will have 360 more hours to get more work done or maybe to go home a little earlier. Wow. That's worthwhile! You can have a little more time for the family, physical exercise, or other life balancing activities. Better life balance means better productivity when at work. All this through just taking a little time now to *"Re-Master the Basics."*

If this message talks to you, then do something about it. Don't just work harder and longer. Take action now to *"Re-Master the Basics."*

Cultural Norms that Limit Productivity

In numerous companies I have observed *"cultural norms"* that severely impact productivity. Here are a few of those norms and what you can do about them:

SOME LIMITING CULTURAL NORMS:

1. Answer the telephone every time it rings. It might be a customer or the boss.

2. We have an open door policy so my door must always be open to employees.

3. I must react to the needs of the work in which my employees are engaged.

4. "Ding!" Another e-mail message just arrived. Check it out!

5. Fix the problem now to reduce negative effects (with usually no thought of focusing on fixing the root cause to prevent the problem in the future).

6. I cannot plan my work; the work just runs my day.

7. I must look and be busy all the time or someone will wonder if I am really working.

8. I am expected to be at work ten to eleven hours each day!

Cultural norms are often established though repetitive communications and behaviors by the leaders, and the desire of subordinates to reach the success level of the leaders by repeating these behaviors. Yet, are the leaders' behaviors resulting in effective, efficient, and productive actions. Often they are not. Old habits and attitudes die hard, especially in organizations. The bigger the organization, the harder old habits and attitudes die. What follows is a description of how limiting cultural norms can be overcome and the organizations become more productive.

OVERCOME LIMITING CULTURAL NORMS:

1. Answering the telephone is an interruption to your planned work. The American Management Association says that for every hour a manager is working, he or she has eight interruptions. Therefore, what could normally take one hour to do will take three hours. Why do leaders and managers come into work early before others arrive? The answer is to get work done in the quiet of the morning or after work when everyone is gone. You need to change what you do so that you can get work done during normal working hours.

2. An open door policy is wonderful. Nevertheless, untrained employees walking into your office whenever they wish are another interruption that steals your time and productivity. Let everyone know that if the issue is an emergency (high payoff activity and urgent) they should just walk right in and tell you. If not an emergency, then they should come when you have scheduled time to share non-urgent and low payoff issues. Respect each others time.

3. Are you in control of your time and work or are you reactive to everything that goes on in your business? Train your employees to respect your time and, by example, teach them the discipline of respecting their time. List non-crucial and low payoff items and mutually share with each other at scheduled times during the day.

4. Turn off the "ding" of the e-mail. Ignore what arrives. Do not let it control you. Schedule specific times during the day to clean out the Inbox. Alternately, when you have a few minutes between scheduled tasks, field the messages that have newly arrived. Deal with e-mails only once and keep a cleaned out Inbox.

5. Take time at the end of the day to reflect on the emergencies you handled (urgent and high payoffs). What was the root cause? What are all the possible solutions to fix the root cause? Which solution is the best one? How and when can I carry out a permanent fix? Then, implement the fix (preferably delegated). What are the results of that application? How can you institutionalize that solution so it never happens again?

6. This is an excuse for not controlling your work. It is an attitude and behavior that are not accountable. Take control, schedule your work, and work your plan. Yes, emergency interruptions will occur. Get them under control, have someone work on the issue, and return to work on your schedule as soon as possible.

7. This is an attitude of exhaustion and burn out. An effective and efficient manager gets work done through his or her employees. An excellent manager or leader normally gets his or her work done in a reasonable amount of time, say eight or nine hours. If you are spending more time than that, you better look at your own attitudes and habits and determine where you need to improve. You are not modeling effectiveness and efficiency. You are not managing so that you can recognize opportunities and think strategically.

8. If you spend eight hours of highly focused work on high payoff activities, then you are making a highly effective and efficient contribution to your company's success. Longer hours are generally a sign of inefficiency, and as more time is spent, the less efficient and productive you become. So, get in control of your work, sharpen your work skills, and attend to the other life areas that enhance your work productivity (exercise, education, family, spiritual, social).

CHANGE & ACCOUNTABILITY: I am sure that if you search your own work attitudes and habits you will discover one or two improvement ideas. The ideas you get from this chapter are lost unless you take action to implement them.

Adding to Your Success

Remember that to add to your success you must venture out and try new things. For instance, try things that are entirely new and therefore may be uncomfortable. Also, retry the things that you may have inadvertently abandoned. Let me list a few of the most valuable productivity enhancing techniques that participants have succeeded at using, and shared with me:

CONFERENCE PLANNER - Schedule and group communications (mind traffic). Then share with others at planned times in the day or week, instead of interrupting often with only one item.

SCHEDULING YOUR DAY - Planning your work day in the evening allows you to go to sleep at night knowing what you will do the next day. Plans change, but you have done your best pro-actively to work on the most important things first.

CLOSING OUT YOUR DAY - People find that fewer commitments and actions fall through the cracks. I used to pride myself on my excellent memory but I will tell you honestly that it did not always work. Now I pride myself on my personal management system and it seldom fails.

PRIORITIZING ACTION STEPS (tasks) - By making a list and deliberately ranking each item according to priority, you have determined what is most important to work on. Then when other less important items come along, it is easier to say "no" because you have already decided what it is you should be doing.

TRACKING YOUR HPA - I used to think this was probably a waste of time. Now it takes seconds to do and keeps me in touch with how effective I am in using my time (my only life resource). The practice motivates me to focus on doing HPA (High Priority Activities) that bring me results.

Improving Work Productivity

While your work may often include emergencies and be reactive in nature, you can always improve the management of your work. Though *comfortable to continue doing things the same way*, this habit keeps you from developing new and improved work practices. Better management of your work tasks and activities can result in increasing your time spent in High Payoff Activity (HPA). HPA are those high value tasks and activities that you are being paid to accomplish. To manage your work more effectively and efficiently, *you must change what you are doing.* The following is a set of activities that if practiced, will positively affect your work and time spent in HPA.

Write all promises and actions / tasks you say you will do into your commitment book (Planning System, PDA, Outlook, etc.). Upholding the integrity of *doing what you say you will do* is imperative for us all.

Close Out each day and transfer all unaccomplished actions or tasks to the next or subsequent day's Imperative or Important Action Step list (or "to do" list).

Set priorities for the next day's action / task list.

Plan & Schedule your next day's work to accomplish the highest priority actions and tasks first. Accomplish these steps usually at the end of the day before you go to sleep (*it clears your mind*).

The next day: *Work* your plan as best you can to accomplish the high priority actions and tasks you have scheduled. *Don't use excuses to hide your failure to manage your scheduled work aggressively.* Recognize that you probably cannot follow your schedule perfectly, but through careful management you can make significant progress and spend more time doing high priority work.

Recognize/Acknowledge that at the end of the day, you made progress toward the important things you wanted to accomplish. Let this step motivate you to continue this process.

Repeat the above steps at the end of each day.

Doing the same things you have always done is easy. Old habits and attitudes die slowly. Still, *who is in control* here? Is the past conditioning you have experienced in control, or *the choice to manage your work better?* Who makes your choices? If you continue to do things the same old way, that is also a choice. What are the results of each of those two choices? What choice will you make today?

P.S. *To enjoy life more fully, you may choose to apply the same steps to manage your personal time.*

Wood Cutting

If you have ever cut wood in the forest or sawed boards, after some time you know that it gets harder to cut or saw, and that the same effort produces less cut wood. Our work skills are the same way. They get dull with use and do not produce the results we would like to have (reasonable effort, reasonable results). We work harder and harder and get only the same or fewer results. How can we correct this problem?

Stop and sharpen the saw! Doing so, you take a little time and work at improving your capacity to do work. Consider taking a little time each week to try new techniques of working smarter, not harder. Adopt the techniques that work and improve your personal management system. If you do not, what will be the result? Not a pretty picture! You will be working harder and harder without getting ahead!

Closing out your day and scheduling your next work day is one of those improvement techniques that can add huge amounts of control to your day (and added HPA). No excuses.

Using a communication planner can group what was at once considered an interruption into effective small communication interchanges.

Using one system to keep commitments recorded - tasks you must do, notes that are important, telephone call notes and other personal management particulars - is highly efficient as it allows you to work on your tasks anytime, in one place. This system can include MS Outlook and a PDA (if it is available for use most of your waking hours.)

Decide the priority of your tasks, to dos, and action steps, before you schedule your day. This allows you to schedule the most important tasks first in your day (Imperative, then Important). When you do this, it's easier to say no to the insignificant things that fight for your time.

Everyone is a Teacher

THE PROBLEM: The American Management Association completed a study and found that managers are interrupted an average of eight times each hour. Work that would normally take one hour to accomplish, now takes three hours. You have heard people (managers and workers) say that by coming in at 6:00 A.M. they get more done before 8:00 A.M. than they get done all day. Why is this? Because repeated interruptions devastate their productivity. Your goal should be to get work done during normal working hours!

EXCUSES: I hear many excuses for allowing this to happen. My customers demand my immediate attention. I have to respond to the e-mails. I have to answer my telephone. People need to see me when they have a problem. I have an open door policy. The list goes on and on. Let me seed the idea that maybe you have trained other people to interrupt you while you are working. Yes, that's right, by allowing interruptions, you have inadvertently trained the people you work with not to respect your time.

REALITY: You are a teacher. Teach people to respect your time. Teach them that you have important blocks of time that must be spend in what you call High Payoff Activity (HPA, activities you engage in to earn your compensation). Reciprocally, respect other people's time. The following are a few ways to accomplish this:

1. CUSTOMERS: Educate them that you will respond within two hours (or any period you choose) if they leave a voice mail or send an e-mail. Then do it!

2. E-MAILS: Schedule time to process e-mails every two hours. Responsiveness can save huge amounts of wasted time (for you and others). However, do not let the sound of an e-mail arrival control you like one of Pavlov's dogs.

3. TELEPHONE CALLS: Use a voice mail greeting that says you will return calls at 10:00, 2:00, and 4:00. If the caller has an emergency (urgent & High Payoff Activity), tell them to call your receptionist or assistant who will then notify you.

4. WALK-INS: Ask immediately, "Is this urgent? Is this a HPA?" If the answer is yes to both, stop what you are doing and handle it. If the answer is no to either, ask the person to come back at the specific time you have scheduled to handle non-urgent items or low payoff activities. If no one has issues or problems at this time, handle existing e-mails and voice mails.

5. OPEN DOOR POLICY: You can have an open door policy even if the door is closed. Place a sign outside your door that says, "I am working on High Payoff Activities, unless this is an emergency, please come back at (time scheduled for that type of interaction)."

ACTION: The important thing is to manage your interruptions. Train people to respect the time you are spending on important work. In return, respect the time of others. Make mutual agreements on how you can work more efficiently together. Don't allow every unexpected happening to control your work and time!

The Nature of Productivity

Productivity is the springboard to success. A basic part of human nature yearns *to achieve, to attain, and to do better in the future than in the past.* The term productivity captures the essence of this human need to become better and better. Productivity in the broad sense is concerned with the overall effectiveness and efficiency of getting things done by working smarter, by using resources better, and by continuously improving your process of doing things. No matter what you do, you are always looking for ways to do it faster and more effectively. From mowing the grass, to shopping, and to obtaining your business goals you keep looking for ways to make it easier, faster, and better. This is true whether you are aware of it or not.

EIGHT Elements: The following are eight primary elements that will separate mediocre performers from high productivity achievers:

1. Time Management

The first key resource to increase your productivity relates to the way you use your TIME. The saying "time is money" is so often repeated we forget that it is literally true. Good time use cannot give you more time but it can help you use your time more productively than you have in the past. When you understand the worth of your time, you are better able to concentrate your efforts on items that offer the highest payoff.

2. Goal Setting

The quickest and most effective route to increasing productivity is to spend time on tasks that advance the things that are important to you. In other words, concentrate your efforts on achieving your goals.

3. Self-Discipline

The ability to exercise self-discipline keeps you focused on any task, working steadfastly through its completion. Establish your priorities and refuse to allow distractions, interruptions, or the happenings of the moment to destroy your concentration. Being persistent, with careful planning, goal setting, and determination will help you to realize your goals. These efforts are vital to personal productivity.

4. Getting Started

The best way to complete a project is to get started on it - now! Seems simple, doesn't it? People fail to finish jobs for only two reasons. They either never start or never follow-through and finish. Both are unproductive time patterns.

5. Continuous Improvement

Strive for results, not perfection. Overemphasis on perfection nearly always renders negative consequences, to you and to others who help you. Productive people distinguish between what is important and what is not. Approximately 80% of the results you obtain stem from 20% of the tasks you do (80 / 20 rule).

6. Self Confidence

Confidence in yourself and in others is essential to your productivity. The attitude you display toward others is a reflection of how you feel about yourself. As you strengthen a belief in yourself, your belief in other people naturally grows stronger. Self-confidence is critical to strengthening effective interpersonal relationships.

7. Positive Attitude

Attitudes toward external circumstances and the company's practices and procedures have a bearing on your performance. By committing yourself to an attitude of positive expectancy, you not only help yourself but those around you as well. True synergism occurs. If you view your company's current practices and procedures as a good starting point to improve upon continuously, your positive attitude will allow progress to take place.

8. Focus on High payoff Activities

The 80 / 20 rule applies to high payoff activities. If you practice the process of continuous improvement on just 20% of the tasks, you are affecting the outcome of your work in a highly productive way. So, identify the most productive activities (20%) in your daily schedule and devote most of your key hours to that 20%.

Improving personal productivity provides immense benefits. You will have more control of your life and all that matters to you. You will accomplish more in less time and use more of your potential. Improving your personal productivity will provide a profound sense of achievement and enhance your self-image and self-respect.

■ CHAPTER TWO ■
GOALS

"Whatever You Vividly Imagine, Ardently Desire, Sincerely Believe, and Enthusiastically Act Upon, Must Inevitably Come to Pass." - Paul J. Meyer

If you are not taking planned actions toward your goals then what are you taking action for? Most of us say we have goals and in fact we do. However, goals may be vague, dimly visualized, lost in the background noise of life, or only faintly dreamed. The bustle of life seems to consume all of your time and when you do have a break, the last thing you want to do is *think*!

If you analyze this last statement you will find that the most important things in your life will never be acted upon. The demands of a modern life crowd out the proactive thinking, planning, and actions needed to realize your goals and dreams. You must break the cycle of not making the progress you are capable of by taking time to think, set priorities, plan, and take action toward your goals and dreams. Failure to break the reactive cycle of life may result in frustration, feeling unfulfilled and stuck at what you are doing, and unhappiness with your life.

Making progress toward your goals and dreams is simple. Yet it involves self-control and discipline (sometimes hard to do). Just follow the steps below (self-control) and then apply self-discipline to realize your goals and dreams.

1. Block out the time to dream again. List all the things you want to do and accomplish in your life.

2. Prioritize your goals and dreams.

3. Completely fill out a Goal Planning Sheet on the highest priority goals. *If you don't have a Goal Planning Sheet, contact me for some.* This one step crystallizes your goals and dreams in a way that they become visually alive, clear, specific, and impressed upon your subconscious mind.

4. Schedule the actions you identify from your goal planning sheet into your personal management system.

5. Take action on your plan and make things happen to advance you toward your goals and dreams.

6. Track the results you get. Celebrate the progress you make. Enjoy reaching your new life destinations.

Life long goals are a great motivating force in any person's life. For three or four years I had a goal to refurbish my 1959 single-engine Comanche 250 airplane. In October 2004, I decided to begin that goal and started the planning process. On December 1, I wrote a check for the Avionics, and in February 2005 the airplane was grounded and work began. The entire interior, all the instruments, and the instrument panels were torn out. What a mess it was with only a terrible gaping hole left. Next came new instrument panel fittings and hundreds of modifications and installations lasting through July 14, 2005. Finally, the work was completed and the first flight scheduled. What was to be a six-week job became six months of challenging work.

Achieving the goal taught me two major lessons. They are:

1. Your acceptance of the conditions as they are, is critical to your happiness. Try to fight or get upset about the existing conditions and your life will be miserable. Accept each challenging condition as an opportunity to solve a problem. Try something new to learn and grow. Acceptance of the conditions as they are, made my life a whole lot happier during those six months.

2. Perseverance is necessary to achieve the major goals in a person's life. Many worthwhile dreams do not come easily. We made many steps forward and backward, but over time and hundreds of problems solved, we won. Keep taking actions every day toward your goals, and your dreams will become reality.

My refurbished plane was a dream. Now it is a reality. What dream do you want to become reality? Pick one now. Decide and start planning. Take steps each day with acceptance and perseverance and your dream will come true.

■ ■ ■

Just as there are two types of lessons there are two types of goals. One type is "To Become Goals." The other type is "To Get Goals."

TO BECOME GOALS: These goals are focused on increasing your capacity to work and live. They improve your knowledge, skills, productivity, and efficiency. They are personal growth goals that enable you to get more out of life and work, with less and less effort. An example goal is, "To develop the skill of holding me and others more accountable for what we say we will do." Another might be, "To become more empathetic with people." To Become Goals are very important in increasing your future success and creating a satisfying and happy life. Without them, you may stagnate in your development, and your value in the marketplace and effectiveness in life will slowly atrophy.

TO GET GOALS: To Get Goals are set at obtaining something you want. You might want a new car, new home, raise, promotion, vacation, or any number of tangible items. To get the many things you want, it is often necessary to establish and achieve "To Become Goals." An example goal is, "To be promoted to the manager position in the technology department and get a $4,000 raise in pay." Another is, "To achieve financial security (set specific measurable & tangible targets)."

Now is a great time to think about your year. If you have a Dream List & a Goal Plan, then revisit them to set priorities and focus on what you want To Get in this year. If you do not have a Dream List & a Goal Plan, take time to create them. Then, establish the To Become Goals you need to facilitate achieving the To Get Goals you want. Of course, when you have completed these steps, taking action each day to achieve each of your goals is necessary. As you might surmise, the To Become Goals are essential in adding to your future success. Take time now to *schedule a block of time to accomplish the planning* described in this section. If you do not, you will languish in the land of insanity, described as doing the same old things and expecting something different!

One of the Few – Written Goals

Are you one of the few people? One of the few that write their goals, spend time each day studying to improve themselves, and strive daily to develop more of their potential? Are you the one who has set thirty minutes (ok, fifteen minutes) aside each day to learn about something new and add to your knowledge, to your understanding, and wisdom? Are you the one who knows that you cannot develop those in your care unless you develop yourself first? Are you one of the few that has a written list of dreams, actively works on several of those dreams currently, and is making progress in chosen and specific areas of your life? Are you a person who is in control of your life? Do you know your purpose for living, your vision for the future, your mission, and your values (fundamental guiding values)? Or, are you so busy that you don't have time to do the above, and use excuses to justify not doing so?

Personal leadership is about developing you to use more of your potential. Without personal leadership, people will not enthusiastically follow you. They will languish in mediocrity. It's all about developing personal leadership. Think about it! If this message talks to you, take action now to develop more of your personal leadership. With personal leadership, life can be Joyful. Without it, life can be just an existence. What do you choose? Remember, you do have a choice!

The Power of Written Goals

There is something special about writing down your goals. Before you write down your goals you have to think about them in precise terms. You need to form a picture of it in your mind before you can write a clear concisely worded description. Crystallizing that picture of your goal does magical things. For instance, it communicates with your subconscious mind and mobilizes it to help you achieve the results you want. It communicates your intentions with the universe, and you call on forces far greater than yourself to help achieve your goal. You engage synchronicity and inform all areas of your life of your desire. Soon miracles begin to appear.

One woman wrote down her goals at the beginning of the New Year and didn't look at the list until the year was over. Guess what happened? Reviewing them at the year's end, she found that 80% of them had been accomplished. This could happen for you!

It's the beginning of a New Year. All it takes is a little thinking to make a written list of the goals you wish to achieve for this New Year. Write them down, make it happen!

Written Goals – A Winner

All companies succeed or fail based on its employees achieving or failing to achieve the goals that they and the company set. What are your goals? What are the contributions you will make to achieve your goals? Your success and your company's success are totally dependent upon the aggregate of achieving all of your goals.

People's financial success was studied and recorded by Mr. David C. McClelland in an article entitled, "The Achieving Society" (New York Press, 1967) and later verified by other studies. His article provides the following information:

3%: Three percent of Americans are independently wealthy. They can live off the income from their investment capital.

10%: The next 10 percent live comfortably, the way most of us would like to live.

60%: Sixty percent barely make a living. They live from one paycheck to the next.

27%: Twenty-seven percent need support from others or the government just to survive.

What is the difference between these groups? The top 3 percent have written specific goals. The next 10 percent have their goals in their mind but they are not specific or written. The next 87 percent have no goals except to get to the end of the day or week or to the next paycheck.

How does this information affect your life? Maybe it is time to write those goals down. If so, you know what to do. It will take time, but you can join the top three percent of Americans by just writing your goals down. Do it now!

Chunking Down Your Goals

Are there things you want to accomplish but are not making any progress toward? Are those dreams and wishes in your head? Only about 3% of people write down their goals. That one action of writing down your goals is a huge step toward accomplishing them. You can write down your goals any time you wish. This month is a good time to start writing them or visiting written goals to assess progress. Consider adding to your list and reestablishing your priority and commitment to your goals for the remainder of this year. Once you have a prioritized list, then it is time to "Chunk down your goals."

"Chunking" down your goals means to divide them into smaller more manageable action steps. Chunking down yearly goals provides monthly goals that are easier to achieve. Chunking down monthly goals supplies weekly goals that are even easier to accomplish. Chunking down weekly goals identifies daily actions that you can easily complete. Daily actions become those tasks that take little time and effort but that advance you one step toward your weekly, monthly, and yearly goals. *Using only minutes each day*, over a year, you can have a total of 365 daily actions that advance you far toward achieving your goal. That is called progress!

If you are not chunking down your goals now, then start with one goal and chunk it down to daily action steps that you can easily complete. Once you see how easy it is, then chunk down another goal. Continue this chunking down process until you are comfortable with the progress you are making toward your highest priority goals. According to Frederick Herzberg, achievement of your goals is one of the highest motivators. You'll feel good about the progress you make toward your goals and dreams. Write down a goal and begin chunking now!

Communicating Your Goals

Communicate Goals. The first step in proactive personal or business management is to "Set Goals & Plan." The second step is to "Communicate Your Goals." You communicate your goals to enlist the help of others to accomplish those objectives. If your goals or expectations are never or poorly expressed, then others cannot help you get the results that you want. Who do you communicate them too? To the people who can help you achieve the results you want.

SHARING WITH OTHERS – I want to take you one step further in your thinking about communicating goals. Everyone I know has personal goals or aspirations. What they do not do is share those goals with their friends and acquaintances. The special thing about people I know is that they will go out of their way to help a person, even if only a hint of need is felt. I tell someone of a goal and they instantly provide ideas or suggest resources that can help me accomplish it. Logically extended, I should share my goals with everyone I meet.

ASSESSMENT AND ACTION – Think about your goals. What goal have you not shared with those you know? Why haven't you shared that goal? What would happen if you did share your goal? Consciously, share your goal and see what happens. Repeat this sharing with others until it becomes an attitude and habit. See how your progress quickens toward the results you want. If you want to try sharing safely, share your goal with me and see if I help!

Lesson from the Garden

Growing tomatoes is a hobby of mine. I have been working on the Arizona soil in my yard for fourteen years and it is now rich and fertile. For thirteen years I have been planting and enjoying some wonderful, ripe tomatoes from June through the end of July. I bought eight-foot long, one and a half inch wood boards and split them into two pieces to use as two four-foot stakes. The tomato plants climbed up those stakes, and often higher. So, I'd bunch them together and augmented them with a couple of higher stakes and they would grow a bit more. This year I bought eight-foot stakes for each tomato plant. Guess what happened? My tomato plants are all eight-feet tall and still growing. They are producing twice as many tomatoes as before and I just know the plants are happier. What is the lesson?

Set out four-foot stakes and get the plants and fruit of four-foot tall tomato plants. Set out eight-foot stakes and get the plants and fruit of eight-foot tall tomato plants. In other words, set four-foot goals and challenges and reap some results. Or, set eight-foot goals and challenges and reap far better results. Take the time now to see how this lesson can apply to your work and life. If you need to stretch more, set that new goal or challenge, take action, and reap the many benefits from your new goals and challenges.

Why Goals?

We set and achieve goals to enjoy their results. The benefits of reaching a goal therefore need to be compelling, or the goal will not be worth pursuing. If you only have a whisper of a reason for achieving your goals then you will not make the progress required to succeed.

In life, we have two basic kinds of goals. To Get or To Become! Most of us are familiar with the To Get goals but hardly take notice of the To Become goals. Unfortunately, you usually need To Become before you can Get. Think about it. How often do you take stock of your skills and competencies in relation to achieving your life goals and your dreams? Are your skills and competencies sufficient to enable you To Get the things you want? If not, then what do you need to develop more to facilitate Getting what you want?

Here is your assignment. You should schedule fifteen minutes in the next week to take inventory of your current skills and competencies. Answer the question, "What skill or competencies do I need to develop to Get the things I want?" When you have the answer, then take a goal sheet and complete all sections. Schedule and take one action this week to make progress toward your To Become goals. Do this weekly and over a period of time you will become competent and skilled in the areas needed to reach your To Get goals. Don't procrastinate on this assignment. **Do It Now**!

Tracking Progress

Do you know how much progress you are making toward your goals? Businesses track sales, costs, production, services, and many other items to determine how well they are doing. Without those measurements, we would have no feedback, no control, and chaotic work, life, and results. Remember the saying, "What gets measured gets done."

In your everyday work and life, what do you measure? Most people I know measure only what is required of them to measure at work. Still, is that sufficient to achieve the results that you want from life? Usually, people have many things they want but they do not take the time to write them down as goals. Nor do they take daily action to achieve their goals, or measure their progress toward realizing their goals. Measuring your progress is a way to motivate yourself to get the things you want for yourself and others in your life.

Tracking progress toward your goal can be easy and fun. The following are some ideas about how you can track progress toward your goals:

- Counting - 1-31 Day Tracking Sheet (Excel spreadsheet)
- Graphing - Goal Tracking Graph (graph paper or Excel chart)
- Hash Marks - White board, daily planner, note book, etc.
- Thermometer chart
- Bar & Pie Charts
- Gantt Charts
- Marbles in a jar or dish (coins, etc.)
- Water level in any vessel (quantity of water consumed)
- Days marked off on a calendar (other symbols too)
- Completed items in the "Out Box"
- Software that tracks your wealth
- and many others …

Take a moment and write down those things that you want but are not making any progress toward. Then, turn them into S.M.A.R.T. goals (specific, measurable, achievable, realistic, and time bound). Determine how progress can be measured and tracked. Take one action today toward achieving that goal and start tracking your progress. Follow this process of daily action and tracking of your progress and before you know it, many things you wanted but were not progressing toward will start to appear in your work and life. Start with one or two wants (goals) and gradually increase it until you feel you are making all the progress you want and can make. The most important thing though is to START RIGHT NOW!

Tracking & Recognition

If you put $35,000 in the stock market, how often would you check to see how it is doing? I check my investments every Saturday morning. Just a reminder, you may have invested that much in the development of your people and that was a great decision! You have focused them on goals that will deliver between three and possibly ten times that amount of value to your company this year. How often have you checked with your people to see what progress they are making (tracking their results)?

How often have you recognized the improvements that they are making (recognition, the best motivator)? I hope the answer is weekly! If not, now is the time to start. They need the recognition and accountability that comes from their supervisor taking an interest. The following is a five minute check list to help you in this weekly check-in with your participants.

>   *1.* Ask about their weekly business goal and how it contributes to their positive development program goals. What progress are they making.

2. Ask what they learned in the last week's lesson and how they are using those ideas in their daily work.

3. Point out and praise positive behavior change that you have observed.

4. Ask if anything is preventing them from achieving their goals or achieving the results you both agreed upon were important. Take action to help remove any obstacles so that your participant can be successful (you will become more successful as a result).

5. Let me know what I can do to help you. I am dedicated to achieving the maximum results and positive changes that we together can achieve for your company. Only in that way am I successful too! Thanks. I know it will take five minutes a week and you are already busy, but tracking and recognition are positive habits that are critical and essential to "Building on the Success" that your company has already achieved. Thanks for your active help.

Tracking for Results

WHY TRACKING: Every business tracks critical or important goals regularly, if not daily. Goals can include sales, production, service, waste, revenue, receivables, consumables, and a host of other items. Everyone is largely comfortable with the necessity of tracking those parts of their business. Tracking allows you to see if you are achieving the results you want and if not, making the adjustments and taking the actions needed to hit your target. It motivates you to take the actions needed to achieve your goals!

TRACKING AT WORK AND IN LIFE: This tracking technique, when applied to your work and personal life, can act as a motivating force to

29

get the results you want. At work you might want to track the number of calls made to customers, contacts with your network, times you coached your reports, number of times you mentioned on-the-job safety, times you practiced a developing skill to make it a new habit, or the number of invoices you handled today. Instead of letting your results to chance (unmeasured), you can track the actions you take toward the results you want and make the corrections that inevitably are needed to reach your goal. In your personal life, you may want to track the quality time spent with each child, times you rode your bicycle, running or exercising, reading for self-development, new skill development practice, hours spent in spiritual work, or any other area in which you wish to achieve new results. To get the results you want, you can turn wishes into real results by tracking your actions and motivating yourself to make the course adjustments you need.

How to Track: Tracking normally involves counting numbers, line graphs, bar or thermometer charts, electronic signs with status, and a host of other tools and displays. Nevertheless, tracking can be fun. Try using a jar with marbles, calendars with marks, tracking charts in your organizer (electronic or paper), a liter container of water (for measuring consumption), tick marks on anything, smiley face stickers on a goal visualization picture, scores on your personal scoreboard (white board), candy you eat for tracking and reward, and a host of other creative methods. Once I had a woman who wanted to lose weight to fit into her blue jeans but she would not weigh herself. With a little creativity, she chose to put herself into the jeans and note the number of pressure points. Then she tracked the declining number of pressure points until she fit into them comfortably. Let your imagination go wild but choose a method of tracking and motivate yourself to get the results you want.

ACTION: If there is some result in your work and life that you are not making steady progress toward, then tracking can help create the motivation you need to succeed. Take a moment right now and pick one of those results or goals and set up a tracking system. Then commit yourself to use it for a month. If at the end of a month, you have not made more progress toward that result than you would normally have, quit. However, I promise that you will see dramatic progress toward achieving your goal. If it works, then try two or three goals. But, do it now!

■ CHAPTER THREE ■
WORK AND LIFE PLANNING

There is a Tibetan story about an old, blind turtle that lives in the depths of the ocean. Once every thousand years, the turtle swims to the top of the sea, and sticks its head up through the waves, surfacing for air. Now imagine that there is a wooden ring floating somewhere on the surface of the ocean, and think of how rare it would be for the blind turtle, coming up for air once every thousand years, to put its head through the wooden ring. It is just as rare, say the Tibetans, for a being to gain human birth.

- Chop Wood, Carry Water

If it is truly that rare, then you have been given a great opportunity to live on this earth. Taking that opportunity and guiding your life in positive directions takes on new meaning. Planning the upcoming month and setting new HPA's and goals are positive actions that will keep you on an effective and productive life course. Planning your day and your month will help you make the most of your opportunity and produce the very best results for yourself and others.

Monthly planning is necessary to stay on course in your life. Progressing toward your dreams is necessary. If you do not have a planned course, then the winds will blow you wherever they will. You will live an uncontrolled and unguided life. I don't know about you, but I do not like being pushed around. Life is too precious to let that happen. If you don't take time now, tomorrow will soon be here, then the next day, and the next, and so on until the end of the year, with no progress toward your goals. Exercise Effective Personal Leadership, get into action, and complete your monthly planning now!

Visions of the humanitarian cargo ship arriving in the Iraqi port reminded me of a valuable personal leadership activity. For a ship to arrive, it needs a destination, a navigation plan, some form of position tracking, corrective steering, and propulsion. For an airplane to arrive, it needs the very same information and functions. If you want to arrive at some destination (goal), then you need a navigation plan (action steps), some form of position tracking (tracking results), corrective steering (activity corrections), and propulsion (motivation & action).

A new month is almost here. Today is a good day to reflect on the progress you have made toward your goals this month, and for this quarter of the year. The following are some questions to ask yourself to "take stock" of where you are and where you want to go. After reading this list, form your goal, activity, and project plan for your new month. It's called "monthly planning."

- Has your monthly (or life) vision, mission, purpose, and values changed?

- Are your high payoff activities still on target (activities that you do to earn the money you receive or guide the life you live)?

- Are your goals still the destinations you want to achieve?

- Are you on course to realizing your goals (check results achieved vs. planned results)?

- What activity corrections must be made to get you back on course?

- What new or repeat actions will you take in this month to progress toward your goals?

- Are there new goals you wish to set in any area of your life (social, physical, spiritual, educational, family, or career)?

- What are the other correction activities, imperative projects, and important projects you wish to complete in this month?

- What are the priorities assigned to your goals, actions, and projects?

Before an airplane takes off from its airport, it has a flight plan that the pilot has calculated and approved. After takeoff, and with a series of course corrections, it will follow that flight plan within established airway parameters to arrive at its intended destination. Without those corrections and the original flight plan, who knows where the plane would land.

Just like the pilot of the plane, we need a flight plan for our work and life (goals). That plan is broken down into monthly segments that are realizable (even to weekly or daily action steps). That means you must take time to plan what you want to achieve during this next month so you will travel toward your intended life and work goals. If you have not planned your month, Do It Now!

What are your goals for this month? It's easy to arrive at work Monday morning and just dive into work because there is so much of it. That is a great reason to stop yourself and take the time to plan your work for this month. Without planning you will not have identified all the important things you need to do. And what you do know might not be in any priority order. Listing all the tasks, projects, and goals for your new month, and ranking them, will focus your energies and work to get the most important things done first. Won't that be of value to you?

How: In planning your month, first consider not only your personal vision, mission, purpose, and values, but also review the strategic plan for your business, department, or work function. Consider all areas of your work and life (work and career, physical, health, financial, educational, family, home, and spiritual) and determine what you wish to accomplish this month in each area. With your list, separate them into two categories, imperative and important. Imperative items must be accomplished this month while important items could move to another month if necessary. Then in each category, rank the items. Develop and use criteria to help you order them. With your prioritized lists, you are ready to tackle your month with the confidence that you will be focused on the most important work, projects, goals, and tasks.

Without Planning: Without a plan your work may wander from task to task or turn to whatever grabs your attention at the time. Things that are easy may be done first. Things that are hard may lie undone at the end of the month. You may forget some tasks and others may be ignored.

Call to Action: The results you get may still be good but if you plan now, just think how much better your results will be. Take the time now to do your monthly plan. Then, daily, review your plan and use it to focus your work and actions. At the end of the month, you will look back and be glad you did. Do it now!

Choose Your Ship

If you had the opportunity to take a relaxing cruise, you would have to choose the ship on which you would like to travel. Consider the following two choices and decide the ship you would choose.

SHIP 1: Leaves from a specific port, has a detailed illustrated itinerary and activities, and identifies the port that you will arrive at the end of your trip.

SHIP 2: Has no specific departure point, has no planned route or itinerary, does not identify the port of call at the end of the trip.

You see, Ship 2 is like the person who does not plan their month. Ship 1 is like the person who does plan their month. Only if you take the time to determine where you are, review where you want to go, and plan how you will get there, will you have any chance at all of arriving at the destination you want (your wants and dreams). This is your reminder to plan each new month. No excuses now, choose the ship on which you will travel. Do not let the tides of time choose where you will land.

The Trap!

The trap of not planning your month is that the next month will not be planned either, then the next, and then the year will not show the results that you truly want. They say that if you "fail to plan, you plan to fail!" If you are exercising personal leadership in your life and work, then you plan how you are living your life this month. You plan both work

37

goals, and personal goals, for each month to achieve your yearly goals. *So what is your excuse for not planning?* There is no excuse, only choices. If you choose not to plan your month, you choose to experience results that may not be aligned with your wants and dreams. You know what to do. Take time now to schedule and take action to plan your month. Enjoy advancing and achieving your wants and dreams this next month.

Planning is one of the most important ways you can use your time. Without it, things prioritize themselves piecemeal, as you encounter them. Without it, goals are achieved much more slowly and many of your dreams will go unexplored. Without it, you will look back over the day and say, "I don't know what I achieved today." And do you know what? You didn't get anything important done!

The time you spend planning returns four to ten times that amount of time in execution (getting important things done). It ensures you are working on HPA and action steps that move you toward your goals. It ensures that you spend your time focused on your priorities. It ensures that you take an organized approach to living that reduces chaos, frustration, and stress. It ensures that you remain in control!

Today is a new month and planning is a serious productivity tool. Is this month planned in your Personal Management System? If not, you have a task to accomplish your monthly planning. It will give you a progress check on your goals and dreams, and commitment to the work that needs to be done to move you along your path in life. This monthly planning might also reveal a goal that needs to be placed on the back burner or a goal that needs to be redirected. In any case, IT IS WORTH YOUR TIME! Block out time and plan each new month. Short and sweet, when you do, you will be exercising Effective Personal Leadership.

There Is Something Special About Planning

- What was once a cloud in your mind, becomes more **clear and doable**.
- What was once left to chance, becomes more of a **reality**.
- What may never have gotten done before, now has a **much greater chance of getting done**.
- Where time was not accounted for in the past (white space in your schedule), a **High Payoff Activity is now scheduled**.
- Where you once felt out-of-control, now you feel **more in control**.
- Where there were no priorities, now **priorities are decided** so that the most important actions get done first.
- Where once there were few or no goals, now there are **clearly written S.M.A.R.T. goals** that crystallize your thoughts.
- Where once the mind wondered without aim, now it is **focused on an outcome** with distinct actions identified to achieve your desires and dreams.

Gee, isn't planning a worthwhile activity?

Intentions are wonderful thoughts but without planning how to realize your intentions, or without scheduling the tasks to accomplish them, there is no progress toward manifesting them. When you show up at work, do you have great intentions? Do you have a clear plan in mind with specific actions to take to get what you want?

One of the greatest productivity and effectiveness techniques that you can practice is planning your work and working your plan. Repeatedly, the people I work with say that planning and scheduling their work day and then working the plan as best they can, are the greatest productivity techniques they can practice.

Don't believe them or me. Try an experiment. Today just do what you have always done as far as planning and scheduling your work. Then tonight before you leave work or go to sleep, sit and plan and set priorities for the tasks you need to accomplish in the next day. Schedule your workday according to prioritized tasks starting with either wake-up or arrival at work. When you start this planned day, do your best to follow your plan. Then compare what you accomplished during the unplanned day, to the planned day, and note the difference.

Guaranteed, you will have accomplished more important tasks in the planned day than in the unplanned day. Try it, you'll like it.

While supervision and work can sometimes present emergencies and be reactive in nature, it can be managed. Only a person's comfort in doing things the same way keeps them from developing new attitudes and habits that lead to better management of their activities, thus increasing their time spent in HPA. So, to manage yourself more effectively and efficiently, you must change what you are doing. The following are the new activities, that if practiced, will dramatically and positively affect your focus and time spent in HPA:

1. **Writing** all commitments down in your commitment book (Personal Planning System).

2. **Closing** each day and transferring all unaccomplished actions (tasks) to the next day's Imperative or Important Activity Lists.

3. **Setting priorities** for those activities that are on your Imperative and Important Activity lists.

4. Planning your day's work to accomplish the highest priority activities (tasks) first.

5. Working your day as best as you can to accomplish the HPA's you have scheduled (**not using excuses to mask your failure to manage your schedule**; recognizing that you probably cannot accomplish your day perfectly, but through careful management you can make progress and spend more time in HPA).

6. Recognizing that at the end of the day you did make progress toward the important things that you wanted to accomplish.

7. Repeating the above steps for the next day.

It is easy just to keep on doing the things you have always done. Old habits and attitudes die slowly. Nevertheless, who is in control here. Is the past conditioning, or the choice to manage better in control? Who makes choices to add to your success? Of course, you make the choice to become more effective and productive. If you choose to do things the same old way, that is a choice too. What are the results of each of these two choices? Which choice will you make today?

Prioritization & Planning Your Work Day

TYPICAL DAY: Some people show up at work on the first day of the week, scan their desk and piles of papers, find the quickest, easiest thing to do, and start to work. A quick easy task completed is psychologically satisfying but may not be important. That process is repeated during the entire day. Mixed with unexpected fires to fight, and interruptions, their work day quickly progresses, but nothing valuable seems to get done. For example, a project due tomorrow must be completed. So, at 3:00 P.M. work is started and almost completed before departing for home, a meal, and rest. "To finish the work tomorrow morning" is the commitment made. Look back over the work day and nothing important seems to have been completed!

PRIORITIZATION & PLANNING: Without a work plan that is exactly the result you will get. Without ordering the work you must do, planning your day to complete the very most important tasks / projects sequentially, and then working your plan as best you can, it will be haphazard whether you will get anything important completed. The best time to plan your work day is before you retire for the evening (or before you go home if you wish). List all the work that is to be completed, and set priorities within that list. Plan each minute of your next day starting with the highest priority tasks / projects. Go to sleep with the knowledge that everything is arranged as best it can be for tomorrow's work day. Sleep undisturbed by the mental stress and turbulence that occur from not having a plan. Then wake to the new day knowing that you will be working on the most important task first and that you will make the most of the time you have at work that day. Manage interruptions and fires and work your plan. Be content at the end of the day that you have worked on the most important tasks / projects even thought you might not have accomplished everything that was planned. Complete the cycle once more and every day. You will be pleased by all the important work that you complete.

■ CHAPTER FOUR ■
TIME MANAGEMENT

"Nine-tenths of wisdom is being wise in time."

- Theodore Roosevelt

TIME: Your only asset is your time. How you spend that asset determines what you experience in life. Every person has the same 24-hours each day. You cannot make more time and you cannot save time. The only thing you can do is spend time wisely.

TIME EXCHANGE: Some of that time you spend in work activities and exchange it for a paycheck or money. Usually that is eight hours. Then that paycheck can be used to meet your needs and wants. Another eight hours are spent in sleep to allow your body to regenerate for the next 24-hour period. That leaves eight hours each day to spend on other activities. Eight hours each day and sixteen hours on weekends gives you seventy-two hours of time to spend in creating the personal life you want. Seventy-two hours gives you many opportunities on how to spend your time.

TIME USE: Look around at your life and possessions, take an inventory, and see how you have spent your time. What possessions do you have?

43

What is used and what is idly wasting away? What personal relations do you have? What personal relations are growing stronger and which are growing apart? Now my question is, "Are you making conscious decisions on how to spend your time or are you allowing your time to go wherever it may be demanded?" **"Are you in control of spending your only asset, your time?"**

TIME USE CHANGE: Take a moment and think about what you really want out of life. What do you really want to possess? What relationships do you really want to build? What experiences do you want to experience? What kind of life do you want to live? With answers to these questions clearly in mind, list and then prioritize all these ways of spending your time. Set some goals and create action plans to achieve them. Then plan how to spend your time. Schedule this time around your priorities and the kind of life you want to create and live. Finally, spend your time according to your schedule. Before you know it, you will experience more of the things you want in life. You will find greater fulfillment, satisfaction, and happiness. Try it, you'll see!

As I view my own world, knowing that I created it, I must ask myself, "Is this really what I wanted to create? Is this what I really value? Are the things I have bought, the relationships I have built, and the life I am experiencing what I really wanted?" I don't know about you but I am making changes!

Time is your only possession! You may trade it for money, building relationships, health, or any number of items. But time is your only resource and it is finite. How you spend your time speaks volumes about what you value. How you spend your time determines your quality of life. So, **how do you spend your time**? Do a time study and track the time you spend on activities and analyze the uses you make of your time (at work and at home).

Time is wasted in minutes not hours. The following are some **time wasters**:

- uncontrolled interruptions
- office distractions
- messy cluttered desk
- stacks of work in sight
- unscheduled time blocks (white space)
- to-do lists in memory
- not finishing work
- poor work focus or discipline
- too much TV

The following are some techniques that can help to improve the use of your time:

- form a complete written to-do list
- prioritize your day's to-do's
- schedule priority to-do's in daily time blocks - work your plan (leave no white space with unscheduled time)
- schedule a time block(s) for employee conferences to manage uncontrollable interruptions and respond only to emergencies (urgent & important problems)
- keep a list of items to communicate with people - cover all items at one time
- return phone calls all at one time
- let e-mail and voice mail accumulate - schedule a time block(s) to handle them - exercise discipline
- eliminate distractions from your field of view when working
- have one work item on your desk at a time

- complete the work you start
- give others a chance to learn and grow by delegating and training
- record every commitment you make on your to-do list
- take an Personal Development program.

ACTION: Take three minutes of your time right now to think about the most important long term goals, work, people, or activities in your life. **Are you investing the appropriate amount of time to each of these important areas**? If not, why not? Then take actions to change how and where you are spending your time. If you do not, you will not achieve the results you seek in your life. Success in work and life is your choice! Make the choices that will bring you the life you seek. Invest your time resource wisely.

Time, an Investment?

Everyone has the same amount of time, and time is your only asset. What you do with your time determines the kind and quality of life that you live. What you enjoy or do not enjoy today is a direct result of the time investment you made in the past. It pays to stop and reflect on where you made, and make, your time investments.

To stimulate thought, I will list a few high and low value time investments.

HIGH VALUE :)	LOW VALUE :(
Quality time with significant other	Watching TV (most programs)
Quality time with children or family	Playing solitaire

Meditation	Frivolous conversations
Setting goals and planning	Bustling around without planning
Reading books	Responding to every interruption
Studying subjects to improve knowledge	Complaining
Listening to educational CD's in your car	Making excuses
Taking a course	Two hour-long telephone calls
Developing a positive attitude	Wallowing with a negative attitude
Practicing and developing new skills	Doing the couch potato thing
Making to do and commitment lists	Trying to remember all commitments
Being and staying organized	Living with clutter
Loving	Embracing fear and associated emotions

Yes, I know. It's impossible to be perfect. Perfection is not the goal. Improving how you use your time to improve and enjoy more of your life is the goal. Invest a little time today to assess how you are using your time. Then take action to eliminate low value uses of your time and bolster the high values investments of your time.

32 Ways to Save Time & Accomplish More

1. Make a daily list. Set priorities and work priorities. Schedule your work.

2. **File, respond to, or trash mail** as you open it. Do the same with e-mail!

3. Eliminate needless interruptions.

4. **Manage non-emergency interruptions**.

5. Utilize the slingshot principle: Go on a vacation to rejuvenate.

6. **Finish one task** before getting involved in another.

7. Consolidate errands, and try to delegate them to someone else.

8. Clump similar tasks together and do them all at once.

9. **Organize work and living spaces**. Eliminate unnecessary items.

10. Listen to educational tapes & CD's in your car.

11. Create a **University on wheels.**

12. Use waiting time. Create and use a **Read File**.

13. Schedule your recreation and do it.

14. **Procrastinate AFTER you finish doing what you want done**.

15. Read only the first sentence of newspaper paragraphs.

16. Learn to navigate your city better.

17. Invest in the proper tools needed to get your job done more effectively.

18. Reduce unproductive schmoozing.

19. Start a greeting card file (birthday, thank you, get well, etc.).

20. Shop for gifts year round and start a gift closet.

21. Take a speed reading class.

22. Utilize delivery and professional services.

23. If you must have a pet, get a low maintenance pet.

24. Don't let clutter accumulate.

25. Avoid People who "**Drain You**."

26. Exercise for energy. Eat for energy. Rest for energy.

27. Communicate your goals. Let people help you achieve them.

28. Study the habits of productive people.

29. Get a digital camera. Eliminate film developing and printing.

30. Learn to say "**NO!**"

31. Clump checkups, dentist, and renewals together in your birthday month.

32. Blow up your TV!

Increasing Productivity through Managing Time

Improved time management does not just happen. The best way to get more results from your time is by *conscious, deliberate goal setting,* followed by *planning for achievement* of goals, and then *taking action* to bring these goals into reality.

YOUR SELF IMAGE

The mental picture that you have of yourself or the picture you would like others to have of you, dramatically affects your productivity. Your self-image controls how you use your time. **You act like the kind of person you think you are.** Doing otherwise for any length of time is impossible. People who think they are failures, inevitably fail despite how much time they spend working. Simply trying hard is not enough. People who expect to succeed focus their attention on constructive activities that produce the results they want.

PERSONAL & ORGANIZATIONAL GOALS

To gain full mastery of your attitudes, your time, and your life, you should immerse yourself in a program of setting personal and organizational goals. Many personal goals involve items money can buy. Your work is the means for earning that money. Other personal goals satisfy such intangible needs as security, ego satisfaction, and self-fulfillment that are closely tied to the work environment. When you recognize this relationship both intellectually and emotionally, you realize that goal setting and its associated increased productivity lead to the satisfaction of both your personal and your professional wants.

One element to consider is the *time investment* required for personal and professional goal setting. Companies make calculated decisions on projects to spend time and money. Why should we be different when it comes to *our time?* In other words, our *time, money,* and *career* deserve a well-thought out plan.

VALUE OF WRITTEN GOALS

The goal setting process coupled with careful planning provides a sense of direction that will keep you focused on your most important activities. Goals serve as a filter to eliminate extraneous demands. They bring order and meaning to life. Goals keep you focused on high payoff activities that mobilize your energy toward the best use of your time. *Written goals* ensure that you identify achievements that will prove most meaningful to you. Writing them down *crystallizes* your thinking better than any other method. Crystallized goals mobilize the forces needed to create reality.

SCHEDULE YOUR TIME

Your time is valuable. There is no more time. What you do with it is important. The process of planning and goal setting are powerful time savers.

Wasted time is like generating scrap. Time spent on activities that do not meet your specific goal directed needs, is wasted. You cannot make time. You must schedule time for accomplishing your important goals!

SHARPENING YOUR SAW

You have just completed a tough year during some trying economic times. Nine, ten, eleven, or even twelve hour days were the norm, and you were tired at the end of the year. Holidays are now over and you are back at work. Do you wish you could change some things to work smart and not have to work ten, eleven, or twelve hour days?

If you never take time to find out what to change, then your new year will just be a repeat of the past year. Take some time and sharpen your work skills. They need the same sort of sharpening that a saw does after cutting several cords of wood. Your work skills can get dull just like the teeth of that saw.

HERE IS HOW TO SHARPEN YOUR WORK SKILLS!

1. Sit with your supervisor, discuss, and agree on the six **High Payoff Activities** (or tasks) that make up your work and job. These six tasks provide the greatest value to the business from the time you spend at work. Get them in writing.

2. Make five copies of the *Personal Productivity Analysis Worksheet*. Place one on your desk each day and record your tasks and how much time you spend in each task. Tasks are listed across the top, and a line placed vertically along the column represents how much time you spend in that task. Update the worksheet every hour. Use impeccable honesty. Do this for five days (every day is typical, no excuses). Total the time you spend in each task at the bottom of the page.

51

3. List your tasks along the side of the **Personal Productivity Summary** sheet. Record the total time for each task in the day block that you engaged in the task. Total the hours spent on all tasks each day at the bottom. Then total the hours spent in each task at the right. You are now able to find the percent of your total time spent in each specific task during this study period.

4. Compare the amount and percentage of time spent in each task to the six High Payoff Tasks you and your supervisor agree are what you are being paid to do. Where do changes need to be made?

5. Simplify your work, delegate, or say no to those tasks that are not your High Payoff Tasks.

A time study like this each six months will help keep your saw sharpened. Without this critical analysis of how you use your time, wasteful habits can creep in, expanding the time you work to some unhealthy numbers and rob you of your best work productivity and satisfaction. **Parkinson's Law** says that, **"Work expands to fill the time available."** Do not let this phenomenon creep into your work life. Sharpen your saw today.

Dull Saw

There is a story about a man struggling to cut down enough trees to build a fence. An old farmer came by, watched for a while, then quietly said, "Saw kinda dull, isn't it?"

"I reckon," said the fence builder.

"Hadn't ya better sharpen it?"

"Maybe later. I can't stop now - I got all these trees to cut down."

BUILDING PERSONAL LEADERSHIP

Misconceptions about Time Management

1. Time management is nothing but common sense. I'm doing well at my job, so I must be managing my time just fine.

2. I work better under pressure; time management would take away that edge.

3. I use an appointment calendar and a to-do list. Isn't that enough?

4. People take time management too seriously; it takes all the fun out of life.

5. Time management takes away from your freedom - and I'm a spontaneous sort of person.

6. Time management might be good for some kinds of work, but my job is very creative. I can't be tied to a routine.

7. The stuff they teach you in time management is a lot of work. I don't have time to do all that.

Interruptions

Time is your only resource. You have twenty-four hours each day and how you spend your time determines the results you get and what you enjoy in life. Spending time wisely on the goals and planned priorities of your work and life is essential if you wish to realize your wants, desires, and dreams. And you possess the potential to realize all your wants, desires, and dreams.

THE PROBLEM: It is important to your productivity to train people to respect your time and for you to reciprocally respect the time of others.

The American Management Association says that the normal manager is interrupted eight times during each hour and work that would normally take one hour to complete now takes three hours. That's why many managers come to work before their subordinates, to get more done in the quiet uninterrupted time of the early morning (or after everyone leaves). These managers often have to spend ten, eleven, or even more hours at work each day just to keep up (ugggggggg ... !).

HANDLING INTERRUPTIONS:

1. **Emergency Interruptions**: If the issue or problem is a **High Payoff Activity** (HPA) and **Urgent**, then it is an emergency. Emergencies are valid reasons to interrupt your planned non-urgent HPA work. Handle the issue or problem as quickly as possible and return to your planned non-urgent HPA work.

2. **Non-Emergency Interruptions**: If the interruption (issue, problem, or communication) is a **low-payoff activity** or is **non-urgent**, then it is an activity that interrupts your planned HPA work. You recognize this interruption when someone walks into your office to share information that is not an HPA, or is not urgent. When I coach managers, I look for someone who is interrupting us and ask them, **"Is this communication a high payoff activity** (important)? **Is the communication urgent?"** If the answer is **NO** to either question, I instruct them to come back at a specific scheduled time for the manager to deal with that non-HPA or non-urgent communication. It works! Try it!

THE FIX: The real "**root cause fix**" is to **train the people who interact with you** to respect your time. Ask them to list their issues, problems, or communications and to share that list with you during a block of time you schedule. During the scheduled visit, share your list of issues, problems, or communications with them. In other words, instead of interrupting each time an issue or problem surfaces, you and your employees schedule times during the day to communicate non-HPA and non-urgent issues and problems. As a model of productivity, you must also respect your employee's time and not interrupt them except during mutually scheduled blocks of time, or for emergencies. Always remember that **Emergencies** are always valid reasons for interruptions. Instruct your employees that for emergencies you will stop whatever you are doing and help them.

RESPONSIBILITY: As a manager or supervisor, it is your responsibility to manage interruptions by training yourself and those who interact with you. Finding and fixing the root causes of all interruptions will prevent them in the future. It is the manager and supervisor's responsibility to manage interruptions both effectively and efficiently to optimize the productivity of both themselves and those they supervise. Don't neglect your responsibility! **What will you do today to manage interruptions more productively**? Do it now!

Procrastination

Procrastination is the lack of a decision and action! Think about it, if you don't make a decision and if you don't take any actions, what is the result? If you do decide to do something and you take action on your decision, what is the result? I would say it would mean progress toward your goal. That's all that it takes, a decision and action, and you will make things happen.

Fixing Problems

Are you responding to problems and fixing them or are you going deeper and discovering their root causes and fixing them? **That is the big question!** Just fixing the problems leads to more of the same kinds of problems. Fixing the root causes of problems leads to a smoother running operation. On a daily basis, which approach to work and problem solving do you choose?

No excuses now. In whatever position you work, you need not only to solve problems but it is necessary to take the actions needed to prevent them. It's called continuous improvement of your work processes. This approach to work can make your work experience easier and more interesting. Not approaching problems in this way can cause your work to become drudgery and frustrating.

Approaching your work processes is only half of the equation. Looking and improving your own working skills and knowledge is the other half. Do you spend time to look at how you do work, take time to assess the knowledge you need to become more effective, and evaluate the skills you must develop to advance in your chosen field of service? If not, why not? Now don't use the tired excuses of there isn't any time, I'm too busy, I can't right now, etc. These are self-limitations to your future advancement and success.

Take control of your future and schedule time to improve both your work processes and your own skills and knowledge. Create the future you dream about. Invest in developing your life passion and becoming successful.

■ CHAPTER FIVE ■
PRIORITIZATION

*"The key to setting priorities, the order in which
you must accomplish things, is to ask yourself,
What is my payoff in doing this activity? How does
this fit in with my long-term objectives...?"*

- Success Magazine

By observing or recalling the tasks you start and complete you determine your actual priorities. That's right, what you work on each day is a direct reflection of where you have actually placed your priorities.

Efficiency experts say you should prioritize your tasks, plan your work, and work your plan. But what you give your attention to and actually accomplish, show your real priorities. This begs an important question.

Is what you are doing each day contributing to getting what you want, helping you achieve your work / life mission or vision, and creating what you want to create? If not, why not?

Could the answer be that you have not taken time to think and set priorities? Have you failed to plan the actions you must take to get what you want? Perhaps because you are afraid of failure, or success, you hesitate to start. Maybe you are not quite as focused on actual priorities as you might be? ***You decide.*** Tune up your planning, step out in the direction of your dreams, and realize the results you want.

Prioritizing the Important

If you observe what you do, then you can identify what your priorities are. Many things are vying for your attention and action. In the world of business there is usually more work than a person can do. But if you list each piece of work and then prioritize them according to the value they add to the product or service you provide, you might find that some work is not so important and should be completed by someone else. Notice. I said list each piece of work. Without listing you must depend on your mind to keep the list and I don't know about you, but if I don't write my commitments and tasks down, I sometimes forget.

What are your most important priorities in work and life? Of course they will be different for each person but I want to seed one idea with you today. That idea is, "**If you don't take care of yourself**, then how can you give your best to others (at work or in your personal life)?" If you don't prioritize and take time to eat healthy foods, keep in good physical condition, pursue more knowledge, develop new skills, and sleep in appropriate amounts, then what are you giving to those you serve (customers, fellow workers, friends, or your family)? To give your best you must take care of yourself and develop more of your potential.

Taking care of yourself is something we often neglect. Learning about and eating healthy foods, exercising to keep your body healthy, and sleeping until you are rested are critical elements to performing at your best. Pursuing knowledge and developing new skills are fundamental activities in developing more of your potential, understanding more about work and life, and advancing in your vocation.

You see, the better you take care of yourself and develop more of your potential, the more you have available to give to others. And that is what we live to do, serve others and contribute to the world around us. But if you are fatigued, weary, tired, and consumed by your duties and commitments, what do you give to others? So what must you do? You must **set priorities**, take care of yourself and develop more knowledge and skills. It is not being selfish. It is about prioritizing what you do so that you have more of everything to give to those you love, care about, and serve.

Don't let life and work, trap you into not taking care of yourself and stagnating you in your knowledge and skills. Set the goals you need to take care of yourself and develop more of your potential. Then take action to achieve those goals. Take at least one action every day for the rest of your life.

Priorities & Motivation

What or who sets your priorities? Is it the customer, supervisor, co-workers, work orders, environment, corporate headquarters, or is it *you*? When everything else sets your priorities all of the time, you will feel like you are out of control. Feeling out of control will drastically increase frustration and stress while reducing your productivity and motivation.

Many of us must respond to emergencies (HPA & Urgent situations) and that removes some control from our work and life. But, you need not let all your time be controlled by others and urgent situations! If you plan and schedule just one hour a day to work on prioritized action steps, keep that commitment to yourself, and work on the highest priority items, you will complete high value tasks regularly.

Completing high value tasks will regularly result in feelings of accomplishment, progress, increased self-worth and self-esteem, growth, and satisfaction with work and life. I call these feelings Self-Motivation (the best kind). Self-motivation is one characteristic of successful people (goal directed and positive mental attitudes are the other two).

In summary, set your priorities, block an hour a day to work on the most important tasks, and keep the commitment to yourself to control at least part of your day and work. At the end of the day, acknowledge and celebrate the progress you are making toward the most important goals in your work and life.

Too Busy

SITUATION: How often have you heard someone say, or felt yourself that you were "Too Busy" to do something that you really wanted to do? It's a national phenomenon! Often you feel like you just cannot find the time to do the things that you want because you are too busy. Get ready. Because I am going to tell you that being "Too Busy" is just an excuse for not setting priorities and taking action on your important tasks. That's right, being "Too Busy" is just a convenient expression for not taking responsibility for accomplishing your important tasks. Instead, you assign the blame for not doing what is important to the phenomenon of being "Too Busy."

CHOICE: Everything you do is a choice. If you choose to neglect doing something for any reason, then that is a choice. What you do, expresses your priorities. List what you do and see if it accurately describes what is important to you in your work (and life). Once you discover that what you do does not accurately describe your priorities, then it is time to change what you do.

TAKING CONTROL: If you wish to take control of your life and not be "Too Busy," you must become conscious of the important activities in your work and life. You must focus your time on those activities. List your priorities and consciously rank them from most important to least important. Then plan the use of your time around your priorities. Knowing that you are focused on the most important activities in your work and life enables you to dismiss the lesser priority tasks that don't get done. You are accomplishing the most important tasks in work and life and not missing anything important.

LESSON: Consciously set your priorities. Plan and schedule your time to accomplish those priorities. Never use the excuse "Too Busy" because you are focused on what is important. Become more able to respond to how you spend your time.

■ Chapter Six ■
ORGANIZATION

"Disorganization is the playground of inefficiency, mental burdens and added stress..."

Quick! What do you think when you walk into a person's office that has piles of paper on the desk, a full trash can, moldy coffee on the table, and an overall sloppy appearance? If you are like most, you probably walk away, feeling that this person is **out of control**.

Now, how do you feel when you walk into an office where the desk is relatively clean, things seem to be in order, and there is no sign of panic in sight? Which of those two people do you think have things in control? Which person do you think would be the obvious choice to lead others, assuming all other factors are equal? Sure, you would choose the **neat freak** - the orderly desk of the person who is **obviously in control**.

Fair or not, people determine your organizational skills by what they see around your workspace. A cluttered desk is not a signal of being a busy, important person. The cluttered desk is a **signal of confusion and inefficiency** that **creates stress** for most people. The obvious choice is a well-organized work space that transmits an effective and efficient appearance.

Another thing: Organization isn't confined to your desktop. Look at your calendar. Is it booked to the max or do you have time to handle daily paperwork, routine tasks, and last-minute meetings? Check your e-mail inbox. Does it have hundreds of once read e-mails still languishing? Do you have the time to complete the important things that pop-up every day? Do you have time to take advantage of the opportunities that come your way each day? Get yourself organized so that you will convey a sense of control, efficiency, and pride that others will want to follow.

Clutter is the result of not deciding to take time to clean up your messes. Not deciding is a choice you make. The consequences and perception of that decision are a lack of self-control, inefficiency, and not caring. Conquering clutter is as simple as making a choice and taking action. These ten organizational tips will help you decrease the clutter:

1. **Know how you spend your time**. Keep track of how you spend your time for two or three days. The results will show you where your time is invested. Delegate, simplify, eliminate, or say **"NO"** to the **Low Payoff Activities** (LPAs). Use your newfound time to get and stay organized.

2. **Create a "Conference Planner"** for your boss, subordinates, and peers. Unless it is a real emergency (urgent & high payoff activity), wait until you have at least two or three written communication items before interrupting that person with your thoughts or questions.

3. **Take a speed-reading course**. The time you save can be spent doing high payoff activities related to achieving your work and life goals.

4. Become a person of decision. Decide and act now on papers, e-mails, and other communication or work items you receive. Don't procrastinate!

5. Take small steps to handle the mountains of lifelong clutter. Bite the bullet and do one small organizing task every day. Over a period of weeks, the steady progress you make will motivate you to conquer the remaining stress-mountain.

6. Always finish what you start. Take the extra few minutes it takes and finish the job. Make sure that the work is complete and that there are no undone messy leftovers.

7. Throw things away. Ask yourself, "What is the worst thing that could happen if I throw this away?" Most of the time, you can live with your answer. So start filling your wastebasket. Are you not comfortable with throwing things away? Find the office "pack rat" that has every memo and letter for years and become their new best friend. Love that person - but throw your trash away!

8. Keep the paper and e-mail moving! Act on the paper or e-mail and move them to your pending file / folder, your out basket, filing system, "to read" folder, or to your trash can. Don't let paper or e-mails sit. Handle them!

9. Analyze your attitude toward staying organized. Has a habit of thought conditioned you to tolerate clutter or reject organization? Question the underlying assumptions and logic. If your present attitude somehow limits your success, reject the old attitude and use affirmations to establish a new habit of thought for getting rid of clutter and staying organized.

10. Plan tomorrow's work! Do these things before you leave the office:

- Clear and organize your desk & computer.

- Close out your day. Transfer all items not accomplished today to tomorrow's to-do list and check your goals for action steps you want to take tomorrow.

- Prioritize the next day's to-do list (action steps) and plan your next day's work schedule in detail.

Then, go home.

Planning the next day before you leave reduces stress and allows you to enjoy your time away from the office and get a quick start in the morning. To un-clutter allows you to focus on the important things in work and life. After all, that's why you clean out the garage from time to time, isn't it? Un-clutter.

Love It or Use It!

This time of year is the right time to simplify your life so that you can focus on the things that are important. We all gather clutter throughout the year or years. One thing is certain about clutter. Clutter distracts you. The brain is forced to process more data than it should, and this is mentally draining. It robs you of productivity and mental space for thinking! It wastes precious materials and resources and it limits using more of your potential for work and life.

The following is a simple rule to help you handle clutter. It is extracted from writings about Feng Shui. Consider each item that you have and ask yourself, "Do I **Love It** or **Use It**." If you **Love It** or **Use It** then keep it. If it falls outside these categories get it out of your life! No matter how long or good you think you are at living with clutter, those people who eliminate clutter sense a load lifted. They have more energy, increased productivity, and because of the freedom that comes with an uncluttered life, they experience more joy. Even if it takes you a whole day to un-clutter, you will still have 364 days to enjoy the liberating feeling.

The "5 S" for Your Work Space

The "**5 S**" is a process for creating and maintaining an organized, clean, high-performance workplace. It creates a work environment where people can focus on their work undistracted by clutter and unnecessary materials and tools. It leads to more effective and efficient work, and greater productivity. There are five steps to the 5 S process. They are as follows:

1. **Sorting**: This separates the necessary from the unnecessary. Unnecessary tools, equipment, and procedures need to be removed from the workplace.

2. **Simplifying**: This puts everything in its place and organizes material according to how frequently it is used. Visual aids are encouraged to aid understanding and reduce complexity.

3. **Sweeping**: This makes everything neat and clean. By identifying potential problems with a regular physical and visual sweep, unsafe and inefficient conditions or damaged equipment can be dealt with early in the process.

4. **Standardizing:** This defines how a task should be done and lets everyone involved in the process know what is the "best way"

to do something. Process changes are documented and shared as they occur.

5. Self-discipline: This ensures that all 5 S policies are adhered to in daily work. It will pave the way for success in other continuous quality improvement efforts.

All five steps are equally applicable to your office, work cubicle, or work area. Now, here is your assignment. Schedule one hour this week and apply the 5 S process to your work area. If you do eliminate the clutter and get better organized, your mind will become more open to the important things of work and life. In addition, you will sense a great load lifted from your mind and you will feel more alive and happier. Don't believe me, try it!

Desk Stress

North America produces more than thirty billion documents annually each year. At least 80% of that ends up in the trash can. After checking some work spaces in your business, you know where the other 20% goes. All the office clutter causes increased thinking and data processing and sometimes causes frustration, energy drain, and brain overload. Indecision or procrastination, clutter and confusion, and frustration / anxiety over clutter will cause a syndrome known as **Desk Stress**. Desk stress can lead to reduced productivity, ineffective work periods, workers becoming ill and thus increased absenteeism.

Desks are typically littered with notes, files, items that need to be filed, phone message post-it-notes, fax messages, important projects, unimportant projects, objects scattered around, newspapers, magazines, trade journals, and executive toys your mother-in-law gave you for your birthday.

68

Keeping an organized and uncluttered desk can easily save you thirty minutes each day. If you spend three minutes a day looking for something ten times, you spend thirty minutes each day times 240 workdays per year or three weeks a year looking for things. With a typical salary rate of $25 per hour, the cost of disorganization is $3,000. The payback for every minute spent in organizing is three to one. Don't use excuses like, "but that is the way I am." *Take action now and get organized.* Remember that many people perceive your workspace as a reflection of your work habits and mind. If you are a leader, how do your people perceive your model of productivity?

The E-Mail Curse

Curse those e-mails. We are all living with the curse, the e-mail curse. Many people get between seventy-five and 100 e-mails each day. Some people find it difficult to keep up or just plain cannot!

CURSE: I have seen more than 800 e-mails in a person's inbox. Wow! It made my mind tumble out of control. I felt like dealing with the e-mail workload was impossible (the person did too). However, habits and procrastination kept them from taking control and managing their e-mail. Their excuses were, I look for the bolded ones, I use the find function, I need to keep them for reference, and I know where the important ones are. It was so interesting, I asked a person to find an e-mail I sent a week or so ago. After using the find function multiple times for about five minutes and failing to find the e-mail, I asked them to stop wasting their time and my time.

TIPS: The following are some tips on managing e-mail:

- Handle each e-mail once - decide
  - o Delete it (no action needed)

69

    o   Handle it now (quickly take action to complete the item)

    o   File it (store in a folder created for storage)

    o   Schedule it for future action

• **Schedule for future action** - Set up a daily tickler file of electronic folders (one to thirty-one days). Click and drag the actionable e-mail into the day folder that the action is to be started. It will be stored there until the day before when you will visit the folder, prioritize the work for the next day, and schedule the item to be worked on. If the work is to be done in another month, set up monthly folders for January through December. Visit the monthly folders at the beginning of the month and move items into the start days (one to thirty-one day tickler file). Alternately, you could print the e-mail and use a paper tickler file system.

• **Schedule several short time blocks** during the day when "low payoff activity" can be accomplished and handle all the e-mails that arrive in your inbox. Alternately, when you finish a task early or come back to your office early, take the available time you have till your next scheduled activity start time to clean out your inbox.

• **Keep your inbox empty** but do not respond to the sound of arriving e-mail. Pavlov's dog experiments resulted in conditioning with electricity or food rewards. Do not become the conditioned dog of your e-mails!

• **Allow yourself to feel good** about great e-mail management (inbox empty). Being "**In Control**" and having a well-managed inbox is a model of workplace efficiency and productivity!

70

ETIQUETTE: One last thought. In my opinion, there is e-mail etiquette. Great communication practices require that you *acknowledge e-mails that affect or could positively affect your work and the results you desire.* Take a few seconds to keyboard an answer or respond to the sender. Acknowledging the person who sent you e-mail completes the communication and builds rapport and trust. Failing to do this is disrespectful of the person and of the value they are hoping to add to your results and success. You can build goodwill by valuing and respecting the people who are trying to help you. Or, you can ignore them and suffer the loss of good will you could have created. I observe many executives and people who are unaware (or lazy, busy, in crisis, procrastinating, etc.) of the benefits that could come from good e-mail etiquette. Valuing / respecting people and modeling productive e-mail habits and attitudes will pay great dividends and results. It is always your choice!

Handling E-mail Effectively and Efficiently

About time, huh! Ninety e-mails a day and two to three hours of work. Not HPA or fun in my book. The following are a few ideas to speed up your handling of e-mail.

Have incoming e-mails screened if possible. Train, and trust someone else to:

- Handle it (give authority to answer, discard, delegate, or decide for you).

- Delegate (give to someone else who can handle the issue for you. If important, have the person handling them keep you informed).

- File (if not HPA or Urgent, file in electronic folders that form your thirty-one days and monthly tickler files. Keep other historical or archival information filed in appropriate electronic filing folders).

• Forward (those e-mails that require your personal attention remain in your inbox or are forwarded to you).

NOTE: When you train and trust an assistant, they will be motivated, feel valued, and develop better job skills. You will both benefit, and win.

If you do not have an assistant to screen your e-mail, help yourself out by making a decision about each piece of e-mail as soon as you read it. Take these actions:

• Delete it!

• Move to review / work on it later (thirty-one day tickler and monthly folders).

• Send it to someone else for action or information (create a tracking system so you can follow up, move to a to-do-list).

• Respond to it. Do it now!

• Once you look at the e-mail, handle it. Give it a final disposition, if possible.

Keep your inbox empty. Hundreds of e-mails in your inbox psychologically is depressing and makes your feel "out of control." When it is empty, you feel gooooooooooooood!

■ CHAPTER SEVEN ■
COMMUNICATION

"Everything we do or don't do communicates a message."

Feedback is the breakfast of champions. It is a Gift that each person can use to grow or discard as she or he chooses. It is essential to life. The more we get, the better we will become. Without feedback we would be lost. Here is why. Without feedback, we would not:

- be able to drive to work.
- know how much money we have spent or saved.
- know how we affect the people with whom we interact.
- know if we were working on the right things or the wrong things.
- be able to choose our favorite food to eat.
- be able to guide our children in growing up.
- be able to correct mistakes we make.
- be able to grow as a person.
- be able to care for ourselves (live).

Our attitude over receiving feedback will greatly affect our performance and rate of growth as a person and leader. A productive attitude for feedback is realizing it as a Gift given to you by someone who cares for you. You can choose your attitude, so no matter how it may be given, you can receive it in a positive way. Receive it as a true and welcome gift, as it can be extremely valuable to you. The more feedback you receive with serious consideration, and take action on, the more competent, effective, and productive you will become. Ultimately, this attitude will make you more successful. I want to be more successful, don't you?

Giving Feedback

The following is a simple formula for giving the gift of feedback. It is called the **STAR technique**. STAR stands for:

1. **ST**: **Specific Target**. The *specific situation* that you are giving feedback about. Describe the situation and time of your feedback.

2. **A**: **Action**. The *action or behavior* that you are giving feedback about.

3. **R**: **Result**. The *effect on you* of the specific target situation and action.

Like any new action you take, it takes practice to become good at a new endeavor. Likewise it takes practice to give great and valuable feedback. I promise that if you practice the STAR technique fifty times and learn from your mistakes, you will become great at giving the gift of feedback. You will make mistakes, but risking and learning, and finally becoming competent at the skill of giving great feedback will be worth it. People will value and seek your gifts. Thanks to all of you who consider me valuable enough to give me the **Gift** of feedback.

Feedback is a "Gift"

Effective feedback is one of the most difficult things to give. It is even more difficult to receive. Have you ever experienced defensiveness, hurt feelings, or attack when someone gave you feedback? Do you ever grumble to yourself about the person who seemed to lashed out at you with that misinformed observation?

In systems theory, feedback is absolutely essential to the proper operation of the system. Error signals provide the input to devices that correct deviations and ensure proper operation. Humans are complex systems. The body is a complex system. It operates many subsystems like metabolism and temperature, blood chemistry and flow, heartbeat and exercise, and much more. Each of our many systems utilizes automatic feedback mechanisms to make life-sustaining corrections that keep our bodies functioning normally. When changes can't be made, we become ill, needing a doctor's help (correction). Without needed corrections, the body will expire and cease to function.

Our mind needs feedback! The feedback comes as data from our environment. Unfortunately, that data is filtered through our world view and much of it can be lost before it ever gets to our mind. Our world view is made up of ingrained and habitual thoughts we have accumulated over years of processing data, and making sense out of that data. It manifests itself in what we call our beliefs and belief system. If we believe that feedback is often incorrect and an attack to our ego, then that feedback can be severely filtered to prevent it from hurting us. If we believe that a person wants to harm us, we may avoid the feedback or block it before it is given. If we believe we are right and the other person is wrong, then we may be blinded to the data as it is presented to us. Our beliefs, attitudes, and habitual reactions to feedback can become huge blocks to the corrections our mind needs to function.

Our attitude toward feedback. For our mind to get quality feedback, it must be completely open to receiving. All limiting beliefs, habitual thoughts, and attitudes must be set aside and our mind must receive and process the data by our mind, unencumbered. A thought that may help you do this is to think of the feedback coming from any source as a "Gift." You normally enjoy receiving "Gifts," don't you? Place yourself into the frame of mind that you are receiving a "Gift" from someone. Receive it unfiltered and without judgment. No matter what the history you have with that person or how it sounds as it is received, suspend judgment and receive the message. Then, thank the person for giving you the "Gift." Really show appreciation for your "Gift." Then, take some time to think about the feedback. Look for the gems of information that can help you make the corrections to get the results you want to get. It is all about attitude. It needs to be an "Attitude of Gratitude" toward receiving feedback. Without feedback, you will live a life "out of control." Without feedback, you will not get the things you most want in life. Seek out feedback to accelerate the progress you can make toward enjoying the things you want.

Improve Your Accountability

You can improve your own ability to remain "**Above the Line**" (accountable) by watching for the following clues that indicate "accountable" attitudes and behaviors. You are accountable if you:

- **Invite candid feedback from everyone about your own performance**.

- Never allow anyone, including yourself, to hide the truth from you.

- Readily acknowledge reality, including all its problems.

- Don't waste time or energy on things you cannot control or influence.

- Always commit yourself 100 percent to what you are doing, and if your commitment begins to wane, strive to rekindle it.

- "**Own**" your circumstances and your results, even when they seem less than desirable.

- Recognize when you are dropping "**Below the Line**" (unaccountable) and act quickly to avoid the traps of the victim cycle.

- Delight in the daily opportunity to make things happen.

- Constantly ask yourself the question, "**What else can I do to rise above my circumstances and get the results I want?**"

When you think, and act in these ways, you are functioning *"Above the Line."* Rising above your circumstances to get the results you seek is the empowering principle of being accountable.

P.S. Extracted from the book, "The OZ Principle: Getting Results through Individual and Organizational Accountability" by Roger Connor, Tom Smith, & Craig Hickman.

Handling Problems!

When a problem comes to you via an employee who is capable of solving it, the worst thing you can do is to solve it for him or her. If you do, they learn they can depend on you to solve their problems. Your workload goes up, frustration increases, and your stress along with it. If you can train the person to solve the problem themselves, then you win and the employee wins. What follows is a simple step-by-step process to teach problem solving.

1. Ask them, "Clearly, tell me what the problem is?" Paraphrase it back so you know what it is. The trick here is to continue questioning until they learn clearly to state the real problem, not the effects.

2. Ask them, "What are all the possible solutions?" Sometimes it is good to write them down (dry erase board, paper, etc.). Offer a possible solution only if they miss an obvious one. Get creative here and have them list as many as possible.

3. Ask him or her, "Of all the solutions, which one do you feel (or think) is the best one?" Get them to choose. If it is a plausible solution, you go to the next step. If it is not a workable solution, then massage it with the person and help them to choose a better one. The test of the solution is whether it will cause a greater problem. If not, let them try it and it can become a learning experience that does not disrupt the operation too much. Remember, you are training them to problem solve.

4. Tell them, "I think that is worth a try. Go ahead and implement it and see how it works." Have them walk away and still own the problem, solution, and responsibility for getting results.

5. Ask them, "Let me know by the end of the shift (week, or any period) the results you get." Make sure you track the follow-up time and check up if they do not get back with you. If they do

not, then you have another training problem, but this time around it involves accountability.

Try it. After a few times the employee will learn that you will ask the same questions and they will begin to solve their own problems without interrupting or burdening you. You may want to establish control thresholds (dollar impact) around problem solutions where the employee either consults with you before solution implementation or where they routinely inform you of their actions.

Working Better Together

If you choose to do this exercise, you might discover some actions that can improve your working and other relationships. Here goes:

Think of yourself and the people who work closely with you as a team of management specialists who plan and direct your time and activities. List each person who has some effect on your time. These people might be individuals you report to, peers, individuals you supervise, family members, or clients. Then for each person, write your answers to the following questions:

1. What is the effect of this person's behavior on my time?
2. What is the effect of my behavior on the team member's time?

Review your answers and identify a specific action you can take for improving your relationships. You know what the next step is. Take action.

Meetings

Everyone complains about meetings but few people do anything to increase their effectiveness and value. The reason: "that's the way things are done around here." We have allowed ourselves to become conditioned to waste time. The way we normally run meetings (mostly unspoken business norms) perpetuates inefficiencies. Someone must take a stand and "bust the norms." Someone must insist that all meetings are held in an effective and productive manner. One meeting with six participants shortened by fifteen minutes each day over a year will result in a savings of sixty hours per person, or 360 hours per group of six. This is worth more than $7,200 if valued at $20/hour. If you don't save fifteen minutes each day, you are wasting $7,200 of your company's money!

The following are some meeting ideas:

- Complete a Meeting Planner sheet for each meeting. Distribute a copy to all attendees before the meeting so they can prepare.

  o Write a **clear purpose** for the meeting.

  o Identify and write down the **desired outcomes** of the meeting.

  o Propose a **detailed agenda** with specific times in minutes (modify it at the beginning of the meeting if needed). Annotate the person who is responsible for presenting each agenda item.

  o Make sure all attendees are needed (other forms of communication can be used to share results of the meeting). If attendees only need to be there for certain times, let them know so they don't show up for the entire meeting.

- Calculate the **per minute cost** of the meeting. Inform everyone at the start. Make sure the cost of the meeting is in line with the value of the desired outcome. If it is not, explore other ways of achieving the desired outcome at less cost.

• Have a **code of conduct** (meeting norms) and use them. Have a participant volunteer for the role of "**Code Keeper.**" Have consequences for breaking the norms established ahead of time (a company I worked with had code breakers make animal noises. It became such fun).

• **Lock the door** at the start of the meeting. If someone is late, they will not be able to enter and therefore miss the meeting. If they needed to be there, they won't make that mistake twice!

• Establish roles for participants like, a leader, a facilitator, a code keeper, a timer, a scribe, etc. Have the team establish the role responsibilities.

• **Write minutes during the meeting**. Instead of spending an hour or two doing minutes, capture the decisions, important findings, and action items (and a person responsible) as you proceed, on the back of the Meeting Planner. Make copies before the meeting is over and distribute to attendees as they leave.

• After the meeting, **communicate the results** with the people who need to know or should know about the results. E-mail is a wonderful thing.

• If you are a leader, **take responsibility** for running an effective and productive meeting. If you are a leader, **make sure others hold effective and productive meetings**. Insist on not wasting money in unplanned or poorly planned spur-of-the-moment meetings.

Almost every company can benefit from properly planned and held meetings. If you look at the cost in time and dollars in today's competitive environment, holding effective and efficient meetings could significantly add to your competitive advantage. At the least, money saved will add to bottom line profits of the organization. It is everyone's responsibility to ensure that meetings are not a waste of their time. You don't want to waste your life, do you?

Cut Waste in Meetings!

The following is a simplified list of the ideas to help you run a more effective and efficient meeting.

Plan the meeting in detail. Beside the regular information (date, start & end time, place, attendees), include:

- Clear and detailed **purpose** of the meeting.

- Carefully chosen **participant list**. Have only the essential people come. Communicate meeting results to others using alternative communication tools (minutes, e-mail, telephone, etc).

- Preliminary meeting **participant preparation** required (to make the best use of meeting time).

- Each planned **topic, time allowed, and person** responsible for leading that topic (agenda).

- Distribute this plan in writing or e-mail to all participants in time to prepare.

PREP THE MEETING PLACE.

• Meeting behavior **norms** posted (acceptable / unacceptable meeting behaviors and consequence of infractions).

• **Parking lot** posted (record topics not on the agenda / issues surfacing in discussions).

• **Cost** of meeting per minute or hour posted where all can see (summed wage rate of all participants including yourself).

• All **tools/aids** present, in working order, prepped, and ready to use.

CONDUCTING THE MEETING.

• **Start on time**. Starting late **sends a message** that **wasting time is okay** in your meeting. Some leaders lock the door at start time and don't let anyone enter. They know that if the meeting is important enough, people will make sure that they get there on time the next time.

• **Review the agenda** and modify or add if things have changed.

• **Facilitate, facilitate, facilitate**. The leader is responsible for use of time in the meeting. He or she is responsible for the wise spending of time (money).

• Stay on topic and time (by consensus, the time can be expanded if necessary).

• Enforce the meeting norms (or have someone looking for infractions).

• Use the parking lot for stray issues.

• Keep meeting minutes during the meeting (write down action items including person responsible and target date due, decisions made, and other important information or results). Copy these minutes and hand out at the end of the meeting. Alternately, this could be done with e-mail by someone not leading the meeting.

• **Conduct a meeting assessment.** Use the + and **D** (delta) method. What were the good parts of the meeting (+) and what can be done to make better use of meeting time (**D**). Act on the improvements or plan to suffer the same waste in your next meeting.

With proper planning and facilitation, most meetings can be held in a fraction of the time that is usually spent. Spent is a good word, because meetings spend your time and money - time and money that could be used in other activities that can bring you revenue, reduce costs, and accomplish important tasks. Assess your meetings today. If they waste any time at all, then take actions to become a good steward of time and increase the respect for people's time.

A Communication Disease & How to Cure It

Uh-oh! The boss just stuck his head in the room again. Everyone clams up. The meaningful exchange of information ceases. Nobody from the department is willing to say anything of substance in front of the boss. No matter how hard the boss tries to encourage his team members to speak their minds, nobody does. Your colleagues say they do, but they do not. The word on the street is that the messenger gets shot or that the boss doesn't listen to, or value, feedback from his department members. Does this sound familiar? This condition destroys work effectiveness and productivity.

84

How did it get this way? The boss didn't know it, but one day a new employee questioned the details of his work and suggested some improvement that needed to be made. Acting defensively, the boss denied the needed improvement, dismissed the feedback as unimportant, and insisted on his way. Happening several times with the same employee, the employee gives up and now only communicates what he or she thinks the boss wants to hear. The employee is closed down, demoralized, and less productive. Meaningful communication and honest feedback are severely degraded because the boss is not open to learning and acting positively on his or her employees' feedback. The boss and the employee now have a Communication Disease. Is this disease in your company, department, or life?

BOSS: WHAT YOU CAN DO IS ...

- Become aware of how you communicate. Understand yourself and how you react to situations. Learn that your actions are a choice. Choose only positive responses, for they have positive outcomes.

- Seek feedback from everyone, especially your employees. Treat their feedback as a gift. Genuinely thank every giver. Every day, ask for feedback multiple times. Respond only in a positive way. Don't shoot, but thank the messenger.

- Show courage in conversations by revealing what you think, believe, and feel. Risk having to take the time to communicate more thoroughly to understand and be understood. Care about the person with whom you are speaking.

- Develop a burning desire to learn, grow, and develop better communication skills. Become an expert at listening, communicating, trusting, and valuing people. These are the keys to your long term success, effectiveness, and productivity.

EMPLOYEE: WHAT YOU CAN DO IS: EVERYTHING THE BOSS CAN DO +

• Become aware of your closed down condition. Find the courage to change your responses in a positive way. Communicate the full reality of this and every situation. Understand, embrace, and value the long term benefits of more effective communication because, they far outweigh the short term risks.

■ CHAPTER EIGHT ■
GETTING CONTROL

"If you don't run you own life, somebody else will."

- John Atkinson

Putting Out Fires

FIREFIGHTING: Friday I called a potential customer and was told that the President was putting out fires. I know that firefighting is a common activity of executives, managers, and supervisors. But, is firefighting the best use of their time?

HEROES: Putting out fires is psychologically satisfying. A problem surfaces, and the executive takes it on, fixes it, and becomes an instant hero. Having many fires to fight during the day lets the firefighter become a hero often, and it makes them look invaluable to the functioning of the organization. Yet, is firefighting the best use of their time?

REAL FIREFIGHTERS: I will bet that even firefighters responding to a real fire take a more planned approach to their work. They arrive on the scene of a fire, respond to the immediate needs, then develop a strategy to beat the flames. Then they pro-actively and systematically extinguish the fire. Of course, a major part of their work is associated with preventing fires. That's more worthwhile, isn't it!

HANDLING FIRES: Some fire fighting in business may be unavoidable. When a problem is urgent and a High Payoff Activity (what the person is getting paid to do), then it must be handled right away. Get the problem under control and immediately get back to the planned work that brings the most value to you and your company.

PREVENTION: At the end of the day, set aside some time to do the following. Look over the fires fought and fixed. Identify the root cause of the biggest problem. Then, identify a permanent solution that will prevent it in the future. Implement that solution, and check to see if the problem is permanently fixed. Finally, institutionalize the solution. By institutionalize, I mean to incorporate the solution into a work procedure, work instruction, check sheet, employee manual, or other document that ensures that the problem does not happen again. How wonderful work would be if problems were prevented rather than just fixed for today.

MODELING PREVENTION: Executives, managers, and supervisors all have the responsibility to model and create a work environment where people prevent problems rather than just fix them. To create that environment, executives, managers, and supervisors must "walk-the-talk" when it comes to preventing problems. Are you modeling the behavior of problem prevention or are you only firefighting? You know the change to make!

More Control!

Getting caught up in the hustle and bustle of work, business and life is so easy, that we sometimes just react to events, instead of managing events for the best long-term results. Our reactions are sometimes survival tactics that when used often become habits. These reactive survival habits are often so automatic and ingrained in how we work that we don't think about them or scrutinize them for their long-term effect on our work or life. Often we are unaware that we have developed unproductive habits and so we see no need to change how we handle our work or live our lives. You can recognize this situation in yourself if you feel like you have lost or have no control of your work or life (stress, the bad kind). You might feel overwhelmed. What is a person to do to get back in control? The following are a couple of ideas:

- Stop what you are doing! Take a few minutes and list all the tasks you need to do. Then, set priorities within the task list. Start work only on the highest priority task. When finished, move onto the next highest task and so on … If you don't get all your tasks done, at least the most important ones are completed.

- Manage interruptions so you have uninterrupted blocks of time you can work on your prioritized task list. **Train people** who interact with you to **respect & protect your working time**.

- Take the time to **fix problems** (crises, issues, etc.) **at the root cause level**. Prevention is the best proactive approach to taking control and improving your productivity.

- Change what you are doing to get the results you want. Ask yourself, "**What more can I do to rise above my circumstances and get the results that I want?**"

- At the end of the day, take five minutes and reflect back on your work looking for ways to improve how you work. Apply your lessons learned to making your next day go even better. This is called, "**Continuous Improvement**." Take time to do it!

Remember that "If you do what you have always done, you will get what you have always gotten." We live in a cause and effect world! Choose to make the changes you need to make to give yourself more control over your work and life.

Who is in Control?

My boss is in control, my husband or wife is in control, my parents are in control, my customers are in control, but I am not in control! How often we feel that other people control our lives and determine what happens to us, or that our economic plight often controls what and where we work and what we do. Who really is in control?

The answer is that we are in control of our life and work! However, our childhood experiences, beliefs, and conditioning provide guides for our living that determine success or the rightness of what we do. So we follow the guidelines to success that others have imposed upon us as we grew up. Our behaviors are closely managed to remain within the "acceptable limits" of living taught by your extended family and work group. But is that really what you were put on this earth to achieve or do? My belief is that we are endowed with unlimited potential and only we can limit the development of that potential. So we thank our past coaches for the past successes they have brought us.

If our past has limited our growth and potential development, then we can choose to discard those limits, take control, and develop into the person we want and were meant to be. We can choose to follow our heart, our aspirations, and make the unique contribution we were placed on this earth to make. Yes, it may not be instantaneous or at the rate we would like, but choices to control where we are going in life and the contributions we make are ours alone. We can give the control to others or we can seize it and guide ourselves in determining our destiny. **Who is in control**? Are we in control or are others? Are we determining our destiny or are other people with limiting beliefs or influences? It's our choice and no one can take it from us. We can decide to give control away or to take control. It is always and forever our choice.

Tyranny of the Urgent

Do you picture what the **Tyranny of the Urgent** looks like? That is where other people and / or your environment are controlling your actions and thoughts. It's the things that are urgent and either important (High Payoff Activity (HPA) and thus an emergency) or unimportant (Low Payoff Activity (LPA)). Purposeful and planned work advancing you toward achieving your important goals in work or life is not being accomplished. When you are engaged in emergencies and urgent LPA, you will feel like you have little control over your work or life and stress is normally high. In these quadrants a person will say at the end of the day, "I just didn't get a thing done today."

Proactive personal management is the answer to reversing the effects of emergencies and urgent LPA. Proactive personal management is exercised when you:

1. **Set Goals & Plan**
2. **Communicate Your Goals & Plans**
3. **Manage the Results**
4. **Roll up Your Sleeves and DO**

Crisis management is just the reverse order of the four steps. Remember, you get in a "DO" loop that never ends until you just take the time to Set Goals & Plan.

To live a life where you are engaged in activity that leads to achievement of meaningful milestones in your life, follow the four steps and live more of your time in HPA.

1. Set Goals & Plan (aligned with your work or life vision and mission)

2. Communicate Your Goals & Plans (people want to help you achieve your goals)

3. Manage the Results (track your progress and take corrective actions when straying off course)

4. Roll up Your Sleeves and DO (take action)

Even if you can only find thirty minutes a day to work in HPA, at least you will be making progress toward the important things in your life. More time is better, and staying in that productive activity is best. But please, don't use the excuse that you don't have time to Set Goals and Plan. That's a cop out! It's a mental excuse to take the easy way out! Take control of your work and life.

Strategic Opportunism

Strategic Opportunism is defined as, "the ability to remain focused on long-term objectives while staying flexible enough to solve day-to-day problems and recognize new opportunities." This state of flexibility can only be achieved if the person, manager, or executive is in control of his or her schedule, work, and life. They have time to pro-actively plan and work toward their long-term goals. When they are too busy to think about the future, they have lost the ability to recognize opportunities as they present themselves. And opportunities present themselves repeatedly every day. Just think about this question, "What opportunities have you passed up because you were too busy to become aware of and respond positively to them?"

Effective Personal Management requires that you efficiently manage the time and resources that you have available. With effective management, you can block and schedule time to think about the future, work on long-term goals, and respond to opportunities as they present themselves. Without this focus and commitment, you will be caught up in the everyday business battle that consumes your entire reservoir of time and energy. You will have no time or energy left to invest in developing and assuring your future success.

Management Habits form as you develop routines of work. Some are good habits. Some are mediocre habits. Some can be counterproductive habits. Habits don't require thinking. They are hard to change. It has been estimated that 95% of our actions come from habits. Your thinking can also become habitual and result in attitudes. Attitudes aren't easy to change. You are often unaware of the changes that you can make that can lead to the better management of your time and resources. We often resist changing our habits and attitudes. They worked in the past, why change now?

Your Continuing Success requires developing more effective and efficient personal productivity, habits, and attitudes. Continual development can significantly increase your performance and business success. You can choose to break out of your less productive routines by engaging a coach or enrolling in one of our development program. Only with effective and efficient personal management can you have time to recognize and act on Strategic Opportunities.

Strategic Opportunism is the condition by which you have and take the time to recognize the opportunities that could result in long-term positive benefits for you and your company. Many opportunities present themselves each day. To take advantage of them you must have the time to perceive them, determine their value to you, and act accordingly. Without the time to accomplish these actions, they will pass you by as if it were night and they never existed. *"But, I am so busy! How can I ever find the time?" you ask.* Proactive management of your work and life is how! Remember that the steps to proactive management are to:

1. Set goals and plan
2. Communicate your goals and plans
3. Manage the results you are getting
4. Get busy and take action

You can recognize crisis management as the reverse order of these proactive steps. The problem with crisis management is that you get trapped in a "do loop" and never get out because you never have time to set goals and plan. So, setting goals and planning are essential in protecting some of your time to ensure that you don't miss the strategic opportunities that come your way. If you are a leader, and everyone this message goes to is a leader, you must schedule your time every day so that there is some time dedicated to the important functions of work and life. Important functions like, setting goals, planning, prioritizing work and actions, reflecting / learning from the days events, problem solving at the root cause level, reading / studying, or just communicating with your intuition. Allowing time to do these functions will result in a higher probability of having the time to take advantage of the strategic opportunities that come your way. And that's what you want, isn't it?

Proactive Management – Work & Life

Everyone's wish or dream is to be in complete control of their work and life and to avoid the stress of emergencies and crises. But how can that happen? Well, it can't! But, you can take charge and manage yourself to reduce the emergencies and crises in your work and life. Reactive work and life management is characterized by: Doing tasks, managing results, communicating what needs to be done, and then if there is any time left over, setting goals and planning (*there is never enough time to set goals and plan*). The proactive person reverses the reactive management steps. They:

1. Set goals and plan
2. Communicate goals and plans
3. Manage the results
4. Then they get involved in the doing

It's your choice which order of steps you take. We have several development programs that help you develop new habits and attitudes resulting in effective proactive management of your work and life.

People are Helpful

Proactive Management is the result of following four sequential activities. They are:

1. Set Goals & Plan
2. Communicate Your Goals & Plans
3. Manage the Results
4. Get Busy & Do!

Of course, we know that when these activities are in the reverse order (4, 3, 2, & 1) there is never time to set goals and plan because we are too busy DOING (called crisis management). After setting goals and planning how to accomplish them (completing a goal sheet), we then communicate them. To whom do you communicate?

You communicate your goals and plans to your employees at work. You can share them with your family, friends, and associates. In fact, you could share them with almost anyone, anywhere. Why would you want to do that? Because you might be surprised where help can come from, that will assist you in accomplishing your goals. I've been helped in grocery stores, banks, at concerts, movies, restaurants, and in some most unsuspecting places. Most people want to help and will voluntarily do so! Especially in America, people are helpful! But if you do not communicate your goals and plans, you will not receive any help.

The Easy Way

THE EASY WAY IS TO:

- Let everyone access your calendar for meetings or any other purposes they wish to make of your time.

- Have "white space" in your day so interruptions and random occurrences fill the time that you do not plan.

- Allow interruptions to stop you from doing "High Payoff Activity."

- Not take the time to prioritize the tasks and actions you should accomplish during the day.

- Not take the time to plan and schedule your day.

- Allow every crisis to take control of your time (firefighting can sometimes be self initiated).

THE PROACTIVE AND PRODUCTIVE WAY IS TO:

- **Schedule a block of time each day** so that no one can rob you of the time to work important actions leading to the completion of important goals.

- Have the **day completely planned** so that you know exactly what comes next at all times (no white space).

- Ask questions like, **"Is it important (HPA)?"** and, **"Is it urgent"** before managing the interruption. Only HPA and Urgent items are **emergencies** to be handled now!

- **Prioritizing actions each day** enable scheduling of the very most important items first in your day. It also gives you the ability to say **"NO!"** too lesser important issues / items.

- **For every minute you spend planning, you will save four to ten times that amount of time in the execution** of your work. That means more time for family or other HPA.

- Take responsibility for what is occurring around you. **Manage crisis to return to a planned HPA schedule** as soon as possible. Contribute the highest value to the business and life that you can. **Your only asset is your time, and how you spend it will determine the results that you enjoy!**

■ PART TWO ■
PERSONAL LEADERSHIP

"To be what we are, and to become what we are capable of becoming, is the only end of life."

- Robert Louis Stevenson

■ CHAPTER NINE ■
LEADERSHIP

*"Personal Leadership is the self-confident ability to
crystallize your thinking and establish an exact direction
for your own life, to commit yourself to moving in that
direction, and then to take determined action to acquire,
accomplish, or become whatever you identify
as the ultimate goal in your life."*

As far as you are learning, growing, developing more of your potential, and creating your future, you are developing and exercising personal leadership. You are effectively using your time to create happiness and joy in your work and life. **Personal leadership** requires self-confidence. It is the ability to crystallize your thinking and establish an exact direction for your own life. It is then committing to moving in that direction, and taking determined action to acquire, accomplish, or become whatever you identify as the ultimate goal of your life. Think about it! Are you on this road to happiness?

In an article in the February-March 1997 Fast Company, Dee Hock, founder and CEO emeritus of Visa, observed, "Control is not leadership; management is not leadership; leadership is leadership. If you seek to lead, invest at least 50 percent of your time leading yourself - your own purpose, ethics, principles, motivation and conduct. Invest at least 20 percent leading those with authority over you and 15 percent leading your peers. If you don't understand that you work for your mislabeled 'subordinates,' then you know nothing of leadership."

Leading yourself is the foundation to leading others. Knowing and living your purpose, using principles to guide your actions, engaging in behaviors that lead to producing the results you want, and keeping your own motivation positive and high result in a healthy leadership model to others and your organization. And we are all models of leadership. Only when you are living a life of integrity, developing yourself, and growing can you help others live a life of integrity, help them develop, and fulfill their potential. People who live a life of integrity are developing and using more of their potential and are usually happier, more effective, and highly productive in their work and life. Think about it! Don't you want the people who work for you to be more effective, productive, and happy? It's your choice!

The Most Important Person

Who is the most important person in your life? Why, you are, aren't you? Now, examine how you treat yourself and see if your actions support that answer. In the busy world of work and life people sometimes become trapped by all the competing activities and persons trying to control what they do. Your time is often managed, taken, and controlled by outside sources that seemingly cannot be controlled. People feel out of control and that leads to stress, loss of energy, ineffective actions, and reduced motivation to work and live up to your potential. How can you break the hold that this situation has on you? Here is how!

First, you must take time to better know yourself. That's right. You must set aside time for your own rejuvenation. Remember who is most important and take the time! If you do not get more control and focus in your life, then you will not have the vitality, energy, and focus to give your best in serving others in your work and life. Set a few hours aside each week for three or four weeks and focus on determining what your Vision, Purpose, Mission, and Values are. Create written statements of your life destination, reason for living, what you do, and what guides you in your life. Without Vision (life destination), Purpose (reason for living), Mission (what you do), and Values (your guides to living), you will be operating like a ship without a rudder. Any port you arrive at, any outcome, any actions you take, and any routes you travel will just have to do! This purposeless state of existence is a bummer and a losing way to live.

Once you know your Vision, Purpose, Mission, and Values, then you have the guidance you need to work and live on purpose with meaning that brings you joy and happiness. This guidance will keep you focused on your work, activities, and life in a way that you can say "NO!" to those things that do not fit into your directed life. Doing tasks that are in harmony with your direction in life will be rewarding and bring you great joy. You will feel that you are making progress in your life journey and those around you will notice something different. You will be more joyful and filled with the light of love and service to mankind. You will make the difference in this world that you were meant to make. And everyone has a special mission and contribution to make. So, take action now, plan some time to think about and write your Vision, Purpose, Mission, and Values statements. Then make sure your activities and actions are in harmony with living those statements. Over time, you will realize some astounding benefits that include more peace of mind and contentment with life. Don't wait, schedule and take the time NOW!

Personal leadership is about leading you. It is about knowing whom you are and where you are going in your life. It is about setting goals and applying the discipline and self-control to take the steps necessary to realize your wants and dreams. This process is not easy. However, it is a precursor to great happiness and satisfaction in your life and work.

Knowing who you are. Thousands of books have been written about this subject and I will not attempt to capture their essence here. The most important thing about knowing yourself is realizing that your search for self understanding should never end. There are assessments (for example Myers-Briggs), people (therapists, psychologists, & friends), processes (performance evaluations and feedback), meditations, and reflection that can yield clues and useful information and insights. The more we seek to understand ourselves, the more we will be in tune with whom we are, the more effective and successful we will become. Take regular time and actions to get to know you better.

Knowing where you are going. There is only one way to establish your destination in life. That is to take time from your "busy doings" and think about it! I know that thinking can hurt! But taking time is necessary to rekindle the flames of your passions and dreams. As a child you were filled with passionate dreams. As an adult, we need to reignite our dreams, crystallize them, and enjoy pursuing the actions that will advance us boldly in the direction of our goals. Schedule the time now and keep the "dream date" with yourself.

Set aside thirty minutes today to think about what you want to achieve in each area of your life (Physical, Health, Educational, Family, Spiritual, Social, Financial, and Career). Set a goal in each life area (it can be a small one, later you can go after the big ones). Write up a goal sheet for each and set priorities. Then, schedule the first action step to advance in your life journey. The trip of a thousand miles begins with the first step. Take that step today!

The Basics of Leadership

Every team, when they get into game losing trouble, goes back to practicing the basics. Players miss shots and make mistakes when they forget how to execute the most basic moves of their game. So it is with business. Only in business, we learn the basics from imperfect models. We fall into bad habits and do not know it. We get caught up into activity and work that produce little or no value added results. Business systems reinforce the wrong values and behaviors. Leaders & managers are providing imperfect examples. Things are changing so fast we cannot adjust without working harder and experiencing more stress. Sound familiar? By the way, when I mention business, you know that businesses are made up of the employees and so this applies to every individual in your company. This applies to you!

Knowing how to execute the basics of your job in an excellent way is absolutely necessary for success. What are the basic competencies for performing excellently in your job? Most people do not know the specific skills of their job or the competencies they must master to become excellent. One might think that a good job description might be important in creating excellence. But, who is creating and maintaining an excellent job description? If you could evaluate how well you do against the basic competencies, then you could target areas for improvement. You need feedback, not just any feedback but effective quality feedback in a positive environment that encourages and facilitates personal development planning and growth. And the feedback needs to be often, not just once a year.

The next level of detail dives into specific competency areas. Do something for me. Before each item that follows assess you on how well you are doing using the scale (one unsatisfactory to ten excellent). Once you have your assessment, it should be obvious where you want to take action to improve. Set one goal and take that action. Skills and competencies to consider are:

- Proactive personal management, setting goals & planning

- Knowing your High Payoff Activities and managing your time around them

- Prioritizing your work and working on your priorities

- Evaluating your effectiveness and productivity and taking daily action to improve

- Identifying changes and taking actions to get the results you want

- Being accountable for results (asking, "What more can I do to rise above the circumstances and get the results I want"). Then do it!

- Taking time each day to develop more effective skills or knowledge supporting your work results

- Constantly seeking feedback to avoid being trapped in your habitual way of seeing things

- Practicing an attitude of gratitude with everyone and everything

- Acting each day to change the attitudes that keep you from getting the results you want

- Doing what you say without fail when you say you will do them (practicing total integrity)

- And finally, work skills
  - o Communicating (writing, speaking, modeling, e-mail, telephone, etc.)
  - o Delegating & empowering
  - o Training & developing
  - o Motivating yourself & others
  - o Problem solving & decision making, applying specialized knowledge in an effective way
  - o Selling (products, services, or just yourself)
  - o Honoring organizational values in all your work
  - o Giving feedback in a positive caring way
  - o Interacting with people in an emotionally intelligent and effective way
  - o Many more

There are twenty specific items on this list and a perfect score would be 200. I didn't get a perfect score, did you? So, set your goal and get busy. With small efforts every day, you will remain sharp in the basic competencies, win in work and life, and become the greatest person you are capable of becoming.

The Least Risky Investment

The least risky investment you can make is investing in you. That's right, investing in you! What do I mean by investing in yourself?

You can invest in yourself in many different ways. Here are just a few. You can:

- Take a course of instruction
- Read a book that will help you develop new knowledge
- Practice new positive behaviors that develop more effective skills

- Listen to educational CDs in your car
- Seek out a coach to sharpen your productivity and effectiveness
- Exercise to enhance your health
- Solicit feedback and make changes in your life
- Take time for meditation
- Find a confidant who can help you develop insights into work, life, and happiness
- Enroll in a leadership development program
- Reflect on what works and doesn't work in your life (learn and change)
- Dream again and list all the things you want to do in your life, then start to do them
- Energize and balance your work and life by engaging in a special hobby
- Get the rest that you need to be 100% ready for work and life
- Always stay positive
- Make a new positive friend
- Regularly schedule time to nurture yourself
- Treat yourself to something special
- Say no to things that would detract from working and living your personal mission
- and the list goes on ...

Who better to invest in than yourself? The investments you commit to will greatly enhance your self-esteem and life satisfaction. You will be happier and the people around you will be happier. With the right amount of investment in yourself, you will have more to give others.

Take a moment and assess how much investment you are making. *Is it too little?* Review the investments listed above and identify ways you can increase your personal nurturing, growth, and development. Set goals and take the actions necessary to increase your investment. Do it now.

The Hardest Thing about Leadership

Keeping yourself focused on the most important activities of work and life is the hardest thing to do. There are so many distractions. Becoming distracted by glittery things that beckon your interest and time is easy. Pleasurable activities that will not help to achieve the vision of our lives, often tempt us. Other distractions are urgent things that grab and steal your attention or things that are important to other people yet thrust upon you. *How can I stay focused on my most important life roles and goals?*

It takes self awareness, control, and discipline to stay focused on what is important.

AWARENESS: You must know what is important to you in living a happy and rewarding life, and have an overriding awareness of your High Payoff Activities. Strive to have an awareness of what your goals are. Ultimately, be sure to have awareness when choosing your thoughts and actions and knowing that no matter what your choices, they always produce results (toward or away from your goals).

CONTROL: Choice can give you control or can result in loss of control. Staying focused means you must make choices that result in more control of your thoughts and actions. Planning your day and working your plan are excellent choices toward controlling more of your time.

DISCIPLINE: This is needed to keep you on the track to your goals and persisting. Persistence is necessary to achieve the results that you want. When the going gets tough, the tough get going. Discipline is the ability and process of keeping you on the track to getting what you want.

SELF-DISCIPLINE: This is the tough one. Most of us lack it sometimes. How can I increase my discipline? Try communicating your goals to a friend. Regularly, share with them the tracking of your results. Have them hold you accountable. Consider your friend an accountability partner. You can share your goals with even larger groups if that helps you achieve the results you want. Hire a coach!

TRACKING: We did mention tracking didn't we? This is another month and there is no better way to start this month than by reviewing last month's results and then planning this month's goals and action steps. This planning enables you to make the course direction changes needed to reach your month-end goals and enjoy the results you want. Without this planning, you will surely miss your target because there will be no target!

Life is a Place of Service

"Life is a place of service," Leo Tolstoy said. "Joy can be real only if people look upon their life as a service and have a definite object in life outside themselves and their personal happiness."

If you're not enjoying your work, you should either change your attitude or change your job. And since job change is probably the less desirable alternative, in changing your attitude you should look for ways to serve others while doing your job.

The Advantage

We are constantly searching for distinguishing advantages in our work and life. The advantage could be a product or service discount, sale price, special deal, life enhancement, or other differentiating item such as education, new skill, show home, or a special car. The advantage at work could be a special work experience, relationship with supervisor or peers or subordinates, differentiated service, special loyalty to the company or person, or other distinguishing characteristic. For companies it could be a special feature that offers differentiating benefits. The list can go on and on.

How do we create an advantage in our lives? We do not create an advantage by being mass motivated to fit into the normal life most people lead! Nor do we create an advantage by doing things that everyone else does or by remaining satisfied with the status quo. We do create an advantage when we have a vision and set goals to use more of the potential for greatness that exists in all of our lives.

Developing your Advantage - Reflect on your life and identify the dream or activity that generates passionate feelings in your life. What would really ring your bell? Then develop this dream or activity and realize your passion. Setting a "goal to become" is a great start (develop a skill, or learn more about your area of passion). Finally, *prioritize and schedule the action steps of your goal so you are taking one action each day toward realizing your dream.* Spending thirty minutes a day reading about your passion or practicing behaviors to develop a new skill will make you an expert in no time, and bring great satisfaction and happiness to your life. It's your choice! If you choose to create an advantage starting right now, then you have differentiated yourself from others. If you hesitate, procrastinate, or do not act now, you are joining the ranks of the mass motivated who are engaged in living a mediocre life.

If you haven't figured it out yet, creating an advantage for your life is exercising personal leadership to grow, to learn and to become all that you can become. You are engaged in developing a leadership advantage in your work, life, and relationships. Now you know the rest of the story. **Leadership Advantage is about creating your future!**

■ CHAPTER TEN ■
TODAY MATTERS

*"The secret of health for both mind and body is not to
mourn for the past, nor to worry about the future, but to
live the present moment wisely and earnestly."*

- Buddha (563-483 B.C.)

You have been given this day to do with it what you will. Yesterday is
gone forever. Tomorrow has not yet arrived. Today is the only resource
you have to invest. How you invest in today determines the life you
live and experience. Your experiences can bring you happiness, joy, and
fulfillment or it can bring you hopelessness, despair, worry, doubt, and fear.
Think about it. How you manage and invest your time today determines
your experience. Managing, investing, and living today matters. How will
you live today?

WILL YOU:

- Set goals that are meaningful, uplifting, serving, and contribute
to humanity
- Plan your day's actions to achieve steps toward your most
important goals

- Stay 100% present and focused on your daily plan
- Manage to limit interruptions and invest your time only in what is important
- Live the day with integrity, enthusiasm, and positive anticipation
- Cherish every moment, person, challenge, and opportunity that comes your way
- Give thanks, show gratitude, and appreciate every moment and what it brings you
- Let love flow toward everyone and everything you encounter
- Give your very best
- Do something to nourish, develop, or grow yourself
- Recall the day's progress, show yourself appreciation, and celebrate your progress

OR WILL YOU:

- Assume that you will have a lifetime to do what you might want to do
- Take this day for granted and just let it happen
- Do whatever comes your way
- Work on whatever you feel like in every moment
- Follow distractions that consume your time with no purpose
- Become suspicious and fearful of changes from what you normally do
- Scowl at people and things you dislike or hate
- Defend yourself against the unfair working environment
- Complain about things and people you don't like
- Do only what is enough to get by
- Go home exhausted, worship TV, go to bed, only to repeat the cycle tomorrow

It's easy to see which approach to living is going to bring you a greater measure of happiness, joy, and fulfillment. We don't always live fully in each positive item above. Here is your assignment. On a scale of one (never) and ten (always), how do you rate in each of the positive approaches to life? Now set priorities in the areas that need work. Take the top priority and set a goal today to take action to make it a ten in your life. Continue creating tens in each area until you are happy, filled with joy, and feel fulfilled. You see – today matters.

Giving 100% Today

If you are not giving 100 percent today, you cannot make it up tomorrow. If you are giving only 75 percent today, you can't give 125 percent tomorrow. There are only twenty-four hours in each day and how you use them determines the quality of your life. The hours (or minutes) you waste today are never retrievable or recoverable in the future.

In other words, every day and every hour counts and the best way for you to realize success tomorrow, you must make the most of today. Make every day your masterpiece and your life will become a masterpiece.

Today is a Gift

Everyone is so busy that we almost never spend a moment and reflect on the importance of today. So let's take that moment. Think of the world and the great eco system in which we live. Think of its grandeur, its preciseness, its abundance, and its orchestrating elements that ensure that life can exist on this planet and no other known planets. Think of our great nation and the abundance we have, the wonderful way everything works together to provide for our needs, wants, and dreams. Even when disaster strikes, there are abundant resources to rescue those affected, provide for their continued living, and for rebuilding their lives. Think of your home, family, car, loved possessions, and all the things you possess and enjoy. Think of your work or job and how it provides for you. Some people of this earth do not have that opportunity. Think of the freedoms you enjoy exercising every day. Think of your body and all the systems, complexities, and miracles that continuously function to keep you healthy, alert, and wonderfully alive. Think of this glorious day you have been given to live in this paradise. Today is truly a gift. Use it well.

Yesterday, Today, & Tomorrow

YESTERDAY: Oh, yesterday was fun, filled with achievement, significant progress toward goals, and included a significant event that was gloriously memorable. Or yesterday was filled with harmful stress, personal attacks, worry, meaningless work, futile efforts. Either way, yesterday was yesterday never to be repeated. It can never be relived. It is gone forever. So let it go. Save and remember the positive memories but do not try to relive them because you cannot. Don't let the negative memories control your today! Release the negative memories from your life. They are a poison that will bring misery, distress, and disharmony. Let yesterday go and live today.

TODAY: Today is new, a gift filled with many positive opportunities, a time to create and love and laugh. Today is a time to change, grow, and serve others to make a positive difference in your world. Today is life, filled with the living, a place of unbounded wonder filled with the wonderful. Today is a place of beautiful plants, trees, birds, pets, people, and constructions. Today is a time of precious moments. In this glorious time of today, make the most of your precious moments.

TOMORROW: Tomorrow is not here yet. It may never get here. It is not promised to you or me. Tomorrow is a wish, a hope, a possibility. We often assume that we will have a tomorrow, but it is not a promise. If you don't believe me, look in the obituaries or newspaper headlines and you will find many people whose tomorrow never arrived. To worry or fret about tomorrow is to waste time and energy. To delay doing today what you should because you can do it tomorrow is foolish. To wait until tomorrow to tell someone that you love them today is acting stupid. Let tomorrow go and live today.

Do It Now!

Everything you do, or do not do, is a choice. The results of your choices are what you experience in work and life. What are you experiencing? When faced with all the possible things you can do, you can be overwhelmed with all the options. And don't get me wrong. We live in a wonderful country, with all the things you can imagine, and possibilities beyond measure. I am grateful. However, we often find ourselves faced with choices and we back away from them or we just don't choose to follow some course of action that we really want to follow. We just don't want to take the risk or make the decision since it might upset the way things are. We procrastinate, hesitate, and let the moment of action slip away.

In the motivational world you have heard the phrase, "Do It Now!" What that means is to take decisive action now. Don't languish, do not hesitate, do not procrastinate, and do not put it off until tomorrow what you can do in this moment. Take decisive action now. Do It Now! With this attitude of action to achieve the results you want, you will find life-changing progress toward the work and life you desire. Think about it.

What if you internalized and practiced the attitude of "Doing It Now!" What progress would you make toward the dreams, desires, and the goals you imagine? Don't just sit there. Identify the action you need to take right now in this moment and "Do It Now." In every moment, identify the actions you can take to progress toward your work and life goals and "Do It Now!"

Success Happens One Day at a Time

Every day you live, you are in the process of becoming. What you become depends on what you choose to do. If you want to succeed, take a moment and consider these seven steps carefully:

1. Make a commitment to grow daily and it will not be long before you begin to see a real change. Robert Browning said, "Why stay on earth, except to grow?"

2. Value the process more than the events. Certain events may be helpful in making your decision, but it's the process that matures you into what you want to be.

3. Don't wait for inspiration. Sometimes you can run on excitement; but most times only discipline will carry you through.

4. If you pay now, you will enjoy greater rewards later, and those rewards always taste sweeter.

5. Dream big. When you think of limitations, you create them, but when you preserve your dreams you will always go beyond them. Why? It is because the universe-given potential within you is limitless.

6. Learn to master your time or you will never succeed. Henry Kaiser said, "A minute spent in planning will save you two in execution." You can't get back lost time, so make the most of every moment.

7. Life is filled with critical moments when you'll trade one thing for another. Always trade up, not down! Your recognition and your rewards may come slowly at first, but don't lose heart - you'll succeed in the end!

■ CHAPTER ELEVEN ■
SELF-DEVELOPMENT

"The quality of a person's life is in direct proportion to their commitment to excellence, regardless of their chosen field."

- Vince Lombardi

Conscious personal development does not end with High School or with the first job you take. It doesn't stop with marriage or the first child. It doesn't stop with that promotion to the executive team. It doesn't stop when you reach the age of forty-five or fifty-five or sixty or sixty-five. It doesn't stop until you stop living! Mental toughness and agility come from being engaged in work and life and learning and developing more of your potential. If you don't believe me, look around at the people who totally retire or quit being engaged in learning and life. They decline, atrophy, have more illness, have less mobility, and suffer debilitating health challenges.

The individuals who know their vision (destination), purpose for living, mission (what their work is), values, and who take daily actions to realize progress toward these guiding principles experience great happiness and joy. They are people who are growing daily and developing more of their potential. These people are taking the actions necessary to enjoy life, experience happiness, and find pleasure in all the gifts that life has to offer. They never stop looking for ways to contribute to life and the world and to be of greater service to humanity. Self-development always leads to abundant success in work and life. It is the key to greater service, longevity, happiness, and joy. Can you possibly ignore your own "self-development?"

Self-Development requires that you know who you are. It requires that you set goals to develop more of your potential, and that you take actions to achieve those goals. Self-development requires that you motivate yourself to attain those self-development objectives. Anything less is to choose a mediocre way of living, an existence that is less than what your maker has chosen for you to enjoy. Self-development is simple. Just take one action each day on one area you wish to develop, and that action can take just a few minutes each day. Over time, you will be surprised at what you can achieve. However, it takes the discipline to take those several minutes each day without fail. It's your choice. Don't wait until tomorrow. Do it today!

Human Doing or Being?

Are you a "Human **Doing**" or a "Human **Being**?"

Many people today are very busy doing the many things that they think their work and society expects them to do. They are so busy doing things that they rarely take time to reflect on the results of their doings. Time to ponder the results they are getting and it's affect on their work and lives rarely exists because there are so many things to do. Therefore, they fall into the rut of doing the same things repeatedly again without change. And you know the saying, "If you do the things you have always done, you will get what you have always gotten." They do not change because they don't have the time to consider the changes that could bring much better results and longer term happiness. They are just too busy doing things! Exhaustion, hopelessness, drudgery, fatigue, and depression often result from doing all the time. Sounds like a hopeless rut, doesn't it?

Human Beings take time to consider the results they are getting from their doings. They reflect on important subjects like their purpose on this earth, their mission, things they value, and their vision for the future. They consider the things that are not working in their lives, discover the causes, and make changes to get new results. They keep open to the possibilities that present themselves daily (often hourly) and they act on them. They review their goals and take frequent actions to progress toward them. Human Beings strive personally to grow more competent, explore more of their worlds, and enjoy every moment that they live. Light beams from their eyes, they are quick to laugh, and they bask in joy and happiness. They have great energy and love the people and world around them. Human Beings are positively contributing to the great world in which we live.

Becoming a "Human **Doing**" or a "Human **Being**" is each person's **choice**. A choice you cannot delegate away. This is a choice that you cannot assign (blame) to another person or situation. In other words, you are responsible for becoming either a Human Doing, or a Human Being. If you feel like a Human **Doing**, then schedule time to sit and reflect on your activities, life, and the results you are getting (consider the long-term consequences). Identify the changes you need to make to become more aligned with your life destination (vision of the future), your purpose for living, your values, and your mission. Prioritize these changes so that you can focus on the most important ones first. Then march out and consciously make them happen. Take more control of your life and become more of a **Human Being**.

Learning & Life's Lessons

The enemy of **Learning** is **Knowing**! Take a minute and think about this thought.

Knowing means that you won't be looking at the assumptions that exist behind what you think and know. It means that the thinking process leading to knowing may never be revisited. The result could be a dogged determination to hold onto a belief in spite of all evidence that it should be changed. A "blind person" like this chooses to reject all new evidence that could change his or her knowing. They become stubborn. This blind condition will prevent him or her from learning life's lessons, lessons that are necessary for personal growth.

What to do? A person growing in his or her personal leadership will choose to become sensitive to his or her biases and "knowing." Recognizing that he or she has a knowing will enable the person to open their minds to new facts, changes in assumptions, and new evidence that their knowing may need to be modified, changed, or let go. In this way, it is possible to learn life's lessons and grow as a person.

One thing we know, and that is we live in a world of rapidly accelerating change. That tells me that we need to be open to new information, ideas, and experiences so that we do not become a "blind person." What **action or goal** will you set for yourself to more fully develop your openness to changing your "knowing" and experience added personal growth?

P.S. There is a great book about life's lesson you may want to read, "*If Life is a Game, These are the Rules*" by Cherie Carter-Scott, Ph.D.

Ten Steps to Building Self-Esteem

Sam Deep and Lyle Sussman offer ten steps to building team members' self-esteem in their book, "Smart Moves." Here they are:

1. "**Document their accomplishments** so they can't pretend they don't exist. Never allow team members to lose sight of their accomplishments and with it their potential for success.

2. Show them how to **find opportunity in adversity**. Every outcome, no matter how negative, presents options that were not previously available.

3. Assign them tasks that will **display their talents**. By transferring important responsibility to team members, you demonstrate your confidence in them and give them the chance to succeed in increasingly challenging assignments.

4. **Teach them to get what they want from other people**. Teach your people to be assertive rather than too aggressive or too passive.

5. Show them the awesome **power of listening**, an active strategy for achieving personal success. When your subordinates become better listeners and begin reaping the benefits, they will feel better about themselves.

6. Teach them the **advantage of being a sieve** rather than a sponge. A sponge soaks up all the water it can hold and, when squeezed, shoots it in every direction. Water passes through a sieve completely; "sieve people" are less rattled by adversity than sponges.

7. **Tell them exactly what you expect** of them and find out what they expect of you. **The reason most subordinates and team members give for not satisfying their management is claiming that they do not know what management expects.**

8. Criticize performance but not people. The spirit of criticism should be, "I don't like what you did in this case, but I do like you."

9. Praise not only them but also their **performance**. You don't want merely to keep your people happy; you want them to know what they did right so they can repeat it.

10. Keep them in **ongoing training programs**. This gives them a vote of confidence, and carefully chosen training will further contribute to their effectiveness and ultimately their self-esteem."

I'm sure that one of these steps spoke to you about changes you should make. Set a goal and take action to make it happen. Remember that information without action is just entertainment!

LAST THOUGHT: **Only mediocre people are always at their best!**

Six Behaviors that Increase Self-Esteem

Following are six behaviors that increase self-esteem, enhance your self-confidence, and spur your motivation. You may recognize some of them as things you naturally do in your interactions with other people. But if you don't, I suggest you motivate yourself to take some of these important steps immediately.

First, greet others with a smile and look them directly in the eye. A smile and direct eye-contact convey confidence born of self-respect. In the same way, answer the phone pleasantly whether at work or at home. When placing a call, give your name before asking to speak to the party you want to reach. Leading with your name underscores that a person with self-respect is making the call.

126

Second, always show real appreciation for a gift or compliment. Don't downplay or sidestep expressions of affection or honor from others. The ability to accept or receive is a universal mark of an individual with solid self-esteem.

Third, don't brag. It is almost a paradox that genuine modesty is actually part of the capacity to receive compliments gracefully. People who brag about their own exploits or demand special attention are simply trying to build themselves up in the eyes of others – and that's because they don't perceive themselves as already worthy of respect.

Fourth, don't make your problems the centerpiece of your conversation. Talk positively about your life and the progress you're trying to make. Be aware of any negative thinking, and take notice of how often you complain. When you hear yourself criticize someone, and this includes a self-criticism, find a way to be helpful instead of critical.

Fifth, respond to difficult times or depressing moments by increasing your level of productive activity. When your self-esteem is being challenged, don't sit around and fall victim to "paralysis by analysis." The late Malcolm Forbes said, "Vehicles in motion use their generators to charge their own batteries. Unless you happen to be a golf cart, you can't recharge your battery when you're parked in the garage!"

Sixth, choose to see mistakes and rejections as opportunities to learn. View a failure as the conclusion of one performance, not the end of your entire career. Own up to your shortcomings, but refuse to see yourself as a failure. A failure may be something you have done – and it may even be something you'll have to do again on the way to success – but a failure is definitely not something you are.

■ ■ ■

"Even if you're at a point where you're feeling very negatively about yourself, be aware that you're now ideally positioned to make rapid and dramatic improvement. A negative self-evaluation, if it's honest and insightful, takes much more courage and character than the self-delusions that underlie arrogance and conceit. I've seen the truth of this proven many times in my work with athletes. After an extremely poor performance, a team or an individual athlete often does much better the next time out, especially when the poor performance was so bad that there was simply no way to shirk responsibility for it. Disappointment, defeat, and even apparent failure are in no way permanent conditions unless we choose to make them so. On the contrary, these undeniably painful experiences can be the solid foundation on which to build future success."

- Denis Waitley

Increase Your Self-Discipline

Successful people typically have more self-discipline than others. They have formed good habits like punctuality, organization, and persistence.

The good news is that you can learn better work habits within three or four weeks, says time management authority Merrill Douglass. "A habit is often simply behavior done so often that it becomes automatic," he says. "Force yourself to keep good records, and you will see the day when you keep them inevitably and as efficiently as you bathe," says management expert Ted Pollock in *Supervision*. "Drive yourself to be punctual, and you will soon keep your appointments on time as naturally as you eat three times a day. Make yourself plan your days and weeks in advance, and planning will become second nature," he adds.

Deliberately training yourself into good habits requires stern self-discipline at first, says Pollock. But once those habits become second nature, the payoff is considerable: "Good habits save effort, ease routine, increase efficiency, and release power."

- *Supervision*, Vol. 59, and *ABC Time Tips* by Merrill Douglass

Get More Energy

It is so easy to get caught up in all the firefights, reports, analyses, data collection, and other activities of a busy person that at the end of the day you feel like you have accomplished absolutely nothing important. But you were busy the whole time and now feel exhausted. Is this the way life is supposed to be lived? One day after another you are so busy that what you know you should do, you never get around to doing.

Here are a few **ideas to energize your life**. If one fits, then write it down as an Imperative Action Step and do it! Otherwise, reading more is a waste of your time.

• Write down all the important things you must do (high payoff tasks or goal action steps). Set Priorities. Work only on the highest priority task first.

• Take time to exercise four or five times each week. Your energy level will soar and you will not feel tired at the end of the day.

• Protect thirty minutes each day to spend in self-development. Take that time and spend it on yourself. You are worth it!

• Listen to motivational and educational tapes / CD's in your car on the way to work.

- Guard your attitude throughout the day. Keep it positive no matter what. Use affirmations and crowd out negative thoughts.

- Practice the "**Attitude of Gratitude**." The obstacles and challenges that come our way help us grow and become stronger. Without them, we would become weak and atrophy. With them we know we are living.

- When you close out your day and plan tomorrow's work, reflect on what you accomplished and the progress you made, and **congratulate yourself**. One step a day and in 365 days you can make huge progress toward any goal!

- Realize that **success is your choice**. What you choose to do and how you choose to live your life will result in the success you enjoy (law of cause and effect). Realize that you are responsible for all the results in your life (good or bad).

- Periodically **get a tune-up**. Don't keep wearing out your motor (mind & body). Take the time to sharpen your saw. Invest in yourself. Do what you need to do to peak your energy and interest for work and life.

Either you control what you do or the world controls what you do. Exercise Personal Leadership, make the right choices for you, and live an energized life.

Accelerated Learning

How can you accelerate your learning? Most people are working and living at warp speed. There seems to be no time to stop and reflect on what is happening. If you do have a little time, then TV, the internet, or the work we brought home captures our attention. We are caught up in the whirlwind pace of living. Often in this mode we do not learn the lessons life presents to us because we are too busy. Here are a few ideas to accelerate your learning.

- **Celebrate**: In the evening, when you are planning tomorrow's work, reflect on the day and acknowledge the progress you made toward your work and life goals. Pat yourself on the back. Say to yourself, "Good work today!" Celebrate your progress.

- **Learning Log**: Establish a note book or journal and start a "**Learning Log**." Create two sections, a "**Success**" section and a "**Development**" section.

- **What Went Right?**: Reflect on the day and identify what events went right. Why did these events go right? What can you repeat (*the lesson*) to make it go right again? Write your lesson down in the "**Success**" portion of your "**Learning Log**." Plan to repeat this lesson and making it a regular part of your behavior.

- **What Went Wrong?**: What went wrong today? Why did it go wrong? What must change to make it go right (*the lesson*)? What must you do, learn, or develop to make sure this event goes right in the future? Write it in the "**Development**" portion of your "**Learning Log**." Then, consider writing a goal and taking action to start your new knowledge or skill development.

Taking ten minutes each night to reflect on what went right and what went wrong, recording your findings in a **Learning Log**, and quickly

131

reviewing the accumulated lessons you have learned, will significantly accelerate your learning. Soon you will find yourself getting new results other people just wish they could achieve. Your discipline of reflecting each night and learning more about what works in life and work will create a significant advantage for you, your family, and your company. Make a commitment to start this accelerated learning process tonight.

■ CHAPTER TWELVE ■
CREATING YOUR FUTURE

*"The best thing about the future is
that it comes only one day at a time."*

- Abraham Lincoln

LOST IN THE FOG: Daily work demands, project tasks, errands to run, and doing things only we think we can do often put us in a fog of endless activity. Our world is not getting simpler and so that fog seems to get thicker each day we live. At every turn in our lives, there are new technologies to master, changes to adapt to, and unexpected challenges to conquer. A person can get lost trying to adapt to all that is going on around them. What can we do?

CLEAR VISION: Life need not become complicated. Only if you choose to embrace all the opportunities it presents to you does it become overwhelmingly complex. So how can you keep it simple? From the list of all possibilities, pick and rank the top six life areas that are truly important to you. Here is an example:

1. Your Health
2. Personal Growth

3. Immediate Family Members
4. Rewarding Work
5. Living Place
6. One Satisfying Hobby

In each of these areas develop a clear view of what you want it to look like or become. Develop a crystal clear future vision of that life area. From magazines, cut out pictures and make a collage that clearly depicts your future vision. Make sure you are crystal clear that this is what you want. If you feel passion for the vision, then you are crystal clear.

PLANNING: Every day, ask yourself, "what one small meaningful action can I take to advance me toward the vision I have in each area of life?" Don't plan big leaps toward your goals, as they may become intimidating. Don't let the magnitude of the final vision or the imagined difficulties dissuade you to the point of inaction. Concentrate on making just one small step each day toward the vision you have of each of your focus areas. You will be amazed at what progress you can make in one year (365 actions) toward each of your visions. A small action could be as small as just a telephone call for information or help.

TAKING ACTION: In every moment, weigh what life presents to you in relation to what your vision is of your six life areas. If what the world is presenting to you does not advance you toward your vision, choose not to get caught up in that activity, opportunity, challenge, or event. Keep focused on what is important to you and the vision you have of your life. Reject all that does not support progress toward your life vision. Take the six small actions you have planned to take this day in your six life areas. At the end of the day, congratulate yourself on the steps you took and the progress you made this day. Remember the story of the turtle and the rabbit. It was the steady small progress of the turtle that eventually beat the fast moving and exhausted rabbit.

You can choose the life you create or you can just go along for the foggy ride. What is your choice? Do it now!

Living is a Choice!
What is Your Destination or Vision?

Everything you do or don't do is a choice. You can do something, you can avoid doing something, you can choose not to do something, or you can ignore the "somethings." All are choices you make. So, if everything is a choice, then why not make choices that propel you in the direction that you want to go?

Choices and actions without a direction will get you nowhere. But, with a direction or destination, your choices and actions can move you along a meaningful course. What is that destination? It's called your **vision**. A personal vision of where you want to arrive. Your personal vision or destination can be a week from now, a month, a year, or even a lifetime in the future. The important thing is to clearly define that vision and hold it out as a homing beacon for your choices and actions.

Is it worth the time and effort to think about your destination in life? You bet it is! Without that effort, your life travel will be like a ship without a rudder. Wouldn't it be better to map out the destination first, chart a course to get you there, and then set sail on the sea of life? Take time now to think about, crystallize, and form your life's destination or vision.

Why am I Living? What is My Purpose?

Sometimes life pulls us down so hard that we wonder why we are living. We suffer through the same old work, challenges heaped upon challenges, and stress over too many things to do. *Why, oh why, am I living?* This is a great and worthy question.

So why are you living? What is your purpose for living on this earth? Why were you born into this world? Would the answer to these questions be important to you in living a happy life? Wouldn't it be wonderful to be living a life that is "on purpose?"

So, why not spend some time to ponder this question, "Why was I placed on this earth?" The answer can give you great meaning to the actions you take and goals you set and accomplish. It might make the difference between being "on purpose and happy" or "just existing!"

What Do I Do? My Mission

Your mission on this planet is important. What are you suppose to do? Knowing your mission is really important because it enables you to use your natural gifts and talents to create the greatest good on this earth and to fulfill your destiny.

In developing your mission statement it is important first to identify your roles. Roles can include being a business leader, team leader, individual contributor, husband or wife, mother or father, provider for your family, friend, son or daughter, colleague, or other important role. Then, in that role, you provide services. What are those services you provide? To what standards do you aspire to accomplish the services in those different roles?

If you can answer all these questions in a few memorable sentences, then you have a mission statement. Knowing your mission can bring contentment and joy to work and life.

What Guides Me? What Are My Values?

You know that different things are important but, what really are your values? Do you ever write down the things you value? Well, its time to start that written list. Take some quiet time over the next few weeks and capture all the things you value in writing.

After that, try organizing them. There are probably several foundational values that form the basis of your value system. Examine each value on your list and see if they might be grouped into a few foundational values. It's much simpler to have a few values to remember than 20 or 30. This will take some time and iterations to achieve so don't worry if it doesn't gel right away.

I'm going to share with you the work I've done in this area as an example. It took many years of thinking and hard work to identify my foundational values. They are, "Integrity, Stewardship, and Love." The challenge is to arrive at your own life guiding values. Start your discovery process now.

Putting It All Together:
Vision, Purpose, Mission, and Values

When you possess a vision for your life, purpose for living, knowledge of your mission, and your guiding values, life becomes purposeful, fulfilling, and happy. It may take some time and effort, it may take several tablets of writing, and it may take a year or two to develop some clear statements, but won't it be worth the effort and time?

Without this guidance, life would be lived without purpose and value. It's your choice. What will it be? Will you live a life without direction and purpose or a directed life that brings pleasure, joy, and happiness? If you choose the latter, then take the time to answer the questions in this book.

Integrity

Every leader I work with believes that integrity is a basic value and that it is one of the most important values of a successful business. Almost every person I talk with states that this is one of their values. Let us explore some thoughts about integrity.

The Merriam Webster Dictionary defines integrity as, "Firm adherence to a code of moral or artistic values; an unimpaired condition; the quality or state of being complete and undivided." There are many moral and artistic values floating around and integrity can be attached to almost any value. Integrity must embrace only those values that cause the positive results that we want to create, positive results created from embracing universal values that enrich the world in which we live. Embracing and acting on values that have **positive consequences** for the person, company, and mankind contribute to success results that bring more joy and happiness to those acting, those receiving, and our world. Acting on values that have negative consequences for the person, company, or mankind, detract from our success and result in decline and destruction of the well-being of both ourselves and society.

Being careful of your self-talk, internal commitments and exercising firm adherence to take action on the commitments we do make will result in high self-esteem, joy, and happiness.

Integrity, Your Core Value?

Every person in every company that I work with tells me that one of their core values is Integrity. Integrity can mean many things to different people. Usually integrity means to "Do What You Say You Will Do" (DWYSYWD). Keeping your word and walking your talk are other phrases that describe integrity. Why is integrity important?

IMPACT OF INTEGRITY

You will lose customers (friends) if you don't **DWYSYWD**! That's obvious, but additionally, you will lose the trust of the people around you.

People will hear what you say but they will know that they cannot count on you to do what you say. Trust will be destroyed. The negative attitude of distrust will have a very negative effect on your relationships. And you don't want to build degenerating relationships, do you? Repeat customers and good friends only develop from trust built through total integrity.

The greatest integrity impact is to your own self-esteem. Not DWYSYWD gradually degrades your self-esteem. Miss too many of your promises and soon your self-esteem will be seriously eroded. Low self-esteem leads to attitudes that are negative, behaviors will reflect your negative attitudes, and the results you produce from your behaviors will fall very short of what you desire. Becoming successful and happy in life comes only through total integrity in everything you say you will do (verbally or internally with your self-talk).

VIOLATIONS OF INTEGRITY

Total integrity is built from everything you promise to do. It is built with the little promises and the larger commitments. Common violations of integrity include:

Some Big Violations

- Missing work or other deadlines (without renegotiation of new deadlines)
- Forgetting to do something you said you would do
- Letting yourself be distracted so as not to remember what you said you would do
- Over committing and not being able to keep all your promises (can't say no!)
- Making a promise (offhand commitment) you know you will not keep
- Actual lying (no intent of keeping your word)

- Behaving counter to what you say (saying one thing and doing another, not living your values)
- When asked for honesty, delivering less than honest information or feedback
- Not taking the actions or making the changes in your life you need to remember and fulfill all your commitments
- Not keeping promises you make to yourself

Some Small Violations
- Not responding to voice mail as you promise on your greeting
- Copying a copyrighted document
- Writing off the small promise as not important (can't keep them all)
- Not sewing on the button when you said you would
- Not taking out the trash when you said you would
- Not cleaning out the garage (closet) when you said you would
- Not picking up your clothes when you said you would do it
- Telling a good friend you would help and then avoiding them
- Using tired excuses why you can't DWYSYWD

INTEGRITY ACTIONS

Every person I know including myself can sharpen their awareness of their integrity. Make promises only that you can keep and write them down (in your commitment book). Don't be afraid to say NO! Saying NO is better than to break a promise. Prioritize your commitments and schedule them to be completed during your day. Then do it! Keep both the Big Commitments and Small Promises. There is no distinction when building self-esteem. A commitment that you can't keep should be renegotiated before the deadline or due date. Keep your integrity squeaky clean and impeccably complete.

Walk your talk; keep your word, and DWYSYWD.

Stewardship, Your Core Value?

After many years of grappling with values in both my life and in business, I came to the conclusion that there are three core values. These core or foundational values were identified through exhaustive brainstorming, categorizing, and organizing of values. We will now explore Stewardship.

Stewardship is the careful and responsible management of something entrusted to one's care.

RESOURCES: In business, things entrusted to our care include the use of our time and sometimes money, computers, information, materials, supplies, facilities, equipment, machines, and the management of employees. Outside business we are responsible again for our time, money, living area, cars, investments, paying bills, maintaining relationships, and a host of other things. Wow! That's a lot of stuff. Also a part of physical stewardship is process improvement which includes both improving how we work and how we serve others in both business and our personal lives.

OURSELVES: Stewardship goes further than that. We are stewards of ourselves. We are managers of our own maintenance and growth. In our care are knowledge acquisition, skill developments, maintaining a positive mental attitude, exercising courage, being willing to change, maintaining a productive work ethic, health & physical fitness, and keeping up a desire to win (motivation). I lump a few other values in this category that are important in my life and those are freedom, choice, truth, and knowing. Being responsible for these things, I must try to maintain and improve myself. With special emphasis on managing my time (the only currency I have to spend).

RESPONSIVENESS: Lastly, it's impossible to talk about being a good steward without mentioning responsiveness. Being responsive in our work and life is a key sub-value that builds trust and productivity. Being responsive in a way that is constructive, dependable, timely, consistent, and that fulfills duty is highly valuable. Being responsive helps others and helps yourself optimize the use of your mental and physical resources. Waiting and procrastinating cause huge problems and waste large amounts of resources.

ACTION: The questions to ask yourself are, "How good a steward am I?" "What areas of life and work do I need to improve?" "What actions must I take right now to start improving my stewardship?" "How do I continually keep improving my stewardship?" With your answers, take action NOW!

I'd like to conclude with something I've written to guide my own work and life. It may provide an example in evolving your own stewardship statement.

STEWARDSHIP: I am a good steward of all things entrusted to me. I am responsible for effective and efficient use of all resources under my control. I do not live with an entitlement mentality but earn the money that I am paid. I am responsive in a positive uplifting way to all the people I meet. I am responsible for my personal growth, development, and success. I am committed to continuous improvement in my work, service, and life. I possess and express an attitude of gratitude.

Love, Your Core Value?

There are three types of love. They are Philadelphus (brotherly), Eros (sexual), and Agape or the unselfish loyal and benevolent concern for the good of another. Agape is the love that is the core of this value.

LOVE: When we practice Agape love for the world, we have an enthusiastic sincere concern for others. We believe others have unlimited potential, and openly communicate in helpful ways. We quickly forgive perceived altercations, empower others to achieve greater successes, build positive productive relationships, and approach the world of people with a passion for our purpose that is to serve. Service is another word I often use for Love.

SERVICE: To serve others is the ultimate expression of Love. In serving others, we need to show a visible willingness, seek to help, and treat others with respect, dignity, and fairness. Serving others without expectation of gain or return is the opposite of being self-serving. One universal law states that, "What goes around comes around." So serving abundantly will come back to you in sometimes magnificent ways. Whatever you seek, give it away first!

WHO: We serve our fellow employees, whether superiors or subordinates. We serve our family, neighbors, neighborhood, state, nation, and the world. One little act of Love can affect all those we serve including everyone in the world (the butterfly effect). We can Love (or care for) our environment and exercise good stewardship or we can be self-serving (neglect) our environment and exercise poor stewardship.

ACTION: The questions are, "How good of an Agape Lover are you?" "What areas of service do you need to improve?" "What actions must you take right now to start improving your service and Love?" "How do you continually keep improving your love of life and the world?" With your answers, take action NOW!

I would like to conclude with something I've written about love to guide my own work and life. Maybe it will inspire you to construct your own service or Love statement.

LOVE (SERVICE): I serve my personal family, business family, and community unconditionally with a loving attitude. I know that "the golden rule" reigns and that "Whatever I want, I must first give it away." I care intensively about the growth and development of every human being I meet. My credo includes the words, "Love God, Love People, Love life."

Commitments

Saying that you will do something is easy. It is often more difficult to remember to do what you say you will do. Doing what you say you will do, is paramount to your success and happiness in business and life. When you say you will do something, it becomes a commitment. Keeping your commitments builds trusting relationships. It shows that you are reliable. Not keeping your commitments breaks trust with others, shows that you are unreliable, and is a serious breach of your own integrity. The worst part of not keeping commitments is that it eats away at your self-esteem and self-image. These effects can cause terrible unhappiness and dysfunctions in your life. It causes a downward negative spiral.

How can you keep every commitment you make? Develop a system of being very conscious of every commitment that you make. The moment that you say you will do something or make a commitment, write it down on your commitment list. That list may be kept in your organizing / planning system, Outlook, or PDA. Your commitment list must be available to you always (except when you are sleeping :)). Every evening or morning when you plan your next day's work, check that list and keep your word by getting your commitments done. Everyone I know values responsiveness. So get it done as soon as possible. There are no good excuses for not keeping your commitments. In special circumstances, keeping a commitment is impossible and as soon as you realize it, let the other person know and establish another date and time to deliver on your word.

Do you keep all your commitments? Listen to your telephone voice mail. I ask again, do you keep all your commitments? Every one of your commitments is important. Become more aware. Start your system of recording every one, and reap the benefits of keeping all of your commitments.

Ben Franklin & Character

In Ben Franklin's twenties, he realized that talent and genius can carry a person only so far. It was a conclusion he reached studying the businessmen who frequented his printing shop. Many were charming enough but fell short of success because they did not have a good plan, weren't hard working, or lacked integrity.

To foster his habits and traits, Franklin realized he needed to develop his character further. To do that, he drew up a plan. He decided to cultivate twelve virtues – temperance, moderation, silence, organization, commitment, frugality, cleanliness, sincerity, justice, hard work, tranquility, and humility. He developed these virtues in sequence.

Franklin felt that temperance, moderation, and silence would focus his mind. Organization would help him manage his affairs. Commitment would keep him on track. Frugality and hard work would lead to wealth and independence. Cleanliness, tranquility, and humility would establish a positive impression and influence on people. That, in turn, would make sincerity and justice far easier to practice.

Franklin worked on one virtue each week for several years and kept a log of whenever he fell short. He kept careful notes and found that the process was eye opening. He was surprised at the number of faults this moral inventory uncovered, but Franklin took a smug pride in seeing them diminish. The rest is history.

Consider developing your character like Ben Franklin developed his. What could be the result for you?

Reflection

A son and his father were walking on the mountains.

Suddenly, his son falls, hurts himself and screams: "AAAhhhhhhhhhhh!!!" To his surprise, he hears the voice repeating, somewhere from the mountain: "AAAhhhhhhhhhhh!!!"

Curious, he yells: "Who are you?" He receives the answer: "Who are you?" Angered at the response, he screams: "Coward!" He receives the answer: "Coward!" He looks to his father and asks: "What's going on?"

The father smiles and says: "My son, pay attention." Then he screams to the mountain: "I admire you!" The voice answers: "I admire you!"

Again the man screams: "You are a champion!" The voice answers: "You are a champion!"

The boy is surprised, but does not understand.

Then the father explains: "People call this ECHO, but really this is LIFE. It gives you back everything you say or do. Your life is simply a reflection of your actions. If you want more love in the world, create more love in your heart. If you want more competence in your team, improve your competence. This relationship applies to everything, in all aspects of life. Life will give you back everything you have given to it." Your life is not a coincidence. It's a "Reflection" of you!

- Author Unknown

■ ■ ■

This short story begs that you reflect on your work and life. What are you experiencing? Is it happiness and joy or is it unhappiness and misery? If it is unhappiness and misery, then something needs to change. Ask yourself, "what needs to change?" Once you know, then you can change it. No excuses now! If you need help finding out, don't you think it would be worth whatever it takes to learn what will create happiness and joy for you?

Here is a prescription for living with integrity that delivers positive results in your life. Live with congruency between your thoughts, feelings, talk, and actions, especially those actions that reflect values that deliver positive consequences for yourself, others, your work, and life overall. Always keep your word!

■ CHAPTER THIRTEEN ■
THINKING AND CHOICE

What each of us is doing this minute is the most important event in history for us. We have decided to invest our resources in THIS opportunity rather than in any other. There are two days in every week about which we should not worry, two days that should be kept free from fear and apprehension.

One of these days is YESTERDAY, with its mistakes and cares, its faults and blunders, its aches and pains. Yesterday has passed forever beyond our control. All the money in the world cannot bring back yesterday. We cannot undo a single act we performed or erase a single word we said. Yesterday is gone.

The other day we should not worry about is TOMORROW, with its possible adversities, its burdens, its large promise, and its poor performance. Tomorrow is also beyond our immediate control.

This leaves only one day, TODAY. Anyone can fight the battles of just one day. It is only when you and I add the burdens of those two awful eternities - Yesterday and Tomorrow - that we break down. It is not the experience of today that drives us mad, it is remorse and bitterness for something that happened yesterday and the dread of what tomorrow may bring. Let us therefore - live this one full TODAY. It is difficult to be depressed and active at the same time. So get active! Live TODAY.

- Denis Waitley

Choose Your Thoughts

Except when we are deeply meditating, our mind is filled with thoughts - thoughts about work, life, kids, wife, bills, problems, you name it. Our minds are working all the time, including when we are sleeping. Some of these thoughts are positive and some of these thoughts are not so positive. Some are affirming and some are harshly judging of both ourselves and others. Positive thoughts usually provide us with pleasurable emotions and consequences. Negative thoughts usually have unpleasant emotions and consequences. I don't know about you, but I like the pleasurable emotions and consequences.

How we think about the world is our choice. Viktor Frankl, in his book *Man's Search for Meaning*, puts it like this, "everything can be taken from a man but one thing: the last of the human freedoms - to choose one's attitude in any given set of circumstances, to choose one's own way." Attitude is a habit of thought. In Auschwitz and three other concentration camps in Germany between 1942 and 1945, Viktor Frankl made a choice to learn about the psychology of the concentration camp. His choice of his attitude gave meaning to his life and enabled him to serve mankind until his death in 1997. If Viktor Frankl can choose in the horrid conditions of a concentration camp, then we can choose how we think in whatever circumstance we find ourselves.

Choose to observe and see the good in the world. Choose to find and use the positive ideas, information, and feedback that will help you grow and succeed. Choose to give and forgive. Choose to see the many right ways that work can be done and life can be lived. Choose to develop a positive attitude that brightens everyone's path. Choose to see yourself as the brightly shining star that you are.

P.S. Viktor Frankl was an Austrian Psychiatrist. His father, mother, brother, and wife all died in the concentration camps or were sent to the gas ovens (he had one surviving sister). He lost every possession, suffered immensely from the hunger, cold, and brutality. Extermination was an hourly expectation. He survived and recorded his experiences and learning in the book *Man's Search for Meaning*. Frankl wrote that one can discover the meaning in life in three different ways: "by creating a work of doing a deed; by experiencing something or encountering someone; and by the attitude we take toward unavoidable suffering."

Thought & Creation

Glance around yourself and notice all the objects that surround you. Notice all the things in your home and in your office. Where did they all come from? What was their origin? Pick up any object close to you and ponder what its origin was. Before you go further, take thirty seconds to think about the origin of the object you select.

After you think about it, you might find that the object was first a thought in some person's mind. Someone thinks it up, crystallizes the idea with copious details, perhaps draws pictures or plans, and then creates it. Every object that surrounds you was first a thought in some person's mind.

Everyone who is living has a future. Your future is what you create it to be. So your future must be thought about first before it is created. The more thought you put into your future, the more likely it will turn out the way you want it to become.

Your future thinking process should include your dreams and personal development areas. Take time and list all your dreams without any bounds like money, age, or time. Set priorities for your dreams. Then think about the six areas of your life and what you want to develop in them (financial & career, physical & health, mental & educational, family & home, spiritual & ethical, and social & cultural). Consider the two types of goals that are "to become" and "to get" goals. From your dream list and life areas, write goals needed to create the future you want to create. From your goals, plan how you will achieve them. Then take action and create your future. It all starts with thinking. Without thinking, what will your future be?

Thought, Cause, & Effect

Look around and notice your surroundings. Pick one item and become aware of it and experience its presence. Now notice another item and experience its presence. Now extend your attention to your entire surroundings and experience that. Everything around you is an effect of some cause. Something caused the effects you experience and that something is you.

You caused yourself to be in this exact location and so you experienced the effects of that location. Where you go and what you do have effects that you experience. You caused them to come into your life. Before the cause, there was a thought. You thought you should go somewhere or do something, you then caused yourself to go there or do that something, and lastly you experienced the resulting effects. You Thought, Caused, and created an Effect.

Who is responsible for the effects you experience? Since you thought it, caused it, and experienced the effects, you have to be responsible for your experiences. You are responsible and accountable for what you experience in your life.

If your experiences in your life and at work are not what you want, then all you have to do is think differently, cause something different to come into your life, and check to see if that is what you want. All you need to do is to change your thinking, change what you are doing, and enjoy your new experiences. If that change doesn't work the way you want, try another change. By making changes, you will eventually find the combinations that will give you what you want. If you are unhappy, disgusted with work and life, or frustrated, then make the changes that will bring you the happiness, joy of working and living, and the peace you wish to enjoy. If you do the things you have always done, you will get what you have always gotten!

The Right Questions

Experts say that 90% to 95% percent of your actions are taken through habit. Much of your mental processing of information is done the very same way. Of the 60,000 or so thoughts you have each day, many originate from "the same old thinking grove" (world view) and are very significantly influenced by your past conditioning and the programming of your subconscious mind (through your self-talk either positive or negative). Often "the same old thinking grove" may be in conflict with where you want to go in your life. If that is true for you, then somehow you need to become aware of the results that your thinking is bringing so that the right choices may be made, enabling you to proceed in the direction of your goals, dreams, and aspirations. The Right Questions will help you become aware of your thinking and choices. After becoming aware of your thinking and choices, you will be able consciously to make decisions that will support creating the future you want. The Right Questions are contained in a book of the same name written by Debbie Ford.

Debbie Ford says, "The Right Questions will give you the power and inspiration to create a life you feel good about, one choice at a time. They will help you to become aware of the important choices and their consequences. They will guide you and support you in making the right choices, and there you will find the most direct route to your dreams."

The Right Questions consist of ten powerful inquiries designed to reveal what is motivating your actions. The answers to these questions will immediately clarify your thinking and support you in making the choices that are in your highest and best interest. They are deceptively simple but incredibly powerful and can be used in any situation or at any crossroads. These, then, are **The Right Questions**:

- "Will this choice propel me toward an inspiring future or will it keep me stuck in the past?
- Will this choice bring me long-term fulfillment or will it bring me short-term gratifications?
- Am I standing in my power or am I trying to please others?
- Am I looking for what's right or am I looking for what's wrong?
- Will this choice add to my life force or will it rob me of my energy?
- Will I use this situation as a catalyst to grow and evolve or will I use it to beat myself up?
- Does this choice empower me or does it dis-empower me?
- Is this an act of self-love or is it an act of self-sabotage?
- Is this an act of faith or is it an act of fear?
- Am I choosing from my divinity or am I choosing from my humanity?"

Wow Debbie Ford!

Past, Present, or Future Person?

We can work and live in three places, the past, the present, or the future. People who live in the past try to recreate the past. They duplicate things that worked in the past. People who live in the future try to create the ideal; only in the future if I have _____ will I be happy. People who live in the present make the most of the time they spend in the present moment. The present living people find happiness and joy in the present moment. They make the most of every moment. They control their thinking.

WHAT DOES CONTROLLING YOUR PRESENT THINKING MEAN?

PAST: Present thinking does not mean thinking that is being controlled by the past. The past is gone, finished, never to ever happen again. Our parent's guidance, schooling, friends, work experiences, and environment have no control over the present unless *we choose to give it control* over the present. The good old days of the past are mainly a recreation of our imagination that will never occur again. Trying to live in the past leads you to unfulfilled hopes to replicate the past and general unhappiness.

FUTURE: To live in the future means to be controlled by our expectations of a perfect future. The future is a dream world of fantasy and perfection, where everything is just right. When our expectations are not realized, we become frustrated, demoralized, and unhappy. "The world did not provide what I expected. If only I had _____, I would be happy."

PRESENT: To live in the present, is to make the most of every present moment. Our repeated thoughts must be to make the most of our time in the present. "How can I spend the time I now manage to gain the most positive results?" "What can I do in this moment to progress toward my goals and create the life I want?" "How can I serve others, my employer, and myself to realize positive win-win outcomes?" Spending our time for the most positive outcome in each moment will ultimately result in happiness. You can choose to live in the present moment. Do it now!

Your Emotional Responses

EMOTIONAL RESPONSE: You automatically respond to many sensory inputs with emotion. Some emotions are very strong and take control of your thinking and actions. Historically, emotional responses have been a protective reaction that mobilizes your physical power to combat primitive external threats. However, as civilization has evolved, many physical threats you faced no longer exist. Your emotional response system (limbic system) doesn't know this historical change and so it automatically responds as if you are physically threatened. When you automatically perceive a threat, chemicals like adrenalin and cortisone flood your body readying it for the state of fight or flight. These chemicals are harmful to your body.

LEARNED BEHAVIOR: Perception of a threat is learned. As you grow up, you learn to assign emotional meanings to many sensory input patterns you receive. Some of those meanings can be positive but many of them are negative. Sensory inputs, like some forms of feedback, are often assigned meanings of a threat to us or our self-image. Perceived threats are usually met with defensive responses and behaviors that are strongly charged with negative emotion (anger, fear, rage, hurt feelings, etc). Negative emotional responses and behaviors are destructive to the body and to the value of the moment you are experiencing.

STORIES: What happens to cause a negative emotional response? When you receive sensory input in any form (hearing, sight, smell, etc.), it is filtered through all the emotional patterns and meanings you have learned. A past story you learned, associated with similar sensory input, is instantly recalled and you automatically respond. If the story is threatening, a negative emotional response is created and felt. If the story is positive, then your response will be productive and pleasurable. The story you tell yourself when you receive sensory input controls the emotional response and actions you subsequently take.

STORIES are a Choice: In your daily communications, you will receive many sets of sensory input containing valuable feedback on many of your actions. The story you tell yourself controls the response you make to any feedback when you receive that input. This story is ultimately your choice. I say ultimately, because the initial momentary response may be automatic with the subsequent conscious thought-controlled response becoming your choice. Your conscious response is a direct result of the choice of the story you tell yourself. Since you choose your story, you are responsible for your emotional response and actions, either negative or positive. Let's look at a common example.

EXAMPLE: When a car cuts in front of you in traffic, a common emotional response is to feel threatened, become defensive, and then respond aggressively because the action is automatically and immediately perceived as threatening your safety. The story you tell yourself is one of threat leading to a negative reaction. If your story is one that describes the person as rushing to the hospital to get medical attention for an emergency, we react in a completely different more positive way.

CHOOSE POSITIVE STORIES: Every life situation is just like this traffic example. We choose the story we tell ourselves and emotionally respond to that story. The story you tell yourself is your choice and your choice alone. Take responsibility for the stories you tell yourself,

157

the emotions you experience, and the actions you take. Consciously tell yourself positive stories and you will respond in a positive, happier way. Tell yourself negative stories and you will respond in an unhappy, miserable way.

You Are Not Defined by History

HISTORY: History is a wonderful thing. Our memory of the past can be filled with rich and rewarding experiences. In fact, our memory of the past is quite essential to understanding and making the most of the present. From the time we are babies, we are socialized into learning the rules of living. There are rules like potty training, behavior in school, obeying the traffic laws, respecting and interacting with other human beings, and discovering our place and role in the world. We learn thousands of beneficial rules. We can sometimes learn things that are very harmful to us.

WOUNDS: Our experiences in growing up are not always positive. If negative situations are presented to you multiple times, often unintended, then wounding can occur. Wounding means that your automatic uncontrolled emotional responses to some situations will dictate your actions in the current moment. In other words, historical events define your life experience now and how you experienced and recorded them. Similar situations throughout your life can surface automatic negative responses and create considerable harm. I know that you don't want that automatic negative emotional response and deep hurt.

CHOICE: The one thing you always have a choice of is your response to any and every situation that you encounter.

RESPONSIBILITY: You can choose how you respond to life situations. You can respond in a positive way every time. What can you learn? What life lesson is being presented to you? How can you benefit and grow through the present experience? How can you interpret it so that you can benefit? How can you help the person who is talking with you? What more can you do to rise above your circumstances and get the results you desire? You are always "able to respond" (responsibility) in a positive way to what life brings your way!

ASSESSMENT & ACTION: Ok, where are you living? Are events of the past defining your present and future? Or are you able to respond positively to what life brings your way. By going with the flow of life, growing, and learning is much easier than resisting, and letting the past control your present and future. Make the changes you need to make to "Create the future you want to enjoy." Do it now!

The Hardest Work

THE EASIEST WORK IS:

- Reacting to problems and issues
- Doing what others tell you to do
- Going along with the flow
- Doing whatever you want in the moment
- Letting the environment you work and live in, dictate your actions

THE MOST PRODUCTIVE WORK COMES FROM:

- Listing all the things you want to do (include goal action steps)
- Prioritizing them according to their importance in advancing your life toward your goals and dreams
- Scheduling the most important actions into your day
- Taking action on your schedule to accomplish the priority actions

159

- At the end of the day, tracking your progress and planning and scheduling your next day

It's called self-management.

- It's about: **taking responsibility for your time and managing it to advance you toward your goals and dreams**.
- It involves the actions of **thinking, planning,** and **exercising self-control** to get what you want.
- It's about **making no excuses** that could limit your achievements.
- It's about **having courage** and **exercising personal leadership**.

The result of exercising personal leadership is to enjoy the goals you achieve. But also, in progressing toward your dreams and growing as a person, you will find great happiness and joy in your journey. The journey of living life fully is found in the pursuit of your goals and dreams and developing more of your potential in the process.

It's not enough to read this and be enthusiastic. You must **make a choice and take action** to rededicate yourself to more effective and productive self-management. The time is now. Do the work that will advance you in the direction of your dreams (it's really not that hard). Do it now!

The Examined Life

HABIT: Experts tell us that 90 to 95 percent of our actions and thoughts are habit. Habit means that we take those actions and think those thoughts unconsciously. Largely we are operating on autopilot. That is a scary thing. Or is it?

160

HABITS HELP: the repetition of actions and thoughts develop our habits and is helpful in lightening our conscious thinking and action workload. Without them we could not accomplish all the things we do. Remember when you first drove a car. How much conscious thought did it take? Therefore, habits help us operate in our busy lives.

HABITS CAN HURT: Unfortunately, when we form habits, various assumptions are made and incorporated into the habit. Assumptions like:

- it's the way I was taught (ten years ago)
- it works for me
- all people are like this
- I'm right, why can't they see it?
- this is the way the world works
- there isn't any other way
- etc.

We live during a time of accelerating change. The world is changing around us constantly. The assumptions we made last week, last year, five years ago, or anytime in our past may no longer be true for us. The habits we tightly hold onto may no longer usefully serve us as they once did. Our habits need to be regularly examined for their usefulness. You can tell when your habits need to be examined by noticing that you are not getting the results you want or that you are experiencing harmful stress. When you are not getting the results you want or are feeling harmful stress, stop and take time to examine your present habits and attitudes. Then make the changes needed to get the results you want.

EXAMINE YOUR LIFE: Take time now to examine your habits of action and thought (attitudes) and determine what you need to change to get the results you want. It is often attributed to Socrates (469–399 B.C.) that, *"The unexamined life is not worth living."* Examine your life today so that it is worth living.

■ CHAPTER FOURTEEN ■
ATTITUDES

"Any fact facing us is not as important as our attitude toward it, for that determines our success or failure."

- Norman Vincent Peale

Our attitudes affect the behaviors that we display and the results that we get in work and life. You can think of your attitude as a habit of thought. As you repeat the same thought over and over again, it becomes reinforced (etched) into your brain and becomes an attitude. The interesting thing is that about 90% to 95% of what we think is directly a result of previous attitudes we have developed.

What attitudes did you create, now possess, and regularly exercise? What habits of thought drive and influence your behavior? Do those attitudes enhance your effectiveness and productivity or do they hinder them. Step back, take a moment, and critically examine how you habitually think, especially your attitudes toward work and life. Are they positive, uplift people and yourself, and lead to improved conditions, performance, and effectiveness? Or, do they drag you and others down, steal your energy, and hobble or limit the use of your potential and life?

Viktor Frankl in his book **Man's Search for Meaning** said, "everything can be taken from a man but one thing: the last of the human freedoms - to choose one's attitude in any given set of circumstances, to choose one's own way." In your given circumstances today, you can choose the way you think. You can choose to think in a fear based negative way toward the circumstances you find yourself or you can think in a positive caring and uplifting way toward the circumstances you find yourself. What is your choice?

By exercising control of how you think, you can create great positive attitudes that are impervious to the challenges that work and life present to you. I know that this statement is true from personal experience. The time to choose the positive, caring, and uplifting (loving) attitude is now. Try developing that positive pattern of thought into a life long attitude. It will serve you well. Set a goal and take action now to reap the benefits of continual positive, caring, and uplifting way of thinking.

Attitudes of Success

ATTITUDE: An attitude is a habit of thought. Ninety to ninety-five percent of our thoughts are habitual. In other words, most of the time our thoughts are not original; we just think the same way that we thought before. If our attitude is positive, then we can expect some very positive results. If it is negative, we can expect some very negative results. Developing a more positive attitude will lead to greater success in your work and life.

EXAMINATION: Pause a second and examine your thought patterns. Are your thought patterns positive or negative? The way you think every second has a great impact on the quality of your work and life. Do you see the world, people, and life with a positive spin or do you see the world, people and life with a negative spin?

WORK: Do you approach work with a "what's in it for me" orientation or a "service to others" orientation? Are you trying to make yourself look good or to make others look good? Is your ego screaming "I'm the best" or is the ego quiet and the spirit of love at work? Are you serving those who serve your clients or are you serving yourself?

LIFE: Are you serving yourself or serving those you say you care about? Are you more interested in your toys than the relationships you maintain? Are you building castles for yourself or are you building enduring relationships with others? Are you serving humankind or are you focused on the "me?"

CHANGE ATTITUDE: To develop more happiness, success, and joy in life, you must change your attitude to become more positive. How can you change your attitude? Why, by changing your thoughts! Be aware of all your thoughts (include judgments here too). Stop and examine them. Are they as positive as they can be? If not, change your thoughts to see your work and life in a more positive manner. The world is really a great place of personal opportunity, growth, and fulfillment. Seeing it as bummer of a place will severely limit your possibilities and happiness. I guarantee that if you control your thoughts in a positive way most of your time, you will find happiness, joy, and success in unbounded measure. It may not be easy at first, but the rewards are beyond measure. Try changing your thoughts to become more positive about your work and life!

SOME SUCCESS ATTITUDES:

- My success is totally dependent on the success of those who work for and with me.

- When I uplift others, I am uplifted.
- Seeing and expecting the best in others is a self-fulfilling prophecy. You will get the best.
- If I love the world, the world will love me.
- What goes around, comes around (love or fear, you make the choice).
- Appreciating others will bring happiness and joy to me.
- To help others grow, I must grow first.
- My work or life perception is a manifestation of my own thoughts and attitudes.
- The world I see is but a reflection of my own thoughts.
- Focusing on others success will bring me success.

Success Habits

The experts say that as we learn how successfully to accomplish tasks we develop habits through the repetition of specific actions. Think about it. What sequence of actions did you complete as you showered this morning? Was it generally the same sequence of actions you have always taken? A rule of thumb says that 90% to 95% of our actions are habitual. Wow! We are creatures of habit.

What if those habits are not effective or efficient in getting us the things we want out of work or life? Well then, we will get stuck and never progress to higher levels of success or happiness. So what must we do? We must change what we have always done. When we change what we do, then we can expect different results. It isn't easy because we must overcome the inertia of "I've always done it this way" and endure a little discomfort associated with change. But, if those different results propel us toward greater success or happiness, then we need to repeat those actions until they become new, more productive and successful habits. If the results are negative, we don't want to repeat those actions.

We are responsible for our own success and happiness, and are fully accountable for the results that our actions produce. We always have a choice of every one of our actions. Therefore, we are in total control of expanding our success and happiness. The challenge we face is changing the actions we take, assessing the results, and creating new habits around the positive action-results we get.

Take a moment and reflect on your habits. Are they getting you the results that you want? If not, why not? Is change needed? Don't wait another moment; make the changes you need to make to bring yourself greater success and happiness. Repetition of actions in a positive way makes new habits of success and happiness. If you are not sure what to change, get a coach to help you decide what to change. Do it now!

Think Your Way to Success & Happiness

1. First, a thought!
2. Repetition of that thought causes an attitude.
3. Attitudes greatly influence your behaviors.
4. Your behaviors create results.
5. The results you achieve determine your success.

If you agree with these statements, then you can see that what you choose to think (and particularly what you choose to think repetitiously) is largely responsible for your success. During one of my presentations entitled "Building on Your Success," a business owner got an insight that he took home and applied with his three-year-old daughter, Tiffany. He used the affirmation, "**Tiffany, you're a smart girl**." He did this for six days, and on the seventh day he came home and his daughter ran up to him and said, "**Daddy, your smart girl is here to see you**." What do you think Tiffany will grow up to become? Perhaps she will be a smart girl.

The repetition of positive thoughts can have great power in your work and life. Think about your work, coworkers, friends, relations, your home, and your life. What new positive thoughts could you choose? If you repeated those new positive thoughts regularly, what new result might you enjoy? Would there be changes that would uplift your spirits and lead to more and abundant happiness? Write these new positive thoughts down and, well, *you know what to do*. Just remember that what you think is always your choice.

More Interesting Thoughts

MAKE YOUR CIRCUMSTANCES: *"People are always blaming their circumstances for what they are. I don't believe in circumstances. The people who get on in this world are the people who get up and look for the circumstances they want, and if they can't find them, make them."*

– George Bernard Shaw

FAILURE BEFORE SUCCESS: English novelist John Creasey got 753 rejection slips before he published 564 books. Babe Ruth struck out 1,330 times, but he also hit 714 home runs. Don't worry about failures. Worry about the chances you miss when you don't even try.

PROCRASTINATION: This means: Living yesterday, Avoiding today, Running from tomorrow.

MAGICAL WORDS: What you consistently speak you will become; what you consistently speak you will create; and what you consistently speak you will find and experience.

The Power of Attitude

One of the most powerful success tools you possess is your **Attitude**. This tool can be developed to help you achieve greater results in your work and life.

ATTITUDE: Attitude is a habit of thought. Thoughts consciously repeated over time become automatic thought channels in your mind. These thought channels or attitudes can create limits to your success or they can add greater levels of success in your life and work. Examples of **limiting attitudes** are:

- I'm not good enough
- I must be perfect
- My work must be perfect
- I'm too busy to invest time in my own development
- I can't
- I can't succeed because _____
- I tried it once and it doesn't work
- On and on and on …

The opposite of limiting attitudes are positive attitudes. Positive thoughts repeated over and over become positive attitudes that help you reach your goals, and add to the success you already enjoy. You can choose to create positive thoughts and repeat them regularly to create new positive attitudes. We call these new positive thoughts affirmations. Affirmations are positive statements describing a desired state in the future as if it has already occurred. Examples of **Affirmations** include:

- Every day in every way I'm getting better and better
- I'm a great salesperson (or any other title)

169

- I'm a smart person
- I look fit, slim, and healthy at xxx pounds and feel great
- I live in a world filled with abundance and enjoy every abundant moment
- Every person I meet is special and filled with unlimited potential
- Challenges I face show me how I need to change to be successful
- I am filled with love for everyone
- Feedback is a gift – thank you
- On & on & on

Affirmations become **self-fulfilling prophecies** in your life. Over time you can develop a highly positive attitude that will bring you great joy, peace, and happiness. Create several affirmations for yourself and repeat them often. Shout them out and put some emotion into them. Try it for six months and see what a difference it makes. I know that this works because I used the affirmation, "I'm a Great Sales Person" and it changed my life. Alternately, repeating positive affirmations with your employees will help shape their working environment and positively affect morale. Positive thoughts and talk in the work environment build up people, which leads to greater effectiveness and productivity.

Attitude is Everything

My mission in life and work is to help people use more of their potential, and to make a positive difference in their lives. You can imagine the many different negative attitudes I encounter in conducting that mission. Self-limiting attitudes exist in us all. The challenge for each of us is to discover and overcome self-limiting attitudes as soon as we can. So ask yourself, "What thought, habit or belief do I frequently use that prevents me from changing and using more of my potential?" Once you have answered this question, decide to change that belief. Engage in repetitive new positive actions and thoughts that will become a self-fulfilling prophecy. Use affirmations and develop a knowing that ". . all things are possible."

Paul J. Meyer was so sure that "Attitude is Everything" that he recorded a program by that name. It includes twelve lessons that build a positive attitude. They are as follows:

1. Gain the Slight Edge
2. Do What it Takes to Become a Winner
3. Cultivate an Abundance Attitude
4. Focus on Singleness of Purpose
5. Winners use the Goal Seeking Power of Their Minds
6. Develop the Desire of a Winner
7. Maximize the Power of Enthusiasm
8. Develop a Tough Positive Mental Attitude
9. Never, Never, Never, Give Up!
10. Choose the Positive Forces of Life
11. Embrace the Pure Joy of Work
12. Become a Total Person

With the above attitudes, it a small wonder that ". . all things are possible."

Your Attitude is Everything

Attitude is the way you view your life: your experiences, your environment, your opportunities, your problems, your choices, and your responses. Attitude is the direction in which you lean on all ideas and issues.

Losers see thunderstorms. Winners look for rainbows. Losers see the peril in icy streets. Winners put on their ice skates. Losers put down.

Winners lift up. Losers let life happen to them. Winners make life happen for themselves and others. Winning and losing is all about attitude.

Attitudes begin as harmless thoughts. Over time, and with practice, they become layered by habit into unbreakable cables that shackle, or strengthen our lives. We're scarcely aware they exist. Like comfortable beds, they are easy to fall into but, once settled in, difficult to get out. First we make our attitudes, and then our attitudes make us.

There is little difference between common people and those who are uncommonly successful. The small difference is in their attitude. The big difference is whether the attitude is positive or negative. How important is your attitude? In truth, "Attitude is Everything."

We are not responsible for what happens out there, what others do or think. We are responsible only for how we choose to think and behave. That's our attitude.

Attitude about Learning

The world is presenting us with lessons to learn each day. We can choose to experience and learn the lessons, or ignore them. When we have learned our lesson, we can move on to the next lesson. Otherwise we will become stuck in a circular experience leading nowhere, until we learn the lesson we are suppose to learn. Life presents us with many opportunities to learn lessons each day.

Your attitude about learning is critical to "Building on Your Success." Being open to new ideas and thoughts indicates a productive attitude about learning. *Exercising quick and negative judgments* over the worth of an idea or thought can severely limit your success. Thinking that *automatically rejects what other people have found works,* could result in learning the hard way what works and what does not work (if you learn at all). *Choosing or allowing yourself to see only what you want to see* will result in missing many helpful ideas that people and the world present to you. You will miss the lessons that will enable you to grow and achieve new levels of work and life success. Be open, and even search for the ideas and thoughts that will advance you in the direction of "Adding to Your Success." Stay open to new ideas in every moment of your life.

A mind closed to hearing or seeing new ideas is a mind stuck in the experience loop, going nowhere. You may feel like you are experiencing the same things over and over again. This will become boring and frustrating. You will feel like you are going nowhere in work and life. You will feel like you are not growing and are stuck. If you feel that way, examine your own attitude about learning! Here are a few thoughts to break out of the loop. Embrace the following thoughts:

- "Life has something to teach me in every moment."
- "I choose to be open to new ideas, thoughts, and information."
- "I choose to learn and become a better person every day."
- "I have a positive attitude toward change and growing."
- "I have no limits to what I can achieve as I learn the lessons that life is presenting to me."
- "Life's challenges are the universe's way of showing me how I must grow."
- "Every day in every way I am getting better and better and better."

As these thoughts become a part of the fabric of your mind, you will create and maintain a positive attitude about learning. With that positive attitude, you take control of "**Adding to Your Success**."

An Attitude of Gratitude

Busy, busy, busy! In these busy days it is quite easy to ignore unintentionally, or forget to appreciate the abundance that surrounds and is available to us. We have this to do and that to do, lists of tasks to accomplish (*prioritized of course*), chores to complete, holiday activities to conduct, and family members to please. We can get so involved that there is no time to stop, enjoy the moment, consider the wonder that surrounds us, and appreciate the life that we live. We are surrounded by abundance in what we own, products and services available, opportunities galore, friends to enjoy, entertainment, freedom to travel, nature and all that it offers, and the list goes on and on. This time of year is a great time to stop and spend a few moments, hours, or maybe a day and give thanks for our abundant and blessed lives. Thinking about the following questions may sharpen your appreciation awareness:

Are you grateful for, and do you appreciate, everything that you possess? How do you show it?

Are you grateful for everyone you interact with? How do they know it?

Is your mind filled with loving and giving thoughts? You will show it!

Do you possess an attitude of gratitude? If not, why not?

Are you grateful for and love yourself? If not, how can you be grateful for and love others?

These are serious questions and the answers can serve to stimulate the goal setting you might do to increase your gratefulness in the New Year. Instead of resolutions, set some firm crystallized goals to develop more appreciation. With more gratefulness and appreciation in your life, you might find more happiness, peace, and joy.

An Attitude of Gratitude is Your Choice

STOP WHAT YOU ARE DOING! Quiet the chatter that is ever occurring in your mind. Reflect for a moment and assess your life experiences. Compare it with the people who live in Africa, China, and other continents and countries around the world. You live in relative freedom. You can work where you choose to work. Within a few minutes you can stop at a store and, using plastic cards, purchase almost whatever your heart desires. You may have multiple TV sets, CD players, many kitchen accessories, and sometimes several cars. You have a nice home (or apartment) with air-conditioning, running fresh water, electricity you can count on, e-mail, and, if you choose, opportunities to attend schools to better yourself. You have a job where you can work in relative comfort. You may feel you have too much work but what is the alternative? Do you have too little work and no job? You can freely interact with others in positive affirming ways. You have the choice and opportunity to help other people make their day. If you have the courage, bravery, and risk enough to dream, you can develop yourself, work, pursue, and realize your dreams. You have the opportunity to share positive thoughts with everyone always. What a wonderful life! But, sometimes people may ignore all that and focus on scarcity, or what's wrong with their situation (in their opinion). Or they may focus on how bad they have it - their life is just a repeat of the dreadful past. Or they cower from the risk of developing more of their potential due to fear of failure or loss. You don't need to think that way! You choose how you think and see your world. The meaning you give to life and work is your choice. You choose how you see this moment. You choose and create your future with your current thinking and choices.

The meaning that you assign to events, experiences, and what you sense in your world is your choice. You can choose to see all the abundance and wonderful things that are in your life. You can choose to celebrate the little successes that you experience. You can honor the fact that you are a "work in progress" and that you are making progress. You can choose to see the world in this moment as a great place to live as a human being and not an exploited human doing. You can choose to see the glass more than half-full. You can choose to think and express gratitude for everything around you. When experiences seem initially to sting, you can choose the meaning you ultimately assign. That chosen meaning can be a positive opportunity to grow and develop. You should take time to try new behaviors that might work better. Use the time to risk and develop more of your unlimited potential, and you can have and express gratitude for those growing opportunities.

Your experience of work and life is your choice. Choice is your birthright and no one can take it from you. Creating meanings that are always positive and expressing gratitude for life's experiences will result in unbounded joy and happiness. Developing this "Attitude of Gratitude" is not hard.

ACTION: Set a goal today to recognize three events in a positive light and to express gratitude for them (to others). Track your gratitude daily and continue for a month. Next month, set a goal to recognize six daily events in a positive light and to express gratitude for them. Track your daily gratitude and continue for another month. Continue the goal setting until you feel that you have developed a genuine ongoing "Attitude of Gratitude." You might just find that the world is a great place in which to work and live. Happy workers and people are more productive and effective. They achieve better results! Best wishes for a happy life filled with gratitude.

PMA

What is PMA? Why, it's **Positive Mental Attitude**! "Yeah, I heard all about that PMA stuff and life just isn't that way. Be realistic. I can't maintain a positive mental attitude all the time." Just look around at all the negative people. Well, I'm about to tell you that maintaining a PMA is possible.

When faced with any situation or problem, you can choose to *react* to it in a fearful way or *respond* to it in a positive way. Notice the words *react* and *respond*. Reaction to situations and problems suggest an unconscious automatic response usually derived from conditioned, emotional responses, based on fear, like defensiveness (perceived attack). Reactive responses based on fear will automatically destroy your PMA and the PMA of those around you - not a pretty picture.

The operative word "*choose*" is the key to maintaining PMA. By choosing a response to situations and problems that is positive, you add to and build on your PMA. Choosing to respond requires that you apply conscious thinking that can break through any unconscious emotional reaction. By choosing to respond, you are consciously looking for and focusing on the opportunities that the situation or problem presents to you. Taking this positive approach to all situations and problems will build and maintain your PMA.

Years of reacting to some situations and problems in a negative defensive way cannot be changed in one day with one positive choice. Consciously repeating a more positive response over time can create for you a PMA that is seldom lost. Set a goal to choose a positive response to every situation and problem you encounter. Then practice, practice, practice until responding with PMA becomes a habit. You can do it. I know you can do it. I believe in your unlimited potential to achieve anything you desire. ". . all things are possible."

Positive Thoughts Are A Choice

Having a positive mental attitude is one of the three characteristics of successful and happy people. Approaching your work and life with a positive mental attitude is sometimes quite difficult. But we do have a choice over our attitude. We can choose to be positive or we can choose to be negative. Attitudes are developed through the repetition of thought. We can choose our thoughts (Viktor Frankl, *Man's Search for Meaning*). So by choosing our thoughts in a positive way and repeating them often over time, we can develop new, more positive attitudes. With new attitudes come more positive results and added success.

SOME THOUGHTS OR ATTITUDES THAT ARE SELF-LIMITING INCLUDE:

- I can't
- That's the way I am
- I was born that way (I can't change)
- **I can't succeed because _____ (you fill in the reason)**
- **I'm too busy**
- **I tried it once and it didn't work**
- **It's not my job**
- **It's not my fault. The reason I'm this way is because … (you supply the reason)**
- and on and on!

REPLACE THESE ATTITUDES WITH POSITIVE AFFIRMATIONS SUCH AS:

- I am...........
- I change, grow, and conquer the challenges of life
- I prioritize and do the most important things
- I do things I never thought I could do
- I take responsibility to … (you fill in the item)

With a positive attitude toward life, you learn, grow, enjoy, and find happiness. Challenges are fun and life is filled with wonderment. It all depends on your attitude. And you choose your attitude!

◼ Chapter Fifteen ◼
PERSONAL GROWTH

"Anyone who stops learning is old, whether at twenty or eighty. Anyone who keeps learning stays young. The greatest thing in life is to keep your mind young."

- *Henry Ford*

If the world is fast changing (and you know it is), what you know and the way you work today will not necessarily be effective for you tomorrow! That means you must change and grow to keep up with the evolving world (or is it a revolution?). But, change what, and how?

Change What? Of course, you should change your knowledge, skills, and competencies. But first you must know what they are and where you are in your personal development. You must also choose and want to grow and develop more of your potential. Some leaders, executives, managers, and supervisors that I work with are unclear about their strengths and weaknesses (effective and ineffective skills and competencies). Blind spots exist in their behaviors that negatively affect their organizations. They are often unaware of how their current behaviors and attitudes affect their organizations' productivity. Unless you know yourself and the reality that

181

you create, you cannot meaningfully grow as a person, manager, or leader. Here are a couple of ideas you can use to learn more about yourself:

- **Read** personal improvement books (tapes, videos, etc.). Record improvement ideas you receive.

- **Beg** everyone you know for specific feedback about your attitudes, behaviors, and performance (thank them for their gift to you)

- **Search** out and take assessments to learn more about yourself (Myers-Briggs Step II, BarOn EQ-i, FIRO-B, 16 PF, and many available others)

- **Engage** an Executive Coach to help you see your blind spots, break through your own resistance to change, and accelerate your learning. Every professional sports player has one! You are a professional, aren't you?

CHANGE - How? It's really not hard, just different from what you are in the habit of now doing. It may seem like some impossible task but once you decide to change, it is simple, easy, energizing, and motivating. However, just like an elephant must be eaten one bite at a time, you change one small step at a time. That means setting small goals aligned with achieving the larger changes or goals you wish to make. A small goal may be asking a subject matter expert to recommend to you a book that you can read (then buy it and read it). Another small goal might be regularly to ask your supervisor or significant other for their insights and ideas. Here are a couple of other thoughts about how you can go about change:

Prioritize your areas for development (or improvement ideas) and set **"To Become"** goals. Complete a goal planning sheet for the top priority.

Start with one development goal.

Take action every day toward achieving your "**To Become**" goals.

Tune-up your personal management system so it is proactive, focused on HPAs, and that you are implementing & tracking action steps to achieve personal growth goals. Ensure that you are choosing and directing your life, not your work and life directing you.

Find a friend to act as a **coach** in helping you and keeping you on track. Alternately, enlist the help of a personal development coach.

If you wish to live an enjoyable, long, and bountiful life, you must grow as a person and develop more of your potential every day. The alternative of stagnation is pitiful in the long-term. Even if you have to pay for it, aren't you worth it? You'll pay a lot more for fewer valuable "things." Think about it! Then, take action to grow and develop more of your potential.

Growth vs. Stagnation

GROWTH: Are you consciously growing as a person every day? Do you take time each day to increase your knowledge, develop new skills, use more of your potential, or increase your competencies? If you are not consciously doing that, then you are stagnating! Stagnated in your work and your life where you are today, where you were yesterday, and maybe even where you were years ago. You are not growing like you could. You are not leading yourself to create a better future for yourself and those with whom you have relationships and responsibilities.

BENEFITS: When you do take action to increase your knowledge, develop new skills, use more of your potential, and increase your competencies each day in some conscious way, you become more able to help others including your family, and members of your work group and company.

STEPS: If you want to grow and choose to grow, here are some steps to get you going:

- **Know yourself** better:
    o **Dream again** and write them down.
    o **Develop a vision** for your life. While you are at it, write a **purpose** statement, **mission** statement, and really get in touch with what you **value**.
    o **Learn about your personality** and how you can interact with others more effectively.
    o **Take assessments** that will help you see your blind spots and where you should change and grow.
- **Assess your satisfaction** with all areas of your life (wheel of life) including:
    o Physical & Health
    o Mental & Educational
    o Family & Home
    o Spiritual & Ethical
    o Social & Cultural
    o Financial & Career

- **Write a Goal**: Prioritize an unsatisfactory area of life you want to improve and set a goal to change. Complete a goal sheet and take action to get new results.

- **Seek feedback** from others about what changes you should make. It's a gift most precious that can help you see yourself more clearly and help you become a better person.

- **Find a coach** to help you accelerate your development. It's many times more efficient than plowing forward by yourself. You will be on a fast track to added success.

184

INSTRUCTIONS: Growth or change happens one small action step at a time (action steps leading to the accomplishment of a "to become" goal). So don't worry or let the fear of making large changes keep you from starting. One small step each day and in a year you have 365 steps. Reflect back on 365 steps and you will see great changes and improvements. Your self-esteem will soar and those around you will see a positive and growing person. Your example and the sharing you choose to do will influence them to grow. So, don't just sit there, write a goal and start the process now!

Surviving or Thriving?

Abraham Maslow, the motivation guru, placed survival (physiological needs like air, water, food, reproduction, etc.) as the very fundamental bottom of the motivation pyramid. Security was the next highest motivational level that involves having a roof over your head, regular means of providing for your survival needs, and provisions for the basic ongoing life functions. Today, with our challenging economy, accelerating change, uncertain business futures, and globalization, we often become uncertain of meeting our security needs and sometimes fear for our survival. Or, perhaps fear and doubt grip us and hold us back from exploiting the opportunities that abound.

Leadership and management in companies are struggling to right size, trim costs, and manage resources to "keep the business going." The challenges are ever increasing. Many are fearful of what the future will bring and are operating in a "Survival Mode." Working in the grip of "fear of survival" destroys creativity, motivation, and depletes the energy needed to recognize and engage the opportunities. Many leaders and managers are trapped in preserving what "has been in the past" and not "what can be in the future." How do you break out from this "prison of fear?"

If you are a leader or manager (and everyone is), then here are the steps that you must take to break free of the fear of survival, insecurity, and doubt. You must:

1. Choose to break free of fear and mediocrity (the way you may have done things in the past)

2. Crystallize your work and life focus (Purpose, Vision, Mission, & Values)

3. Set goals and plan the actions necessary to achieve them

4. Exercise discipline and take daily actions in the pursuit of your goals

5. Dedicate daily time to self-development (develop knowledge and skill areas supporting your work and life goals) - **NO EXCUSES**: Who is important here?

6. Grow, grow, grow, & develop, develop, develop yourself (never-ending)

7. Refuse to fall into the same rut you may have fearfully fallen into before

8. Repeat the first seven steps - keep on track and stay the course

Leaders and managers are often so busy with work that they find no time or energy to develop themselves. The people who work for leaders and managers are watching them as "models" of the "right and successful way of working." Unless, you are setting an exemplary example of personal growth and change, you are leading your employees to stagnant or lower levels of mediocrity and performance in your organization. If you are not growing and developing your skills and knowledge daily, you cannot grow and develop those who work for you. The choice to become a more competent and knowledgeable leader and manager is entirely up to you. By investing daily in developing your leadership and management skills, you can raise yourself above Maslow's survival and security to the "Self-Actualization" level where you can live your life purpose. Hey, it may not be easy, but the rewards are great. If you are unsure how to proceed, get help. **The most important person you can develop is you**!

Learning

Reasonable failure should never be received with anger. Benedict Spinoza announced a principle like this when he said that the highest activity a human can attain is learning, or, in his language, understanding. To understand is to be free. He argued that those who respond to failure of others with anger are themselves slaves to passion, and learn nothing.

Tom Watson Sr., IBM's founder and its guiding inspiration for more than forty years, put that Spinozan principle to work a number of years ago. A promising junior executive of IBM was involved in a risky venture for the company and managed to lose more than ten million dollars in the gamble. It was a disaster. When Watson called the nervous executive into his office, the young man blurted out, "I guess you want my resignation?" Watson said, "You can't be serious. We've just spent $10 million educating you."

Nothing ventured, nothing gained, nothing learned!

Going to the Next Level of Success

What do you mean going to the next level? Many people have worked hard to achieve the success that they presently enjoy. However, at the same time they feel that there is room for improvement and another business horizon to capture. Hard as they try, it is unclear what they must do to get there. They feel stuck and frustrated in their hard efforts to get to the next level. What does it take to go to the next level?

If you do the things you have always done, you will get what you have always gotten. Change is involved in going to the next level. What needs to change? Why do I need to change? Since a company's success is equal to the success of its people, then for the company to go to the next level it is wholly dependent on its people going to the next level. Going to the next level is dependent on the individual's change and growth.

Individual change and growth is personal. It involves an individual understanding where they are in their competencies, attitudes, and habits. It depends on the person determining their strengths and weaknesses and in determining where they desire to go in their lives. Once the tension of knowing where they are and where they want to be is clearly visualized, then a person can set goals and plans to achieve those new visions, desires, and wants.

The process is assessment of where you are, determining new targets of competencies, developing the plans and actions necessary to build them, and then taking the necessary actions to develop these new competencies. This process must be conscious and ongoing to continue to develop more of your potential.

If you feel stuck and frustrated with where you are, don't sit and wish for changes. Take action to seek a coach or someone who will help you add to your present success. I guarantee that the new level of success you will enjoy will be worth all the effort and investment you make in yourself.

How to Win Friends & Influence People

FUNDAMENTAL TECHNIQUES IN HANDLING PEOPLE

Principles

1. Don't criticize, condemn or complain.
2. Give honest and sincere appreciation.
3. Arouse in the other person an eager want.

SIX WAYS TO MAKE PEOPLE LIKE YOU

Principles

1. Become genuinely interested in other people.
2. Smile.
3. Remember that a person's name is to that person the sweetest and most important sound in any language.
4. Be a good listener. Encourage others to talk about themselves.
5. Talk in terms of the other person's interests.
6. Make the other person feel important – and do it sincerely.

WIN PEOPLE TO YOUR WAY OF THINKING

Principles

1. The only way to get the best of an argument is to avoid it.
2. Show respect for the other person's opinions. Never say, "You're wrong."
3. If you are wrong, admit it quickly and emphatically.
4. Begin in a friendly way.
5. Get the other person saying "yes" immediately.

6. Let the other person do a great deal of the talking.

7. Let the other person feel that the idea is his or hers.

8. Try honestly to see things from the other person's point of view.

9. Be sympathetic with the other person's ideas and desires.

10. Appeal to the nobler motives.

11. Dramatize your ideas.

12. Throw down a challenge.

BE A LEADER

Principles

1. Begin with praise and honest appreciation.

2. Call attention to people's mistakes indirectly.

3. Talk about your own mistakes before criticizing the other person.

4. Ask questions instead of giving direct orders.

5. Let the other person save face.

6. Praise the slightest improvement and praise every improvement. Be "hearty in your approbation and lavish in your praise."

7. Give the other person a fine reputation to live up to.

8. Use encouragement. Make the fault seem easy to correct.

9. Make the other person happy about doing the thing you suggest.

Thank you Dale Carnegie.

▪ CHAPTER SIXTEEN ▪
CHANGE

"You must pay the price if you wish to secure the blessings."

- Andrew Jackson

Why do I have to change? It's because the world is changing! Nothing stands still in our universe, least of all the need for improved skills, competencies, and attitudes. If you are not changing (or growing) as a person you are standing still, or even worse, falling behind. When people stand still in their development or fall behind, they cling onto what they know by becoming closed minded, secretive, untrusting, directive, dictatorial, negative, unreasonably confrontational, and fearful. This causes them to be increasingly ineffective and inefficient while interacting with others at work and in life. While I understand the "**easy path**" of staying comfortable with what we now know and do, I also know that without change we become fossils. Worse, our minds and body's atrophy, and use less of our potential as human beings. So **change we must!** Why not change in ways that improve your life and allow you to experience higher levels of joy and happiness?

What must be done to change? The following are nine steps that are essential to the personal change process:

1. You must realize and embrace the fact that **change is the only way to enrich your life**. To remain the same is to die a slow death!

2. You must seek and choose to be **open to feedback, information, and learning new things** about the world, work, and **especially about yourself**.

3. From information you get, you must **look for and develop new personal insights, and identify changes** that could bring new positive results to your life.

4. Insights must be turned into goals for personal change. Planning must occur to identify the new goal action steps needed to break through your past conditioning and change your work and life.

5. Planned **action steps must be scheduled into your day, acted upon, and accomplished**.

6. Completed action steps must be **tracked and evaluated as to their results** (positive or negative).

7. Positive results must be made a regular part of your work and life. In other words, actions and thoughts that work must be **practiced until they become new habits and attitudes** (*spaced repetition*). Make them an automatic part of your work and life style.

8. Reflect and **celebrate your new success** on a daily basis. Take pride in your progress and efforts to grow and become all

that you can be. Acknowledge that you are on the path to being an even greater person. **Realize that your future is unlimited**.

9. Repeat the eight steps.

We are all on different roads in our lives. It makes no difference what roads others are on or where they are in their life because **your road and travel are unique to you. You choose and control the road that you travel**. The important thing to embrace is that by systematically following the nine steps, you are deliberately developing more of your potential. You are growing and not standing still, or worse, "**losing it**." **By following the road to growth, you will encounter greater levels of joy, peace, fulfillment, and happiness**. Take someone along with you! Better yet, take your family, your colleagues, your department, and / or your company! That's leadership!

■ ■ ■

Why do we resist changing ? *Not me you say!* If you stop for a minute and step back to observe yourself, you might find that you are a "creature of habit" (experts say 90% to 95% of our actions are habits). Those habits are repeated with *no thinking* on your part. "No thinking" is associated with habits of thought called attitudes. Habits of action and attitudes are automatic and make you feel comfortable. And some of those **habits and attitudes are getting in the way of realizing your goals and dreams** (if you know what your goals and dreams are). These limiting habits or attitudes can be identified as frustrations, stresses, negative attitudes, or conditions that seem to keep you from making progress toward realizing the things you want in your life. Obstacles, barriers, or limiting habits and attitudes are the Universe's way of telling you **what you need to**

change to get or be what you want. Embrace the changes instead of fighting them. Fighting or ignoring the changes you need to make will cost you more energy than embracing the change and taking different actions to form new enabling habits and attitudes.

Have you ever discovered how some small task that you needed to do and put off for a long time weighed heavily on your mind and drained your energy (**habit of procrastination?**). Once you decided to start it, you discover that it actually goes quickly and feels oh so good that it is now finished (a load off your mind). If you know what your goals and dreams are and take that first step, and regular steps after that, you will find yourself changing, growing, and progressing toward your wants and dreams. You will become energized, and over time the pleasure of realizing and enjoying what you create will fill you with great happiness. Try it, I guarantee that change will not hurt. Please call me if it does.

Life Changes

PERSONAL ASSESSMENT: What is your life like right now? Is it the life you want to live, or is it one that just seems to happen? Is it filled with joy, happiness, and positive experiences, or is it filled with dread, hurt, and negative experiences? The truth is that your life right now is the result of all the thoughts, decisions, and actions you have taken in the past. To change your experiences in life, all you need to do is change your thoughts, decisions, and actions. No one can take responsibility for changing your life except you. So if it is to be, then it's up to you. In this moment right now, you can change your thoughts, make better decisions, and take actions to create the life you want to live.

ACTION: What part(s) of your life needs changing? Take just one thing today and make a commitment to positively change your thoughts, decisions, and actions. Make your commitment in writing on a 3x5 card and keep it with you wherever you go. Refer to it often and make the changes you choose. After seven days, choose another area of your life you would like to change and repeat the process. Every week, continue the choice / change and in one year you will make fifty-two changes. What a life you could be living, if you did that. You can do it. It's your choice. No one can rob you of that choice except yourself. Go for it!

A Life Lesson – You Are Not Entitled to Success

HISTORY: I was motivated to do well in High School. I studied and completed my homework, participated in many activities, and wound up eight in a class of about 160 students. In the University, I again focused on the actions that would lead to success (all but one year, where ROTC interfered with my judgment). I spent twenty plus years in the Air Force doing my best and successfully progressing up the ladder. In 1990 I found myself at a company where my second career began. My boss intimated that I would have a future of more than twenty years to create more success. I thought this company owed it to me to develop my knowledge, skills, and career. How wrong I was!

CHANGE: After challenging the way things were done at this company (my commitment to leadership), the company offered me a downsizing or a job that I could do in my sleep. I chose to be downsized. Then, over a couple of more years, I learned that if I were to be successful, it was totally up to me. I was not entitled to success. I have to develop success on my own. I embraced a Peter Drucker quote, **"The best way to predict your future is to create it."** That is what I decided to do.

SUCCESS: Success is a moving target. Setting goals and achieving them is a part of the process. Learning, developing new skills, and growing as person is all important. Living in the moment, appreciating everything in your life, and always seeing the world in a positive way, will lead to joy, happiness, and love. Serving others with a worthwhile purpose is immensely satisfying. Caring and taking time for you, is essential to developing your long-term success and short-term happiness.

CHOICE: Success is not an entitlement you have because you inhabit this earth. Personal leadership development is about directing your life, making it meaningful, and enjoying the journey. Take time to assess where you are on that journey now. Then set and take one action that will advance you in the path of greater success because you choose to travel that path.

Who Creates Your Future?

The obvious answer to the question is that you create your future. But when I listen to, and observe the people that I work with, I often find them passing off accountability for their development onto others. "The company should sponsor my training & development." "My boss is responsible for training me in the new software." "If they want to have this new system work, then they need to train me." *I fell into the same trap*. At the last company I worked for, I expected them to purchase all the books and materials I should have been reading. So, I passed off responsibility and accountability to the company for my own development. An unexpected change in my employment status got my attention, and in the next year Walden Books received more than $1,200 for books that I chose to read.

What did I learn? You must be proactive in developing yourself if you wish to be in charge of your future. Take stock of your skills, competencies, strengths, and opportunities for growth. Pick an area or two you want to develop more fully. Set goals and plan how to achieve the results you want. Don't be afraid to invest in your own self-development. If you will not invest, then who will? Communicate your goals so that other people may help you achieve them. Ask Leadership Advantage. We will help you in every way possible, because it is our mission and the right thing to do. Track your progress and celebrate both your accomplishments and reaching your goals. Take charge of your life and create your own future.

Listen to Your Resistance

In work and life you will find yourself resisting different people, situations, or encounters. You might resist listening to a person who is offering another view of some part of work or life. You might resist making a change someone has suggested. You might resist changes in how you work or how you live. Resistance can come in many different forms. Consciously become aware of your resistance. Resistance is a "Wake-up" call. Resistance is saying to you, "Pay attention." When you find yourself resisting anything, become aware of your resistance and ask yourself, "Why am I resisting this?" The answer to this question will give you a precious insight that when acted upon can profoundly change your world.

Resistance tells you that you are encountering a situation where there is a life lesson to learn. A life lesson that if not learned now, will repeat itself in different forms until it is learned. If you do not care about learning life's lessons, then ignore the resistance you are feeling and keep on working and living as you have always done. If you want to grow and develop as a person, then pay attention to your resistance. Listen for, and learn the life lessons presented to you. Make changes and take actions to progress positively past your resistance. Set a goal to become more aware of your resistance every day and to learn life lessons instead of ignoring them. Do it now!

■ CHAPTER SEVENTEEN ■
BALANCE

*"Reflect upon your present blessings, of which every man
has many - now on your past misfortune,
of which all men have some."*

- Charles Dickens

I often hear statements like "**I don't have a life**." Often they come from people who are working long hours (and some people want to!). It's when this happens day in and day out over an extended period that it gets **unhealthy,** physically and mentally. And, it can slip up on you without you even being aware of it. It just happens.

GET A LIFE - LIFE MANAGEMENT TOOLS

Crystallize in writing and use your:

1. Life Vision: What do you want to create while you live on this earth (it is limited, you know?)

2. Mission: What life roles are most important to you and what will you do to move toward your vision?

3. Purpose: What is your purpose for living on this earth? What do you have *passion* about?

4. Values: What do you value? What values guide your life during the conduct of your mission?

5. Goal Plan: What goals have you set in each of the six areas of your life? You do have a goal or two written and planned in each life area, don't you? (Financial & Career; Physical & Health; Mental & Educational; Family & Home; Spiritual & Ethical; Social & Cultural)

6. Prioritization: What goals are most important right now in your life? Choose only a couple of the most important to work on at a time.

7. Schedule: You are the manager of your time, aren't you? So schedule your priorities first, and then fill in with the less important things that must be done.

8. Take Action: Take action on your priorities each day to move toward your goal. One small action a day is 365 actions a year and I'll bet you will be surprised, ecstatic, and highly gratified at what you can accomplish in just one year.

Each day, week, month, and year, pause and reflect on how you are using these **Life Management Tools**. Make the necessary changes to use them effectively and efficiently. If you use them well, you will achieve a joyful and balanced life. No excuses now (like "**I'm too busy**"). **Take control of your life!** Don't let life control you.

Work–Life Balance

The amount of time you spend in activities directly communicates your priorities. If the activity is work and you are spending twelve to fourteen hours each day working, then work has a high priority in your life. If you spend eight hours working and eight hours engaged in other non-work activities, then you have what seems to be more balance, but not always.

A person can feel unbalanced in their life when one or two life areas consume most of their time. Normally one area is work and the other can be anything (children, education, hobbies, etc.). Having a consistently balanced life is almost impossible due to different and changing life demands. So what's missing that it seems so "unbalanced?"

A person who knows her or himself and pro-actively manages to engage in activities they choose and prioritize will feel more balanced and in control. A person who knows what their life **Vision**, **Purpose**, **Mission**, and **Values** are will have a solid foundation from which to lead a more proactive, purposeful, and meaningful life. From this foundation, people can exercise their ability to **Dream** and again imagine all the things they would like to do. Turning prioritized dreams into **Goals** and developing a **Plan of Action** to accomplish those goals are vital steps in gaining more balance and control. Using a disciplined process to **accomplish small actions each day to achieve your goals** will make your dreams slowly but surely come true. When you are realizing your dreams, your esteem will soar, happiness will abound, and life will be a joy.

Knowing your life Vision, Purpose, Mission, Values, Dreaming, Setting Goals, Planning, and taking disciplined actions seems rather difficult. However, the alternative of not knowing or doing these things can lead to a meaningless life controlled by others and the environment. This uncontrolled life is tossed to and fro by the priorities of other people and things. Consistently letting one or two aspects of your life use all your time and energy will adversely impact your productivity, energy, attitude, and happiness. So what is it going to be? You can choose balance and happiness or unbalance and despair. The choice is yours!

Stress Management

A lecturer, when explaining stress management to an audience, raised a glass of water and asked, "How heavy is this glass of water?" Answers called out, ranged from 20g to 500g. The lecturer replied, "The absolute weight does not matter. It depends on how long you try to hold it. If I hold it for a minute, that's not a problem. If I hold it for an hour, I'll have an ache in my right arm. If I hold it for a day, you'll have to call an ambulance. In each case, it's the same weight, but the longer I hold it, the heavier it becomes."

He continued, "And that's the way it is with stress management. If we carry our burdens all the time, sooner or later, as the burden becomes increasingly heavy, we won't be able to carry on. As with the glass of water, you have to put it down for a while and rest before holding it again. When we're refreshed, we can carry on with the burden. So, before you return home tonight, put the burden of work down. Don't carry it home. You can pick it up tomorrow. Whatever burdens you are carrying now, let them down for a moment if you can. Relax; pick them up later after you've rested. Life is short. Enjoy it!"

And then he shared some ways of dealing with the burdens of life:
- Accept that some days you're the pigeon, and some days you're the statue.
- Always keep your words soft and sweet, just in case you have to eat them.
- Always read stuff that will make you look good if you die in the middle of it.

- Drive carefully. It's not only cars that can be recalled by their maker.
- If you can't be kind, at least have the decency to be vague.
- If you lend someone $20 and never see that person again, it was probably worth it.
- It may be that your sole purpose in life is simply to serve as a warning to others.
- Never buy a car you can't push.
- Never put both feet in your mouth at the same time, because then you won't have a leg to stand on.
- Nobody cares if you can't dance well. Just get up and dance.
- Since it's the early worm that gets eaten by the bird, sleep late.
- The second mouse gets the cheese.
- When everything's coming your way, you're in the wrong lane.
- Birthdays are good for you. The more you have, the longer you live.
- You may be only one person in the world, but you may also be the world to one person.
- Some mistakes are too much fun to only make once.
- We could learn a lot from crayons. Some are sharp, some are pretty, and some are dull. Some have weird names, and all are different colors, but they all have to live in the same box.
- A truly happy person is one who can enjoy the scenery on a detour.

A Guide to Happy Living

Life just became more precious to all Americans. Precious, because it can be short and there are so many things we want to experience and do.

Often we claim that there is never enough time to do all these things. The reality is that everyone has the same amount of time each day. How we use that time determines the results we enjoy. Each of us has a different number of days to live and we all want to be happy, don't we?

Happiness comes from pursuing worthwhile personal goals and living a meaningful life that contributes to making a difference in the world. W. Beran Wolfe wrote this about happiness, "If you observe a really happy man, you will find him building a boat, writing a symphony, educating his son, growing double dahlias or looking for dinosaur eggs in the Gobi Desert. He will not be searching for happiness as if it were a collar button that had rolled under the radiator, striving for it as a goal in itself. He will have become aware that he is happy in the course of living life twenty-four crowded hours of each day."

The actions we take each twenty-four hour period will produce results that either are positive and joyful, or negative and ruinous. The choice of how we use our time and perceive our experiences is ours to make. The following nine steps can guide you in living twenty-four hours that will be worthwhile and meaningful while enabling happiness to find you.

1. Take time to think and set worthwhile and meaningful goals

2. Write your goals down and plan the actions that will achieve results.

3. Prioritize all your goals. Work only on the highest priority goals first.

4. List all the actions you would like to accomplish this day. Prioritize them.

5. Schedule your entire day to accomplish as many goal-directed and meaningful activities as you can.

6. Act on your daily schedule with enthusiasm and purpose.

7. At the end of the day, reflect back and write down all the things you accomplished.

8. Celebrate your day's success. Allow yourself to enjoy the progress you made.

9. Without guilt, let the things undone go for another day.

10. Start over at step one or step four for your next twenty-four-hour day.

Procrastination is the lack of a decision and action. When we have not decided how to spend our valuable time, events of the day will steal it from us. At the end of the day, nothing important seems to get done. Likewise, if you do not purposefully take action on your schedule, then there are no results. Happiness will never arrive in your life under this scenario. Beat procrastination. Decide to follow the ten steps to happiness and act on them today. Happiness will pursue, surround you, and fill your soul with joy!

Lastly, Joseph Fort Newton said, "To be happy is easy enough if we forgive ourselves, forgive others, and live with thanksgiving. No self-centered person, no ungrateful soul can ever be happy, much less make anyone else happy. Life is giving, not getting."

Natural High's

INSTRUCTIONS: Take a few minutes and read these thoughts. Think about each for a few seconds before going onto the next thought. It feels good to think about life's simple pleasures.

Falling in love.

Laughing so hard your face hurts.

A hot shower.

CHAPTER 17 || *Balance*

Watching a beautiful sunset.

A special glance from someone.

Getting a thank you note.

Taking a drive on a pretty road.

Hearing your favorite song on the radio.

Lying in bed listening to the rain outside.

Hot towels out of the dryer.

Cuddling with someone.

Chocolate milkshake (or vanilla!).

An unexpected phone call from someone you love.

Listening to the oceans waves.

Feeling happy with yourself.

A stimulating conversation.

Beach sand beneath your toes.

Finding a $20 bill in your pocket.

Watching an Eagle fly.

Relaxing in a warm sauna.

Running through the rain.

Having joy and gratitude for life and this moment.

Having someone tell you that you're beautiful (or handsome).

Walking in the woods.

Eating your favorite dessert or fruit.

Feeling understood and accepted.

Accidentally overhearing someone say something nice about you.

Knowing you are an important contributor to the universe.

Your first kiss.

Discovering new things about an old friend.

Playing with a new puppy.

Someone playing with your hair.

Sweet dreams.

Hot chocolate on a cold night.

Loving someone and being loved in return.

Swinging on swings.

Watching hummingbirds fly.

Song lyrics printed inside your new CD so you can sing along without feeling stupid.

Enjoying a great concert or show.

Making eye contact with a cute stranger.

Winning a really competitive game.

Watching a thunderstorm.

Spending time with your close friend.

Seeing smiles and hearing laughter.

Holding hands with someone you care about.

Being promoted.

Getting a message.

Watching a child's face at Christmas.

Watching the sunrise.

Waking up filled with love.

Chocolate Sings

One day I had a date for lunch with friends. Mae, a lady about eighty years old came along with them. Overall, it was a pleasant group of people. When the menus were presented, we ordered salads, sandwiches, and soups, except Mae who said "I would like ice cream, please, two scoops of chocolate."

CHAPTER 17 || *Balance*

I wasn't sure my ears had heard correctly, and the others were aghast. "Along with heated apple pie," Mae added, completely unabashed. We tried to act quite nonchalant, as if people did this all the time. But when they brought out our orders, I didn't enjoy mine. I could not take my eyes off Mae as her pie a-la-mode went down. The other ladies showed dismay. They ate their lunches silently and frowned.

The next time I went out to eat, I called and invited Mae. I lunched on white meat tuna. She ordered a parfait. I smiled. She asked if she amused me. I answered, "Yes, you do, but you also confuse me. Why do you order rich desserts, while I feel I must be sensible?"

She laughed and said, with wanton mirth, "I'm tasting all that's possible. I try to eat the food I need, and do the things I should. But life's so short, my friend, I hate missing out on something good. This year I realized how old I was (She grinned). I haven't been this old before. So, before I die, I've got to try those things that for years I have ignored.

- I haven't smelled all the flowers yet. There are too many books I haven't read.
- There are more fudge sundaes to wolf down and kites to fly.
- There are many malls I haven't shopped. I've not laughed at all the jokes.
- I've missed many Broadway hits.
- I want to wade again in water and feel ocean spray on my face.
- I want peanut butter every day spread on my morning toast.
- I want UN-timed long distance calls to the folks I love the most.
- I haven't cried at the movies yet or walked in the morning rain.
- I need to feel wind in my hair. I want to fall in love again.

So, if I choose to have dessert instead of dinner, and I die before nightfall, I would say I died a winner, because I missed nothing. I filled my heart's desire. I had that final chocolate mousse before my life expired."

With that, I called the waitress over. "I've changed my mind," I cried, "I want what she is having, only add some more whipped cream!"

Be mindful that happiness is not based on possessions, power, or prestige, but on relationships with people we love and respect. Remember that while **money talks, CHOCOLATE SINGS! What new experience do you plan for today**?

– Author Unknown

Love Filled Holiday Season

I want to wish everyone a wonderful Love Filled Holiday Season, filled with all the good things in life. I want to encourage everyone to envision the New Year as the most wonderful time they have ever lived, or imagined. For it will be (if you know it will be). I want to leave you with a series of thoughts to support this optimism. They include:

- If you fill your life with love, there will be no room for evil.

- If you know that you are a unique person with a very special purpose on this earth, then you will never become hopeless or despair.

- If you fill your mind with positive thoughts, there will be no room for negative thinking.

- If you fill your mind with positive self-talk, there will be no room for ruinous negative self-talk.

- If you live with a positive attitude toward all events and take responsibility for your actions and experiences, then every life experience will be positive and contribute toward fulfilling your life purpose. You will find contentment and happiness.

• If you think of your world as filled with abundance instead of scarcity, then you will live an abundant life.

• If whatever you want, you give it away first, your life will be filled with wonderful things. The universal law at work is, "whatever goes around, comes around."

• But the greatest of these is LOVE. And so, I send my heartfelt love to you and yours during this Holiday Season and for all time. I know that this next year will be the greatest of all years for us all if we only fill it with LOVE!

Love & Gratitude

It's easy to get into the holiday spirit. It's a time when families gather to share time and festivities, gifts are given with love, meals are lovingly prepared and enjoyed by all, cookies are baked and devoured, workers share more pleasantries. Special positive events are held in anticipation of the holidays. During these times, lives are filled with more joy, happiness, consideration, and **Love** for one another. And that is the way it should be.

Let us also acknowledge and give thanks for all the blessings in our lives. Blessing like the great freedom we enjoy because people are defending our great country, here and in far away places. Blessings like the people who give, serve, and care for the poor and destitute across America. Blessings like our safe homes, bountiful food, plentiful products, and comfortable lives we live. The only word that acknowledges these blessings is **Gratitude**, deep felt Gratitude for the abundance and comfort in our lives.

This time of year is special and filled with great Love & Gratitude. Our challenge is to carry those great attitudes into the New Year. Every new day filled with the same Love and Gratitude we are experiencing this time of year. Every day filled with the same spirit we enjoy this holiday season. Promise to do just that, carry the attitudes of Love and Gratitude into every day of this fast approaching New Year. What a year it could be if we all did that. I'm committed, how about you?

How Good Is Life?

If you woke up this morning with more health than illness, you are more blessed than the million who won't survive the week.

If you have never experienced the danger of battle, the loneliness of imprisonment, the agony of torture or the pangs of starvation, you are ahead of twenty million people around the world.

If you attend a church meeting without fear of harassment, arrest, torture, or death, you are more blessed than almost three billion people in the world.

If you have food in your refrigerator, clothes on your back, a roof over your head, and a place to sleep, you are richer than 75% of this world.

If you have money in the bank, in your wallet, and spare change in a dish somewhere, you are among the top 8% of the world's wealthy.

If your parents are still married and alive, you are very rare, especially in the United States.

If you hold up your head with a smile and are truly thankful, you are blessed because the majority can, but do not.

If you can hold someone's hand, hug them or even touch them on the shoulder, you are blessed because you can offer your maker's healing touch.

If you can read this message, you are more blessed than more than two billion people in the world who cannot read.

You are so blessed in ways you may never even know. Gratitude is a foundational value worth developing in your work and life. Giving thanks for the abundance that is available and streaming into your life each day is critical. An attitude of gratitude will propel you far, toward the happiness and joy that you seek. Try developing the attitude. It works!

■ CHAPTER EIGHTEEN ■
PLANNING

"Our goals can only be reached through a vehicle of a plan, in which we must fervently believe, and upon which we must vigorously act. There is no other route to success."

- Stephen A. Brennen

In an aircraft, the Flight Management System (FMS) provides the navigation function to include the destination and route of flight. Its guidance signals are fed to the autopilot and the autopilot flies the aircraft along its designated route to its destination. *What does this have to do with you?*

You too have destinations. They are called **goals**. Without goals, the winds of chance blow you wherever they will. Without goals, your destination is unknown and not designated. Where will you land? Knowing the route you will take to achieving your goals is important also. In other words, **you must plan the goals**. Then, to make corrections, just like the autopilot, you need feedback about your progress toward achieving those goals. Only in that way can you land at your chosen destination. **Tracking progress toward your goals** daily, monthly, and yearly can provide you just the right kind of feedback to ensure you achieve them.

213

Taking corrective action when you are off your plan can ensure that you realize your goals.

The "**proactive person (pilot in control)**" will schedule time to review progress made toward last year's goal plan. If you did not have a goal plan, now is the time to set aside time to think of what you want to accomplish in all areas of your life. Write down your goals and dreams. Plan how to accomplish them (goal sheets are excellent forms to use). Develop tracking systems to measure your progress. Then, take action to start your New Year journey. Near the end of December, complete your January monthly planning to ensure that you start in the right direction with the right actions.

I have provided these instructions so that you can be ready for the New Year. Schedule the time now to accomplish the steps in this book. If you do not do that, chances are that December 31 will come and go, and another year may not have the focus it needs for you to start and make progress. Your dreams may only become **New Years Resolutions**, and you know how well those work.

Your Weekend Retreat

Our lives are so busy that we rarely set aside time to think about our future. Life is filled with so many high priority activities that planning where we want to go (vision) and what we want to do in life (goals) is neglected. Happenings of the moment steal every available minute and there is never time just to ponder what might be. There is only one way to get control of your life and set a direction that can become fulfilling. Schedule the time to plan your life direction and goals. Prioritize this time so high that nothing will thwart you from forming your plan. Get away and focus on what is important!

You deserve this time away from the bustle of life and work to think and ponder old and new dreams, don't you? Take the time to relax, refresh your thoughts of the future, and renew your life with new dreams, energy, and enthusiasm. The steps you can take to reinvigorate your life include:

1. Plan an entire weekend away from home and work just to think and plan for your future.

2. Act on your weekend plan. Get away and spend it by yourself. You deserve it. Don't feel guilty about spending this time on yourself. If you do not, no one else will!

3. Start by listing all your past, present, and future **dreams**.

4. Write a future description of what your life will be like in five, ten, or twenty years.

5. Compose a short inspirational **vision statement** for your life. Don't worry about quality. Just do it! Over time it will become polished.

6. Think about the **purpose** of your life. Why do you inhabit the earth? Write it down.

7. Write down all the personal characteristics or things that you **value**. Set priorities. Simplify your list to a number that can be used to guide your future actions.

8. Draft a **mission statement** for your life. What is it that you will do to realize your vision and fulfill your purpose on earth?

9. Brainstorm on paper all the **goals** you would like to accomplish in the next few years. Consider the following life areas:

- Family & Home
- Financial & Career
- Mental & Educational
- Physical & Health
- Social & Cultural
- Spiritual & Ethical

10. Set Priorities for your goals. Then plan how you will accomplish the highest priority goals. Immediately begin to **take daily actions** chosen to accomplish the highest priority goals. Every day, take at least one action toward one goal and watch your life take on new meaning, enthusiasm, and become filled will a greater sense of satisfaction and happiness.

One mantra I hold of great value is the statement written in a popular book, " . . all things are possible." One year and a half ago, I conducted a weekend retreat where I set and planned forty goals. In reviewing and updating my plan this year, I discovered that twenty-three goals were completed, fourteen goals were in work, and three were being planned for initiation in the near future. You can have the same success experience if you follow the ten steps listed above. Enjoy!

Reflection & Planning

When you are a few weeks from the end of the year, it is the perfect time to "block time" to **reflect on the year and ask yourself these questions**:

1. "What were the most important things I experienced this year?"
2. "What made it possible for me to experience this growth, joy, or experiences?"

3. "What goals did I set and what did I accomplish?"
4. "What progress have I made toward my dreams?"
5. "What do I want to accomplish this next year?"

In answering these questions, think of the different areas of your life – Physical, Health, Educational, Family, Spiritual, Social, Financial, and Career – that you can develop by setting goals. The next step is obvious. Set goals that will advance you toward the important thing of your life. Then fill out the entire goal sheet for each of your goals. This planning will crystallize your thinking and program it into your subconscious to help in realizing what you want to accomplish. *The fact that you just plan will make a huge difference in what you will achieve this next year.* So, **do not procrastinate**, take action now by **scheduling time now to reflect** on this past year and **Plan Your New Year**.

■ CHAPTER NINETEEN ■
DREAM AGAIN

"All our dreams can come true -
if we have enough courage to pursue them."

- Walt Disney

Sometimes life has a way of dashing your hopes and preventing progress toward your dreams. Time slips by and the vacations you wanted to take, experiences you wanted to have, places you wanted to travel to, don't seem to get done. Ever feel that way? Here is what you can do to rejuvenate your dreams and make progress toward them.

Take some paper and label one "**My Master List of Dreams**." Then in a quiet place where you won't be disturbed, write down all the dreams, experiences, vacations, trips, and things you want to do yet in your life. Don't let any factors like money or other present limitations keep you from listing your dreams. When you have a complete listing (some people have lists of hundreds of items), then rank your list. One way to do that is to write each dream on a goal sheet (or 3x5 index card), spread the goals out on a table, and then sort them into your priority order.

Now comes the fun part. Take the first few goals and plan the actions you will need to take to accomplish them. Take these actions and write them into your to do list this week. Simply take action on those steps and you are off again following your dreams. It's as simple as that. Every week, list a few more action steps. When you get close to achieving your goals, plan new actions steps needed to achieve a few more dreams (goals). Do this each week and you will make unbelievable progress toward realizing your dreams. Take time to complete this assignment today!

365 Steps to a Dream Come True

What was that special project you always wanted to do but just didn't get around to doing? Did you not have enough time to complete it? Are you too busy to start? Will it take too much work? Think about your **unfulfilled dreams**. What would you like to do but just haven't gotten around to doing? Is it a vacation in Alaska, learning to fly, a special project or promotion at work, a cruise in Hawaii, to climb a mountain, learn to Golf, rebuild / restore that first car you drove, create fifty memories for your family, or build that dream home? Why hasn't your dream come true for you?

There are always "reasons" (or **excuses**) why you haven't started or accomplished your dream. **A legitimate reason** is that your dream is on a list but you have not prioritized it high enough yet to start accomplishing it (that is, if you *consciously prioritize your dreams*). Otherwise conscious or unconscious excuses take over and crowd out starting or realizing them. **Excuses like**:

- I'm too busy to start working toward that dream (start a new goal).
- It's going to be too hard and I don't have the time.
- I've got too many things to do as it is.
- I'll get to it when I retire (or other times).
- **I can't start it because …** (you supply the excuse).

- I don't have the money (and can't improve my financial position to get it).
- It's the fault of someone else (finger pointing).
- It's just not for me. I was born to be a looser in life.
- I don't deserve it.
- and on and on and on and on ...

Choose one dream you want to come true. Crystallize it in your mind by filling out a **Goal Planning Sheet**. Break the goal into **Yearly**, **Monthly**, **Weekly**, and then **Daily Actions Steps** you can take to achieve the dream. Make sure that the Daily Action Steps are something you can do quickly and without too much trouble or sacrifice in your daily life. With 365 days in a year, and 365 Action Steps to take toward one of your dreams, you will make unbelievable progress toward realizing your dream. After 365 Daily Action Steps you will find it hard to believe the progress you are making. You will be energized to see and know that your dream is going to actually come true. One step each day, that's all it takes. Small, simple, quick, painless **Daily Action Steps** toward your dream or goal. Before you know it, it's done.

It doesn't happen until you prioritize the dream high enough and plan it in detail to Yearly, Monthly, Weekly, and then **Daily Action Steps**. Then you step out daily and before you know it, your dream will come true. Do it now. Take action to start realizing your dreams now! **Don't use an excuse**!

Follow Your Dreams

What follows are a few success stories that individuals have lived. I write these to motivate you to stretch and develop the greatness that is in you. Your transition to working toward and following your dreams may take some time and considerable effort. The people I write about have made that sacrifice and hard work. But the day will come when you will be "Following Your Dream." You will be so happy and filled with joy that you will be in continuous wonderment. Work and living will become one. Prepare yourself for this possibility.

His love of wood working and violin music
began in childhood.

- Antonio Stradivari

As a child in England, he spent hours creating cardboard
sets for his puppet shows to entertain the family.

- Andrew Lloyd Webber

At fourteen, visiting state capitals during the summer
vacation, she pondered a career in lawmaking.

- Sandra Day O'Connor

Cut from his basketball team as a youngster,
he still dreamed of playing.

- Michael Jordan

Swimming to gain strength in his two broken arms, the
teenager changed dreams from astronaut to aquanaut.

- Jacques Cousteau

The young boy was fascinated with anatomical diagrams
in the World Book.

- Jonas Salk

At twenty-one, she lived in a one-room flat over her father's
grocery store and dreamed of public service.

- Margaret Thatcher

One of his high-school term papers was on being a cook and owning a restaurant.

— **Dave Thomas** (founder of Wendy's)

This college dropout had ideas about information access.

— **Bill Gates**

" .. all things are possible." Only your **beliefs and choices hold you back** from "Following Your Dream." Change them! Plan and prepare yourself for greater success. Set goals "**To Become**" and take action. Take one small action each day toward your dreams. In no time you will see progress and before you know it you will find yourself on the path that "Follows Your Dreams."

Follow Your Heart

Deepak Chopra M.D., a pioneer in the medicine of the future, has encouraged his children to discover their unique ability and to find a way to exercise that ability in service to humanity. In other words, he has encouraged them to find their purpose in life and to engage in activities that uplift and meet people's needs. What is your purpose in life? Who are you to serve? Your service may change over time but knowing your ultimate purpose and the people you are to serve can make all the difference in how you feel about yourself and the happiness that you experience.

Your heart will tell you what your purpose is. You have to listen to your heart. Your heart will tell you whom you are to serve. When you listen and discover, then you will find the most compelling reasons for living and being. Become quiet and listen to your heart.

You may be trapped in a life of activities that are not now on purpose or in service to those you were meant to serve. Don't fret about that. Start now to take small actions that will lead you toward discovering your unique on-purpose future. Small actions like taking time to become quiet and listen. Small actions like thinking about your unique purpose for living. Listen to your heart, discover your purpose for living, plan and take actions to prepare yourself for the journey you were placed on this earth to make. Travel the new roads you must travel to discover the real reason you were placed here. It may take a few years to find the right road so stay with it. Consciously travel your roads, always mindful of finding your purpose and area of unique service. Remember that life is a journey of discovery, opportunities explored, wisdom gained, a place for serving humanity, a place of loving and being loved. It is a precious gift given to you for a special purpose. Find that purpose and live it fully.

When you are on-purpose and working / living in service to your fellow human beings, then you will find bliss and happiness. You will feel fulfilled and at peace with the world. Take a small amount of time each day to focus on discovering your unique purpose and service. When you find your purpose, then create **New Year's Resolutions.**

I am sure that you have some thoughts of something you wanted to do differently this year. Great intentions to do something new, change something old, or just go after a recurring dream. You might have even **resolved** to make those changes. All these thoughts are good! But they are not good enough to realize the results you intend to get. The things you must do to get results include the following and I promise that you will get results:

> 1. **Goal Planning Sheet**: Complete a goal planning sheet for each intention you are serious about. Do a thorough job and make sure that both sides are done to include affirmations and visualizations. Go and cut out pictures or make sketches and place them around where they will remind you of your completed goal. Use your affirmations often every day.

2. Transfer Specific Action Steps: Transfer your goal's Specific Action Steps for Achieving This Goal to the day you plan to take action. Write it in the Important Action Step area. Reference it to your Goal Planning Sheet. Don't wait, do it now!

3. Plan Your Day: The night before, prioritize the Imperative and Important Action Steps for the next day. Then plan and schedule your day to accomplish the highest priority Imperative and Important Action Steps. Make sure your goals are prioritized high!

4. Take Action on Your Day's Plan: Work your plan as it is scheduled. Remember that you have scheduled and are doing the most important things in your work and life. Don't let **non-emergency interruptions** (not urgent HPA or urgent LPA) drag you off your schedule and prevent you from achieving your prioritized actions. *You can tell the priority you give to things by what you accomplish during the day! Track what you do.*

Procrastination is the lack of a decision and action. Life pressures may have led you to stray from the discipline of the four steps that you need to take to achieve your goals and dreams. ***Getting it back on track is easy.*** I guarantee that if you follow the four steps described above, you will not only achieve your goals, but you will feel really good about yourself. When you think and intend to do things but don't, you violate your **internal integrity** (keeping promises to yourself). When you don't keep your word to yourself, over time you will give up and quit because you can't get things done. A self defeating thinking process creates limiting habits. So counter it now, **make your decision and take action** to realize your intentions and resolutions.

225

■ PART THREE ■
BUSINESS LEADERSHIP

". . . the most successful leader of all is one who sees another picture not yet actualized. He sees the things which belong in his present picture but which are not yet there ... Above, all, he should make his co-workers see that it is not his purpose which is to be achieved, but a common purpose, born of the desires and the activities of the group."

- Mary Parker Follett (1868-1933)

■ CHAPTER TWENTY ■
THE GREAT LEADERSHIP CHALLENGE

"Life is unique. Leadership is unique. The skills that work well for one leader may not work at all for another. However, the fundamental skills of leadership can be adopted to work well for just about everyone: at work, in the community, and at home."

- Excerpt from Leading an Inspired Life *by Jim Rohn*

If you want to be a leader who attracts quality people, the key is to become a person of quality yourself. Leadership is the ability to attract someone to the gifts, skills, and opportunities you offer as an owner, as a manager, or as a parent. What is important in leadership is refining your skills. All great leaders keep working on themselves until they become effective. The following are some specific suggestions:

Learn to be strong but not impolite. It is an extra step you must take to become a powerful, capable leader with a wide range of reach. Some people mistake rudeness for strength. It is not even a good substitute.

Next, learn to be kind but not weak. We must not mistake weakness for kindness. Kindness is not weak. Kindness is a certain type of strength. We must be kind enough to tell someone the truth. We must be kind enough and considerate enough to lay it on the line. We must be kind enough to tell it like it is and not deal in delusion.

Next, learn to be bold but not a bully. It takes boldness to win the day. To build your influence, you've got to walk in front of your group. You have to be willing to take the first arrow, tackle the first problem, and discover the first sign of trouble. Like the farmer, if you want any rewards at harvest time, you have to be bold and face the weeds and the rain and the bugs straight on. You have to seize the moment.

You have to learn to be humble but not timid. You cannot get to the high life by being timid. Some people mistake timidity for humility, but humility is a virtue; **timidity is a disease.** It is an affliction. It can be cured, but it is a problem. Humility is almost a Godlike word. Humility is a sense of awe, a sense of wonder, an awareness of the human soul and spirit, an understanding that there is something unique about the human drama versus the rest of life. Humility is a grasp of the distance between us and the stars, yet having the feeling that we are part of the stars.

Learn to be proud but not arrogant. It takes pride to build your ambitions. It takes pride in your community. It takes pride in a cause, in accomplishment. But the key to becoming a good leader is to be proud without being arrogant. Do you know the worst kind of arrogance? I think, it **is arrogance that comes from ignorance.** It is intolerable. If someone is smart and arrogant, we can tolerate that. But if someone is ignorant and arrogant, that's just too much to take.

The next step is learning to develop humor without folly. In leadership, we learn that it's okay to be witty but not silly; fun but not foolish.

Next, deal in realities. Deal in truth. Save yourself the agony of delusion. Just accept life as it is. Life is unique. The whole drama of life is unique. It's fascinating.

Exemplary Leadership

James Kouzes and Barry Posner began a research project in 1983 to "know what people did when they were at their personal best in leading others." They did not survey star performers because they wanted to ask ordinary people to describe extraordinary experiences to find patterns of success. They published the result of their work in 1987 in a book called *The Leadership Challenge*: *How to get extraordinary things done in organizations*. They have updated the book three times with the latest revision in 2002 and it has passed the test of time with more than 1,000,000 copies sold.

I attended The Leadership Challenge training program with Jim Kouzes in 1993 and it was outstanding. My experience became a solid foundation for my own leadership development. In the table below you will find the five practices and ten commitments of exemplary leadership. Jim and Barry found that they could attribute 80% of a leader's success to the quality of engaging in these practices.

Practices	Commitments
Model the Way	1. Find your voice by clarifying your personal values. 2. Set the example by aligning actions with shared values.
Inspire a Shared Vision	3. Envision the future by imagining exciting and ennobling possibilities. Enlist others in a common vision by appealing to shared aspirations.

Challenge the Process	5. Search for opportunities by seeking innovative ways to change, grow, and improve. Experiment and take risks by constantly generating small wins and learning from mistakes.
Enable Others to Act	7. Foster collaboration by promoting cooperative goals and building trust. Strengthen others by sharing power and discretion.
Encourage the Heart	9. Recognize contributions by showing appreciation for individual excellence. Celebrate the values and victories by creating a spirit of community.

Since we are all leaders and this study consisted of ordinary people, the results are equally applicable to us all. Take a few minutes and on a scale of **one** (poor at this practice or commitment) to **ten** (outstanding at this practice or commitment), assess your performance in these five practices and ten commitments. Yes, that's right, record your assessment on your paper. If you are brave and exercise courage, you will ask others to do the same, and then see what their perceptions of you are in these practices and commitments. It should then become obvious where you might set a goal and start working on improving a practice or commitment to develop more of your own leadership skills. In Jim's Leadership Challenge training program in 1993, I set a goal of developing more skill around Encouraging the Heart. Anyone who knows me today will probably say that this is one of my current strengths. So it can be done!

You can develop more of these practices and commitments and they will result in your being recognized as an Exemplary Leader. Set your development goal, consciously take daily action to develop more of your chosen practice, and enjoy the results of your developmental journey.

Seven Steps of Effective Leadership

1. Leaders help people succeed.
2. They don't confuse management with leadership.
3. They set goals that everyone can understand.
4. They set high standards.
5. They know there is always room for improvement.
6. They take charge!
7. They do what is right.

- General Norman Schwarzkopf

The Leader's Job

The editors of Fast Company recently asked their readers to share their thoughts about the characteristics, qualities, and skills of successful leaders. The most compelling answers, which they featured in the June issue, revealed that the magazine's readers - many of whom are leaders themselves - have a good understanding of what it means to lead effectively. In the words of the Fast Company faithful, here are a few of the most important things good leaders do:

- "Fully delegate.
- Serve.
- Listen and act.
- Find, groom and train his/her replacement.
- Lead, not manage.
- Make leaders.

- Lead with integrity - integrated so that those you lead, know who you are, and that you are consistent from the inside out."

When I ask people if they are leaders, eventually everyone acknowledges that they are. You are a leader in your own life, your family, your community, your work, your team, your organization, and sometimes your company. In those areas of life leadership that you perform (appropriate to the areas), how do you rate yourself in each of these seven important things good leaders do? Take a moment now and assess how well you do on a scale of **one (not like me)** to **ten (always like me)**. This assessment will allow you to identify what area you could improve. Then set a goal to study, learn about, and take actions to develop more of the important things good leaders do. The benefits of developing your own leadership skills transcend the value of almost anything else you can do. Don't just read this, take the action you need to develop more of your leadership potential!

The Leadership Reality

Each Organization uniquely defines success, both for the organization and every person involved. The behaviors and attitudes needed to become successful in an organization are often set and modeled by the organizational leader. People look to their leader and then emulate what they do to fit in, get ahead, and become more successful. Interestingly, a keen observer will notice that starting at the lowest levels in the organization, the employees, supervisors, managers, and top executives often repeat behaviors and attitudes that they observe in their immediate superiors and top organizational leader. **If they don't "fit in," they normally choose to depart the company, are downsized, or are fired.** They "fit in" to have approval and to get ahead in their work and life. Yes, there are some exceptions, but generally one conforms and behaves like their supervisor. In turn, their supervisor conforms and behaves like the person one step over them, and so on to the "**top leader**." Each supervisor in an organization is a model of that organization's behaviors and attitudes. Those behaviors and attitudes determine the success of the organization. Leaders must look into the mirror of their organizations (results and success that they enjoy) and determine what changes they need to increase their present success. The "top leader" must lead, change, and grow to achieve ever increasing success, or choose to wither in the comfort of mediocrity. Remember, each of us is a leader in our own lives. Each of us is a model of success for his or her working contacts, family, and friends.

Whom do you see as a model? What behaviors and attitudes do you model? Who gives you quality feedback to refine your model? What goals have you set and daily actions are you taking to further develop your leadership model?

Answer these questions and you will be on your way to developing even more effective leadership in both your life and your organization. Ignore these questions and accept the mediocrity that comes from complacency.

■ CHAPTER TWENTY-ONE ■
OPEN COMMUNICATION

*"It is understanding that gives us an ability to have peace.
When we understand the other fellow's viewpoint
and he understands ours, then we can sit down
and work out our differences."*

- Harry S. Truman

Openness is revealing all you know and can share, easily expressing feelings and emotions, and being frank and sincere when communicating. "Open" people are characterized by frequent statements of personal opinion or experience, high-risk, self-disclosure statements, and attempts to facilitate openness in conversations. They strive to keep secrets to a minimum. They build closeness and security by sharing things that happen with those who should know. Excluding people and keeping or telling secrets creates distrust, generates jealousy, leads to envy, and often results in harmful conflict. Open communication requires trust, and people learn trust by being trusted. Open communication is an essential factor in becoming an effective communicator and leader. It is essential to your productivity, success, and enjoyment of work and life. How open of a communicator are you?

Dialogue

According to Peter Senge, the discipline of team learning starts with "dialogue," or the capacity of members of a team to suspend assumptions and enter into genuine "thinking together." To the Greeks, *dia-logos* meant a free flowing of meaning through a group, allowing the group to discover insights, not attainable individually. In dialogue there is the free and creative exploration of complex and subtle issues, a deep "listening" to one another and the suspending of one's own judgments. The purpose of dialogue is to go beyond any one individual's understanding and to reveal the incoherence of thought. In dialogue, people become observers of their own thinking.

Dialogue allows participants to enter into a shared thinking that transcends judgments and polarized stances. Dialogue can occur only when a group of people see each other as colleagues in a mutual quest for deeper insight and clarity. To dialogue, we must:

1. See and greet each other as a colleague with caring and acceptance.

2. Use questions and inquiry statements to draw out each other's needs, assumptions, values, opinions, and passions.

3. While the other person is talking, listen without judging or forming a response.

4. Acknowledge understanding by reflecting back what you heard and saw.

5. Contribute and respond with honest advocacy (share "Your Truth" as well as the assumptions and beliefs underlying your truth).

6. Be aware of, and avoid engaging in negative self-talk, labeling, over generalizing, minimizing, or negatively judging.

What's the value of dialogue in the workplace? Where employees are able freely to share and contribute to the pool of shared meaning, make decisions based on complete information, and then act on those decisions with enthusiasm and conviction, the organization develops and maintains healthy relationships. Healthy relationships result in less wasted time and resources, better bottom line and business results, and happy stakeholders. It's a crucial skill to master.

Feedback

Think about it: Two people cannot move a piece of furniture down a staircase without giving each other feedback. How can a company win in the marketplace if its people don't give each other constant feedback? Here is a question you can use to solicit feedback, "**What feedback do you have for me?**" If you want feedback, you must seek it! Make it a regular and daily part of doing business.

Leaders Need Feedback

Employees often comment about their leaders saying one thing and doing another. They call it "**not walking their talk**." Employees are very smart and pick up on the slightest inconsistencies between words and actions. Every action a leader takes, communicates what they value. Interestingly, his or her subordinates copy the behavior of the leader.

After all, that is the behavior that leads to promotion and success. The organization becomes a mirror of the top leader's values and actions.

If you are a leader and **everyone is a leader**, it is essential that you become consciously aware of how your employees (or others) perceive your actions and behaviors. You must know how your organization perceives your "value message." Since business today is a fast-moving engagement, leaders do not always take time to become conscious of the messages they send. That state of being unaware usually continues until there is some negative impact or serious problem. Traumatic change is then required to fix the problem. Sometimes, the change results in removal of the leader. Why let it go on this long?

A leader needs feedback about the employee's perception of their actions, behaviors, and values. They need feedback to make the gradual refinements needed for continuing success and effective leadership. Leaders almost never get quality feedback from inside their organization. It just isn't, or doesn't feel, safe for the feedback giver. The reality is that in today's world, change is an accelerating force that can leave a business behind, or open up opportunities to grow and flourish. The trick is to stay ahead of change and the challenges of business. You must develop your leadership potential and grow faster than the changes.

The leader needs a coach who is interested in the leader's continued and future success. Engaging the services of a coach can literally mean survival of your business or the demise of your business. It can mean **realizing your dreams** or becoming a **victim of the status-quo**. By accelerating your personal development and growth, you assure your future success. Others, just cruising along without growth, will experience great disappointments. It's your choice.

Ground Rules for Positive Confrontation

- Focus on issues, not personalities. Avoid personal attacks.
- Separate your own opinions from the facts, as you know them.
- Acknowledge your own "hidden agendas."
- Make sure you can restate the views of others before you debate them.
- Don't interrupt.
- If you think someone is "hiding out," check in with the person and ask them what they think.
- No "hallway discussions." Openly share your perspectives with the group.
- Wear all of the hats you should be wearing during the discussion.
- Remember, the goal is to move forward as a team - we will not advertise the disagreement, but we will demonstrate our full support of the decision.

> - From the book *Journey to the Emerald City*
> by Roger Connors & Tom Smith

■ CHAPTER TWENTY-TWO ■
PEOPLE

"Nothing great will ever be achieved without great men,
and men are great only if they are determined to be so."

- Charles De Gaulle

There are an estimated six billion four-hundred forty-six million, one-hundred thirty-one thousand and four hundred different and unique people inhabiting this earth. The good thing is that we don't need to understand them all. The challenge is that we do need to understand those who we wish to interact with, in a positive, productive, and effective way. That number may be ten, a hundred, or several thousands. So many differences to discern, understand, and interact with. Help!

Attempting to learn about the psychology of human beings that includes understanding their personality differences is a key skill and knowledge area of effective leaders and managers. It is for all of us as we live and interact with others. Happiness, joy, and great relations with other people will depend on understanding the differences between us. However, I find few people who wisely spend time in developing this skill and knowledge area.

I have been exposed to hundreds of tools that can help a person understand differences. Many of them are good and contribute to the understanding of differences. The best understanding tool comes from the work of Carl G. Jung (1875-1961), Katharine Cook Briggs (1875-1968), and Isabel Briggs Meyers (1897-1980). They call it the Myers-Briggs Type Indicator. While this is an indicating tool to personality type, there are hundreds of books, pamphlets, tapes, workshops, and other resources available to learn more about personality differences in every application you can imagine. Organizations, communication, leadership, teams, relationships, retention, conflict management are just a few areas where there is considerable personality type information available.

I learned of personality differences late in life. I could have greatly benefited from personality type if I had learned it in high school, college or early in my working career. Today it is invaluable to me and to those whom I share it. If you want to work and live more effectively with those you interact with, I highly recommend you set a goal to learn about personality type. I'd be happy to help you in your journey to greater understanding in any way I can. Let me know how I may be of service to you.

People Problems?

Wherever we go, people problems seem to exist. But are they really people problems? The leader has a vision of the future. The manager has a clear goal that will move the organization closer to the vision. The workers need a clear understanding of the results and standards that they need to achieve and meet. When people are placed into a job that they are naturally suited to do, then they are comfortable in working to achieve the expected results. Where can **breakdowns occur**?

BREAKDOWNS CAN OCCUR IN THE FOLLOWING AREAS:

- Having a clear vision of where the organization is going.
- Management goals set to ensure progress toward realizing the vision.
- Worker's clear understanding of the expected results and work standards.
- The worker's personality type matched with the work that needs to be done.
- Knowledge, skills, and work environment needed to successfully complete the work.
- Personal choice of attitude and behaviors to achieve the expected results.

The first five areas are the responsibility of the leader or manager. The last is the responsibility of the individual. Ask yourself the following questions.

- Do I have a clear vision of where the company is going? Do I communicate that vision daily?

- Do I know my business goals and how they support achieving the vision? Do I often communicate the goals?

- Do my subordinates know precisely what results I expect and the work standard they are expected to meet?

- Does the "Type" personality of the people who work for me match the work that they are asked to accomplish?

- Do my people have the knowledge, skills, and work resources, tools, and environment needed to be successful?

Have I creatively removed all the obstacles to their achieving the results that I expect?

• Do I have the knowledge and skills to help my employees develop a positive attitude and make the choice to become more successful? Do I realize that employee attitude is a choice of the individual and out of my control but something I can positively influence?

If the answers to these six questions are "**yes**," then you are an awesome leader and manager. If you are not absolutely clear and confident of your ability to manage these areas, then there is still room for you to grow and develop more of your knowledge, skills, and potential. Leadership Advantage specializes in just that; helping people grow in their knowledge, skills, and developing more of their potential. You can accelerate your growth, effectiveness, productivity, and success with our programs and coaching. **Courage says try it, risk changing, see if it can work, and invest in you because you are worth it. Fear says hold back, wait, better be careful, and don't spend the money because it probably won't work**. It's your choice! Are you worth it?

Finding the Right Person

You have done your homework and have developed a six-page detailed description of the job that needs to be done. Then, you develop a detailed script of questions that will reveal the strengths, skills, knowledge, and attitudes of the participant. Being skilled in personality typing, you know what to look for to perfectly match the person's natural personality to the work you need done.

Personality type – what is that? There are hundreds of different personality assessments and tools. So what do you study and choose to use? Why not choose the tool that more than 2,000,000 people use each year, the one that is more useful and that gives you the in-depth insight you need to make decisions and get results. The Myers–Briggs Type Indicator (MBTI) is by far the best and most useful of all personality tools available today.

The MBTI isolates two attitudes and two mental processes. One attitude is a direction of focus or source of energy (**Extravert** - **Introvert**) and the other attitude is a function used in the external world (**Judging** - **Perceiving**). One mental process concerns the gathering of information (**Sensing** - i**N**tuition), and the other is a way of coming to a conclusion (**Thinking** - **Feeling**).

You have a job that needs an outgoing person who is detail oriented, logical in making decisions, and who is very organized. Here, you look for an ESTJ. If the job requires a quiet person, who builds great one-on-one relationships, sees the big picture, is future oriented, and is very flexible and adaptive, then we look for an INFP. You can take any job and identify a personality type that will be a natural fit. By fit we mean that their preferred type or functions are naturally suited to the needed work. Some words of caution about fit are necessary. Some job candidates may have developed functions that are not of their type and thus can work in a mismatched job with little stress. Or they may be willing to do what is necessary to learn the skills needed to be successful in that job. The MBTI is not a job-screening tool, but MBTI knowledge greatly assists matching the right person to the work.

By learning how to discern personality type and its development, you will vastly improve your decisions, management techniques, and job selection process. Improvements will be manifested **in far fewer management problems, frustrations, and coaching sessions or training**. Simultaneously, you will create **greater productivity,**

increased effectiveness, and **great savings** derived from **less employee turnover**. Knowing personality type may just be the management tool that will help you rise above your peers. Knowledge and skill in using the Myers–Briggs Type Indicator may be just the advantage you need.

Keep Top Employees

We call it job sculpting. And it is what you need to do to keep your best people – the ones who make you look good. The idea is this: Good people will stay only in jobs that "fit their deeply embedded life interests – that is, their long-held emotionally driven passions."

To adopt this approach, spend a lot of effort listening. For each individual, try to identify what life interests are dominant. Then work with them to customize assignments – sometimes that may mean simply adding another assignment to existing responsibilities. In other cases, it may require moving that employee to a new position.

The Big Eight: What kind of interests are you looking (and listening) for? The following are eight identifiable areas of interest for people drawn to business careers. In brief, they are:

1. Application of technology.
2. Quantitative analysis.
3. Theory development and conceptual thinking.
4. Creative production.
5. Counseling and mentoring.
6. Managing people and relationships.
7. Enterprise control.
8. Influencing through language and ideas.

– Timothy Butler, James Waldroop
in *Harvard Business Review*

What People Want

In the book *Enlightened Leadership*, Ed Oakley and Doug Krug created a list of what people want in their work environment. Here are some of those items.

WORK

- ____ Clear, common inspiring goals
- ____ Stimulating, challenging work
- ____ Adequate resources

PEOPLE

- ____ To be respected and appreciated
- ____ Encouragement to express creativity and try new ideas
- ____ Authority appropriate to responsibility
- ____ Freedom to do the job
- ____ Freedom to "fail" or make mistakes
- ____ Adequate compensation and other rewards

LEADERSHIP

- ____ Responsive, caring leadership
- ____ A place where management says what it means, means what it says, and does what it says it will do
- ____ Opportunity for input in decisions
- ____ High priority on growing and developing people

ENVIRONMENT (A LEADERSHIP RESPONSIBILITY TO CREATE)

- ____ A can-do, positive, winning attitude as a way of life
- ____ Honesty and truthfulness as a way of life

- _____ Empowered people open to change
- _____ A sense of team
- _____ A high level of trust
- _____ People taking responsibility
- _____ A solution orientation

TOTAL _____

YOUR ASSIGNMENT: Copy this article. Then on a scale from **one** (not at all like my company) to **ten** (exactly like my company) rate your working environment. Total up your ratings.

> **1 to 60** = Help is needed now!
> **60 to 140** = There is much room for improvement.
> **140 to 200** = Your company is humming along quite nicely.

Whether you are the President of your company or a line worker, **use this assessment as a dialogue starter for improving your working environment**. Please let me know what you find and what you will do about it.

Developing People

The *October 25, 2004 issue of Business Week* magazine headlines what they call "The Unsung CEO; United Technologies George David runs a $31 billion company that out guns GE in shareholder return." In reading the magazine I also came across an article called the "Management Evangelist" who turns out to be none other than Jack Welch of past GE fame. It goes on to say that "under Jack Welch, GE developed the deepest bench of executive talent in US business." How is it possible that George David and Jack Welch were able to create such successful businesses?

The George David article credits him with crafting one of the most progressive employee education programs in the world - even extending benefits to laid off-workers. In the Jack Welch article it states that, "Welch made it his mission to manage and foster top talent with hawk-like attention." Jack judged how well his leaders were leading and nurturing others. It goes on to say that, "Jack put his time and energy into developing people." So both these successful leaders put great emphasis on developing their people. They knew that their own success was dependent on the success of those who worked for them.

You cannot help other people develop more of their potential unless you are developing more of your own potential. My question to you is this, "Daily, what are you doing to develop more of your own skills and competencies?" "Is your own development a habit and are you in the habit of taking the time to develop others?" Stagnation in today's world is like the kiss of death because change is ever accelerating and what we knew or could do yesterday is not enough to ensure our success for tomorrow. It does not take much effort. Choose a skill you would like to develop and spend fifteen minutes a day working on it. As you gain in competency, teach that skill to others and you will grow even stronger. Make your continual development a daily habit and you will find security and success in your future.

Care & Feeding of Monkeys!

In the November-December 1974 issue of the Harvard Business Review (HBR), a classic article was written entitled, "**Management Time: Who's Got the Money?**" by William Oncken Jr. and Donald L. Wass. In that article, the monkey-on-the-back analogy is used to describe "subordinate-imposed" time with their supervisor. Subordinate-imposed time can take the form of a problem the supervisor agrees to solve for the subordinate. But who is working for whom? Come to think of it, problems can be passed from anyone to anyone (children to parents, friends to friends, peers to peers, etc.).

If the supervisor is not vigilant, a subordinate may pass several monkeys onto the supervisor each day. After a few days, the supervisor can be overcome with subordinate gifted monkeys. So, what is a supervisor to do? The article goes on to say, *"At no time while I am helping you with this or any other problem will your problem become my problem. The instant your problem becomes mine, you will no longer have a problem. I cannot help a person who hasn't got a problem."*

The article also says that, "In order to further clarify our analogy between the monkey-on-the-back and the well-known process of assigning and controlling, we shall refer briefly to the manager's appointment schedule, which calls for five hard-and-fast rules governing the 'Care and Feeding of Monkeys' (violations of these rules will cost the supervisor discretionary time):

1. **Rule 1**: Monkeys should be fed or shot. Otherwise, they will starve to death and the manager will waste valuable time on postmortems or attempted resurrections.

2. **Rule 2**: The monkey population should be kept below the maximum number the manager has time to feed. Subordinates will find time to work as many monkeys as he or she finds time to feed, but no more. It shouldn't take more than 5 to 15 minutes to feed a properly prepared monkey.

3. **Rule 3**: Monkeys should be fed by appointment only. The manager should not have to be hunting down starving monkeys and feeding them on a catch-as-catch-can basis.

4. **Rule 4**: Monkeys should be fed face-to-face or by telephone, but never by mail (or e-mail). (If by mail or e-mail, the next move will be the manager's). Documentation may add to the feeding process, but it cannot take the place of feeding.

5. **Rule 5**: Every monkey should have an assigned next feeding time and degree of initiative. These may be revised at any time by mutual consent, but never allowed to become vague or indefinite. Otherwise, the monkey will either starve to death or wind up on the manager's back."

The fundamentals of great management never change. If you feel as though you have too many monkeys on your back, then you need to read this article in full (HBR article reprint 74607, 800 274-3214).

Learning Team

Lifelong learning is the only way to excel and ensure continued success in today's business world. Those who have stagnated in their acquisition of knowledge and skills are traveling a slippery slope of declining competencies. The microchip / communication revolution and its accelerating change ensure that the stagnated learners will drift into mediocrity and eventually into incompetence and failure. Did you know that the average person in America reads less than one book a year? How many books have you read this past year? What follows is a powerful way to create a continuing learning experience.

Learning Team - Form a Learning Team of individuals who are interested in lifelong learning. As a group (any group of executives, managers, supervisors, teams, or employees), choose a book to read (could be articles, pamphlets, CD's, or other materials) that has group appeal and application to work and / or life. Agree on a weekly study schedule and assign the first week's study assignment. At a scheduled time, meet as a Learning Team and have one individual lead the group in a review of the weekly study material. As a group, talk about how they could apply this material to work, or life. Have everyone choose one insight for application the next week as they also prepare to cover the next study assignment. Choose the next week's review leader. At the next scheduled meeting, have everyone quickly state their previous week's application and results. Then quickly have the next study leader review the weekly assigned new material. Again, talk about possible insights & application, individually choose another insight for application, and seek a volunteer to lead the next week's study assignment. If needed, appoint a timekeeper to limit the Learning Team meetings to the time agreed upon (usually ten to fifteen minutes).

Results – It's obvious that the Leaning Team members will be learning and experiencing personal growth and competency development. The accountability built into the ongoing process will facilitate results that could significantly add to current business results. Significant development of the individual's knowledge and skills ensures quality applicants for advancement and leadership in the organization. Ignoring the development of the people in your organization (or your own development) is a choice that will lead to eventual defeat and drastic change. Make a powerful choice, start a Learning Team today.

Ideal Supervisors, Managers, & Leaders

I recently presented to an Arizona industrial convention, a seminar entitled, "**Supervision, Management, and Leadership in the 21st**

Century."The participants participated in developing the ideal profiles of Supervisors, Managers, and Leaders and **What's In It For Me (WIIFM)**. Here are the results:

SUPERVISORS

> Bi-Lingual
>
> Knowledgeable (want to learn)
>
> Self-Motivated
>
> See the Big Picture
>
> Good at Planning
>
> Makes Decisions
>
> Feels Empowered
>
> Teacher
>
> Dependency Free

MANAGERS

> High Level of Education (especially regarding use of money, costs, profits etc.)
>
> Understanding Goals of Company (aligned with them)
>
> Decision Making (and the ability to teach it)
>
> Able to Develop Creative Solutions
>
> Personally Interested & Involved
>
> A Motivator
>
> Not Reactive (proactive)
>
> A Teacher

LEADERS

> Strategic Planner
>
> Able to Successfully Implement Strategic Plan

Good (Great) Coach

Model – Show by Example

Possess Character & Integrity

Live by Their Values & Principles

A Teacher

Take Ultimate Responsibility

Active Role in Industry & Community

WIIFM: The business owners and leaders said if progress toward developing the ideal supervisor, manager, and leader were made, that they would enjoy:

More Dollars ($) Bottom Line Profit

Fewer Complaints

Less Stress

Healthier People (emotionally & physically)

Less Fear

More Leisure Time

Sense of Accomplishment

Sense of Purpose

Two thoughts occur to me from these results.

• The **WIIFM** is certainly worth pursuing for all business owners & companies.

• The competitive advantage that would be achieved by developing toward the ideal supervisors, managers, and leaders would put your business way ahead of the competition.

Now you might not be able to develop the ideal, but you can certainly help supervisors, managers, and leaders **grow & develop toward those ideals**. And that will put you ahead of the competition because they are doing business the same way they have always been doing business. We know that if we continue to do the things we have always done, we will get the things we have always gotten. Developing your supervisors, managers, and leaders involves change. Change is often difficult and not well understood or executed. **You want leader / coaches that are proficient in leading change and have a stellar record of results to help you develop your supervisors, managers, and leaders**.

■ Chapter Twenty-Three ■
IDEAS TO MANAGE BY

*"Never tell people how to do things. Tell them what to do
and they will surprise you with their ingenuity."*

- George S. Patton

Fully 80 percent or more of your success is mental. What you achieve is
determined primarily by the way you think about yourself, your life, and
the people around you. As you change the quality of your thinking, you
will change the quality of everything you do! The great secret of success
is that there are no secrets of success; only timeless principles have proven
effective throughout the centuries. Here are a few of those principles:

- If you change your thinking, you change your life.
- It doesn't matter where you're coming from; all that matters is
where you are going.
- You have great untapped reserves of potential within you. Your
job is to release them.
- Decide what you want, and then act as if it were impossible to fail.
- Learn from the experts; you will not live long enough to figure
it all out for yourself.

- The more reasons you have for achieving your goals, the more determined you will become.

- You are in the people business, no matter what you do or where you do it.

- There are no limits on what you can achieve with your life, except the limits you accept in your own mind.

- You are a potential genius; there is no problem you cannot solve, and no answer you cannot find somewhere.

- Your success will be largely determined by your ability to concentrate single-mindedly on one thing at a time.

- If there is anything you want in life, find out how others have achieved it and then do the same things they did.

- If you conduct yourself as though you expect to be successful and happy, you will seldom be disappointed.

- It is not what you say, or wish, or hope, or intend, it is only what you do that counts.

- Everything you have in your life you have attracted to yourself because of the person you are.

– Brian Tracy

The Extraordinary Manager

The **Mediocre Manager** is an ordinary sort of person. Everyone feels comfortable with the person and there is seldom any conflict (or it's avoided). Their performance is satisfactory but there are some areas of improvement that never seem to develop. The manager is always busy doing things, so busy that there is little time to consider the opportunities that come their way. They work hard for ten, sometimes eleven or twelve hours each day, five and a half days a week and never seem to "get on top of everything."

They take work home to do Sunday. Exhausted at the end of the work day, they acknowledge the wife and kids when they come home, catch a little TV, and then off to bed. The next day they begin the same routine.

The **Extraordinary Manager** knows and practices time and activity management so that they can engage in a well-balanced work and life routine. For instance, they:

- Plan their work day and manage it to accomplish their tasks, goals, and plans.
- Prioritize and delegate work efficiently to manage their workload.
- Take time to exercise, eat regular high energy meals, and get the rest they need.
- Have "**To Become**" goals, and daily work on them to grow and develop themselves.
- Coach others to help them develop and grow their knowledge and skills.
- Have time to explore opportunities that come their way.
- Take time to love their families, friends, and attend to their own needs.

Where are you? Are you an **Extraordinary Manager**? What changes do you need to make? Why aren't you making them? Hey, making those changes isn't easy. Our own habits and attitudes have often trapped and limited us. We have a program that is designed to make the leap to Extraordinary Management. Give me a call and let's plan to make that leap together. If you are committed, **I guarantee the results**!

Get-Along Tools

If you are frustrated in your relationship with someone at work or in your life, why are you frustrated? The frustration and emotional stress are easy enough to identify, but the reason often escapes us. We want to understand the causes of those emotional hooks and rifts, but we just can't quite figure it out. Have you ever been in this situation? I know I have!

Most of us are perplexed by certain people's behaviors that just annoy us and rub us the wrong way. ***How could they be so different from us when we are soooooo right?*** All people are unique and different. These differences can be grouped into sixteen personality types. According to the prominent Swiss psychiatrist, Carl G. Jung, the personality type differences that we observe are predetermined at birth. As we grow up, our experiences further shape and differentiate them. When we don't know or understand the differences, we get frustrated, emotionally upset, and reject cooperation in trying to bridge the gaps. Different personalities have unique ways of behaving in the world. Different emotional competencies combine with the personality to further complicate understanding of behaviors. Each of us possesses different levels of emotional development. Knowing and understanding our own personalities and emotional development can help us bridge these gaps and improve our working and life relationships.

Over two million people use the **Myers–Briggs Type Indicator** (MBTI) each year. It is absolutely the best personality type descriptor with the most useful and reliable in-depth information and practical uses. The **BarOn EQ-i Emotional Quotient Inventory** is a very popular instrument for measuring your emotional development and competencies. Together, these two self-report tools allow us to understand and **Get-Along** with ourselves. Aristotle said it in the phrase, "**Know thyself.**" The understanding we have of ourselves enables us to understand and Get-Along with others. If you are a leader, executive, manager, or just want to learn more about yourself and how you can become more effective with other people, the MBTI and BarOn EQ-i tools are for you. We have these assessments available to help you in your journey. Become a person of action and call us to learn more.

Who is Responsible?

Dr. W. Edwards Deming, the guru of quality, who revolutionized work in Japan, held that 80% of problems and waste were the faults of work processes, systems, and procedures. Only 20% of problems were attributable to people. His focus was therefore on process improvement rather than on blaming people. He also indicated that process improvements were the responsibility of management. In addition, he said that it was management's responsibility to include those who did the work in improving the work and service processes.

Quite often we see managers blaming people for the mistakes that happen in the workplace. Actions are taken to discipline the worker. I'd like to suggest that maybe actions should be taken to discipline the manager. It's his or her responsibility to take actions continually to improve the work processes under their supervision.

Let's extend this Deming attitude to **workers they identify as underperforming**. Let me state right now that maybe **10% to 15% of employees choose an attitude of underperforming and they won't respond to a manager's helpful initiatives**. You should find work where they are comfortable or let them go (so they discover that they must change their attitudes and habits – a good thing). The other underperforming employees, at any organizational level, are not getting either the **feedback they need to change or the coaching required to become high performing**. Whose responsibility is it to do that? Why, their immediate supervisor. The immediate supervisor needs to be skilled and effective in providing the feedback and the coaching necessary to help their direct reports develop and meet the challenges of their work. If their immediate supervisor cannot provide effective feedback or coaching or shirks their responsibility for providing feedback and coaching, who is responsible for the problems? I suggest that the supervisor is not meeting his or her responsibilities for providing feedback and coaching to enable their reports to meet the challenges of today's business.

As a rule of thumb, when I see a supervisor giving an underperforming performance appraisal, or who has multiple turnovers in their department, I look to the supervisor to find the problem. Let's work to solve the problem where it originates. Let's take responsibility for improving processes and the development of the people who work for us. Of course that means that **supervisors at all levels need to be growing and developing** first so they can **help others to grow and develop**.

Are you growing and developing yourself? Are you becoming more skilled and competent at leading process improvement, providing feedback, and coaching your employees to become more successful? If not, why not? **Who is really responsible?**

Employee Responsibilities

If you are an employee, then certain responsibilities go along with the work you perform. Neglect these responsibilities and your work will suffer and your employment may be jeopardized. These work related responsibilities often include:

- Show up - be on time or inform your supervisor
- Eight hours of concentrated work for eight hours of pay each working day
- Manage your time at work effectively and efficiently

- 100% presence and engagement in your work
- Keep your work related commitments & promises
- Actively work to improve your communication skills
- Provide useful feedback in a positive manner
- Enthusiastically support and contribute to the company's Vision, Mission, Values, and Purpose
- Develop productive working relationships with each person inside the company
- When at work, maintain an attitude of service toward all customers
- Offer suggestions and seek to improve your work, work processes, and business systems
- Become a positive fully engaged team member
- Learn and become a teacher of subjects that you master
- Fix problems at the root cause level instead of just patching them
- Develop and maintain an ownership attitude "What more can I do to rise above my circumstances and get the results I want (or company wants)?"
- Remain emotionally stable and productive
- Be a constructive & enthusiastic company ambassador outside work
- Outside of work, pro-actively develop more of your work potential
- Exercise and stay healthy
- Get the proper amount of daily rest and relaxation

Take a moment and consider the different areas where you might improve the conduct of your work responsibilities. Choose one or two areas and set a goal(s) to improve your performance. Only with conscious attention to improvement will you improve your employability. With continuous improvement, you can name the type of work you do, compensation you receive, and the company where you work.

Fixing Problems the Right Way

PROBLEMS: Every day, there are many problems and issues to deal with, and most of them can appear to be - or are - urgent. The natural response of any individual is to fix them as quickly as possible and get back to the important things that need attention. That's what people are paid to do, fix them, isn't it? The answer is of course yes, fixing problems is important. However, if you only fix them, will they not pop-up again in the future? Let me share with you a superior attitude about the problems and issues you face daily.

ENDURING PROBLEM SOLVING: At the end of the day, take a few minutes and reflect over the problems and issues you faced. Which one had the most negative impact? What was the problem or issue that caused you the most inconvenience or caused the largest negative financial impact? When you identify the issue with the most impact, do some permanent problem solving. Look for the "Root Cause" of the problem. When you have identified the root cause, then brainstorm all the potential solutions. Analyze and pick the best solution that if implemented would correct the root cause. Implement the solution and see how it works (do a pilot if it affects a lot of people). If the solution works, then institutionalize it by integrating it into a procedure, process, employee handbook, or other operating instruction that ensures that it is done the right way the next time and every time. Now that's problem solving.

RESULTS: Most leaders, managers, and supervisors I know are so busy handling the daily work that they rarely take time to prevent problems in the future. Nevertheless, that process of problem solving is critical to a smoothly running business. As a result, your own workload will remain manageable and you will feel less stress. Just fixing problems on the spot and not considering the impact of root cause analysis and solutions will result in out of control processes, reaction management, wasteful time usage, and bottom-line lost profits. You must become proactive in solving problems at the root-cause level thus preventing the chaos that results from quick fixes.

It is always your choice. Take time at the end of each day to analyze your most daunting problem and fix it permanently. Do it today and every day.

Effective Execution

Individuals and organizations who are **consistently delivering great business results** are disciplined and deliberate in the performance of their work. They are skilled and committed to:

1. Developing well-defined goals contributing to the success of their business

2. Planning the necessary actions for achieving their goals in writing

3. Taking effective & efficient actions to achieve those goals

4. Tracking and measuring progress toward their goals

5. Being accountable by asking and acting on the question, "What more can I do to rise above my circumstances and get the results that I want?"

6. Making the corrections necessary to achieve the results they want

This "**Effective Execution**" of the management process can be broken down into three competencies: **Planning**, **Organizing**, and **Implementing**. Most people and businesses perform these competencies at one time or another but few people do so as effectively as possible, or in a balanced way. For instance, near the end of the year many organizations create strategic plans for the next year. When the next year comes, there is an initial flurry of actions starting the implementation process. As time passes and the routine of work develops, focus and emphasis on plan execution wanes and sometimes plans are ignored and shelved. Alternately, the year begins and the hustle and bustle of immediate work, fixing things, and serving the customer becomes the focus of almost all activity, and goals and plans are forgotten. **Do you know how well you are Planning, Organizing, and Implementing?**

Making Your Future Work Easier

BUSY WORKING WORLD: In the busy world of completing tasks, projects, and goals, it's easy to get totally caught up in the whirlwind of work, work, and more work. Fix this problem, complete that task, work on this project, take steps to accomplishing this goal. The pressure to achieve seldom lets up. Are you taking the actions that will make your work easier in the future?

PREVENTING PROBLEMS: Making work easier in the future means preventing future problems. To prevent problems you need to take time to do root cause analysis of present day problems, and then implement permanent solutions. Let me suggest that at the end of each day, when you close out your day and plan tomorrow's work, that you also take fifteen minutes to prevent future problems. Those fifteen minutes should be spent reflecting on your day, identifying the most costly problem you encountered, and developing a solution that permanently fixes it. The problem-solving steps to do this are:

1. Write a clear statement of the problem (gap between what is and what should be)

2. Identify all the possible causes

3. Analyze and find the root cause (the one cause that if fixed will prevent the problem from occurring in the future)

4. Brainstorm all the possible solutions to the root cause

5. Analyze and choose the best possible solution

6. Implement the chosen solution

7. Measure the results (if it works, go to step eight; if it doesn't work, got to step one)

8. Institutionalize the working solution (write into a work procedure, incorporate into a check list, include in employee manual, etc. so that the solution doesn't go away)

Taking Action - If you follow this fifteen minute process every day, you will be permanently solving about 240 problems each year. Would that make your work easier in the future? Set a goal and take action to spend fifteen minutes each day to prevent problems. Who is more valuable to your company, a person who is preventing problems or a person who is just fixing them?

Higher Laws of Business

One of the great success stories in business comes from the Springfield Re-manufacturing Corporation (SRC) located in Springfield Missouri. They re-manufacture a variety of motoring products including truck engines, transmissions, and other vehicle related products. I visited there a few years ago and met Jack Stack and heard the SRC story. You can get a feel for their success in his book called, "***The Great Game of Business: The Only Sensible Way to Run a Company***." In the beginning of that book, Jack lists "The Higher Laws of Business." Here they are:

1. You get what you give.

2. It's easy to stop one guy, but it's pretty hard to stop 100.

3. What goes around comes around.

4. You do what you gotta do.

5. You gotta wanna.

6. You can sometimes fool the fans, but you can never fool the players.

7. When you raise the bottom-line, the top rises.

8. When people set their own targets, they usually hit them.

9. If nobody pays attention, people stop caring.

10. As they say in Missouri: Stuff (*my word*) rolls downhill. By which we mean change begins at the top.

Jack's book is worth the time you will spend in reading it. Enjoy learning more about The Higher Laws of Business.

Resilience to Change

In Daryl Conner's book, "***Managing at the Speed of Change: How Resilient Managers Succeed and Prosper where Others Fail***," he says that **resilience to change** is often the single most important factor that distinguishes **those who succeed** from **those who fail**. He goes on to say that resilience is the pivotal clue that allows the mystery of change to be re-framed into an understandable and manageable process. With resilience serving as a reference point, you can influence the circumstances that surround you, prepare yourself and others to better absorb disruption, and skillfully plan and implement your desired future.

Resilient people are: positive, focused, flexible, organized, and proactive. These five basic characteristics of resilience are manifested by certain beliefs, behaviors, skills, and areas of knowledge. Listed below are the attributes that are most noteworthy for each characteristic.

Positive – Views Life as Challenging but Opportunity Filled

- Interprets the world as multifaceted and overlapping.
- Expects the future to be filled with constantly shifting variables.
- Views disruption as the natural result of a changing world.
- Sees life as filled with more paradoxes than contradictions.
- Sees major change as uncomfortable, but believes that hidden opportunities may usually exist.
- Believes there are usually important lessons to be learned from challenges.
- Sees life as generally rewarding.

Focused – Clear Vision of What Is to Be Achieved

- Maintains a strong vision that serves both as a source of purpose and as a guidance system to reestablish perspectives following significant disruption.

Flexible – Pliable When Responding to Uncertainty

- Believe change is a manageable process.
- Has a high tolerance for ambiguity.
- Needs only a short time to recover from adversity or disappointment.
- Feels empowered during change.

- Recognizes one's own strengths and weaknesses and knows when to accept internal or external limits.
- Challenges and, when necessary, modifies one's own assumptions or frames of reference.
- Relies on nurturing relationships for support.
- Displays patience, understanding, and humor when dealing with change.

Organized – Applies Structures to Help Manage Ambiguity

- Identifies the underlying themes embedded in confusing situations.
- Consolidates what appear to be several unrelated change projects into a single effort with a central theme.
- Sets and, when necessary, renegotiates priorities during change.
- Manage many simultaneous tasks and demands successfully.
- Compartmentalizes stress in one area so that it does not carry over to other projects or parts of one's life.
- Recognizes when to ask others for help.
- Engages major action only after careful planning.

Proactive – Engages Change Instead of Evading It

- Determines when a change is inevitable, necessary, or advantageous.
- Uses resources to creatively re-frame a changing situation, improvise new approaches, and maneuver to gain advantage.
- Takes risks despite potentially negative consequences.
- Draws important lessons from change-related experiences that are then applied to similar situations.
- Responds to disruption by investing energy in problem solving and teamwork.
- Influences others and resolves conflict.

To enhance resilience, you only need to replicate what resilient people do. Take inventory of yourself in the five characteristics of being positive, focused, flexible, organized, and proactive. Where there is a need to develop more of that characteristic, set a goal and work toward bolstering your resilience. Armed with enhanced resilience, you will be able to handle change more effectively. And since ever accelerating change will be our constant companion, it makes sense (and cents) to enhance your resilience.

Beware, the Busy Manager!

The *Harvard Business Review* magazine has just hit pay dirt again. In their February 2002 issue on page 62 is an article called, "Beware the Busy Manager." It asks the question, "Are the least effective executives the ones who look like they are doing the most?" What a great question to ask and answer!

To avoid being trapped in the "**activity trap**" instead of engaging in "**high payoff activity**" and the planned mode of managing oneself, each of us needs to regularly answer this question. This great article goes on to provide these statistics about the managers they studied:

- **30%** suffer from low levels of both energy and focus (**procrastinators**)
- **20%** suffer from high focus and low levels of energy (**disengaged**)
- **40%** are well-intentioned, highly energetic, but unfocused (**distracted**)
- **10% were both highly energetic and highly focused (purposeful)**

This actually tracks with what we know about goal setting people: 13% of people are goal setters (3% written & 10% mental goals).

If you feel like you are just spinning your wheels and getting no where, it's time to block time in your schedule to think, set goals, plan, and reflect on the personal management techniques you know will bring you success. Plan your month, plan your day and take action on your high payoff activities. You are the leader of your life.

■ CHAPTER TWENTY-FOUR ■
GETTING RESULTS

*"Get a good idea and stay with it. Dog it,
and work at it until it's done, and done right."*

- Walt Disney

Most organizations no matter how small have definite results or goals they want to achieve with their business. Usually these goals are in the mind of the leader. How well they clearly communicate these goals to the organization, and how well all employees are focused on delivering the desired results, are the important questions. Often people in organizations complain that they don't know how their work contributes to organizational goals - if they even know what the organizational goals are! This uncertainty ensures that some employee activities do not make a valuable contribution to the company's products and services. In other words, **employees waste precious time and money because they are not totally focused on the business results required** for business success. What can be done to solve this problem?

Here are some ideas, leaders, managers, and supervisors can use to align and focus employees to get the results they want:

1. Set and plan goals in detail and in writing.

2. Communicate the goals and plans to employees. Do it every day, week, month, for the entire period they are in effect. Don't miss a day. Let employees know that their performance is important to their, your, and the company's success.

3. Have employees set goals, projects, and tasks that will contribute to achieving company goals. Make sure they are aligned with, and contribute to company goals.

4. Ensure that employees are focused on, implement, and steadily work on their tasks, projects, and goals.

5. Insist that employees track progress toward their goals.

6. Arrange frequent communications to share their progress. Encourage employees and show interest to, and appreciation for, employee results.

7. Coach employees to help them improve their work processes to become more efficient, effective, and productive.

8. Celebrate when they make significant progress toward goals, projects, and tasks.

9. Do it all again.

You might notice that this is a proactive approach to management, and that it will lead to more effective, efficient, and productive work results.

Great Business Results

The latest business book to be published by one of our own right here in Scottsdale, is called *What You $ay Is What You Get: The $ecret*

Language of Great Business Results by Linne Bourget M.A., M.B.A., Ph.D. The book is Volume 1 in The Leader's Positive Toolkit Series. In her book, Dr. Linne uses her extensive twenty plus years of consulting and coaching experience in creating a powerful positive approach for getting great business results. A national pioneer in using the positive approach to developing teamwork, growing leaders, and coaching for dramatic business reversals, Dr. Linne has captured the essential principles and laws that every leader needs to know to add to their present success. There are many specific examples of powerful client stories, tools, their applications, and subsequent results that you can use in your own business. This is an application and results oriented book, not an academic publication. The entire book is delightfully and tastefully integrated with driving powerful cars, and we know who likes to drive powerful cars, don't we? For example, the four wheels illustrate the basic concepts Dr. Linne presents in her book. They are:

> **Wheel 1**: What You See Is What You Get
>
> **Wheel 2**: What You Say Is What You Get: What To Say For Great Results
>
> **Wheel 3**: What You Ask For Is What You Get
>
> **Wheel 4**: What You Don't Say Is What You Get: When The Best Thing For Your Results Is Not To Say It

If you are looking for positive ideas to grow your leadership and get the results you want, you need this book! You can obtain a copy or copies by contacting Dr. Linne at **drlinne@whatyousayiswhatyouget.com** (soon available on Amazon.com). Dr. Warren Bennis, Mark Victor Hanson (Chicken Soup for the Soul series co-creator), and many other noted authors have endorsed her book. I have read it and highly recommend the book. You need every trick you can learn to get Great Business Results. Give this book a try!

How to Create the Unbeatable Team

Whatever the industry, its great leaders share basic qualities. In his book, *Think Like a Champion: Building Success One Victory at a Time*, Denver Broncos' coach Mike Shanahan shares his insight into the principles of creating a winning team on, or in, any field. Here is Shanahan's fifteen point game plan for winning teams:

1. Teams matter more than individuals.
2. Every job is important.
3. Treat everyone with respect.
4. Share both victories and defeats.
5. Accept criticism.
6. Keep the boss well informed.
7. Focus on your work ethic, not others'.
8. Allow for differences in lifestyle.
9. Be more creative than predictable.
10. Let go of failed ideas.
11. Employ structure and order.
12. Reward those who produce.
13. Find different ways to motivate your employees.
14. Keep your employees fresh.
15. Protect your system.

ASSESSMENT: Using a point scale of one (poor) to ten (excellent), assess your performance in each of the fifteen items. Then add your points.

0–30 – Going out of business.

30–60 – Existence threatened.

60-90 – Serious disconnects exist.

90-120 – Growth opportunities still exist.

120-150 – You are doing great!

Simple No Cost Productivity Gains

After interviewing a large sample of managers and their employees, the Gallop Organization found that no single factor more clearly predicts the productivity of an employee than his / her relationship with his/her direct superior. More specifically, Gallop found that the key drivers of productivity for employees include whether they:

- Feel cared for by a supervisor or someone at work
- Have received recognition or praise during the past seven days
- Someone at work regularly encourages their development

In our hustle and bustle to accomplish more and more work, do we neglect to do the simple things that can make a significant positive impact on the productivity of our employees? Take time now to audit your relationship with each person who reports to you and answer each of these three questions. Make notes and take corrective action to increase the productivity of your organization. You will feel good about the choice you make and actions you take.

P.S. Another source has documented that 75% of employees quit their jobs because of problems or unresolved issues with their immediate supervisor.

The Power of Suggestions

Toyota does a great job of involving employees and fulfilling their need for autonomy. They require employees to submit two suggestions per month that they can implement themselves or with a teammate - in other words, something the employee can control. As a result, Toyota receives about 1.5 million employee suggestions for improvement each year. More impressively, **80% of these actually get implemented**! Though many of Toyota's employees perform repetitive manufacturing jobs, this approach sends a strong message that employees have control over their work processes. What kind of impact would this approach to autonomy have in your organization?

If you are the boss, plan for and take action to implement this successful technique.

If you are not the boss, pass this article to her or him and ask for their support in implementing your suggestion.

- Taken from the pamphlet *Passionate Performance: Engaging Minds and Hearts to Conquer the Competition* by Lee J. Colan

Long Term Productivity

WORK "IN" YOUR BUSINESS - **Everyone** works "in" their business. You lead, manage resources, sell, provide services, and produce products, plan, and do all the diverse tasks necessary to make the business function. Completing these tasks and to-dos are essential.

WORK "IN" YOUR LIFE - You might think of your life in the same sort of terms. You have to complete tasks like doing the laundry, cleaning, grooming the lawn, running errands, and doing all the things necessary to live a "normal life." Uggggg, and there are the taxes to do!

ALWAYS DOING - Just doing the things that you need to do may take most of your time. There never seems to be time for anything else. You're exhausted just keeping up with the "things to do." Investing most or all of your time in the "to-do list" can result in burn out, extreme stress, exhaustion, sickness, hopelessness, meaninglessness, and depression. The result is suffering, unproductive, unhappy, and unfulfilled workers and people.

WORK "ON" YOUR BUSINESS – If you work "**on**" your business, then you are working on the systems, processes, and ways of working to make them simpler, more efficient, easier to use, and more productive with less cost. You are improving the way you do business to become more competitive and profitable.

WORK "ON" YOUR LIFE – In your life, you are working "**on**" yourself to become more capable and competent, to use more of your potential, become more effective, and more efficient at living your life. You are working on yourself to use more of your potential to create a better life in the long-term. Building a "better performing you" can result in greater happiness, joy, and satisfaction.

WORK PRIORITIES – Which is more important for your long-term success? Working "**in**" your business furiously cranking out the maximum amount of work or working "**on**" your capacity to complete more work in less time. Well, you can't stop working "**in**" your business but you can *take time to work "on" your business*. If you don't, eventually your business will succumb to those who are working on their businesses!

LIFE PRIORITIES – Which of the following are more important for your long term personal satisfaction and happiness? Spending all your time doing, or taking some time to work "**on**" increasing your competence and capability as a unique and valuable person. Why of course, taking some time for you is essential for your long term success and happiness.

Take some time to balance your life. Take time for regular exercise, time for learning new skills, time for reading, time for feeding your spiritual source of power. It is not selfish! It is essential self-care because if you don't take time to develop yourself and grow, then you won't be at your best or have the resources and energy to help others. You won't have the capacity to work and live as effectively, efficiently, and productively as you could. You will find yourself **working harder** rather than **working smarter** in trying to get ahead in work and life. But you won't be getting ahead! Stop all the doing, and start taking a little time to develop more of your long- term potential for happiness and joy.

PERSONAL ACTION - *Insight without action is only entertainment!* Set a goal now to take short periods of time each day to both work "**on**" your business and to work "**on**" yourself. You will be happy you did.

Engaging People in Work

A Gallup poll revealed that only **26% of U.S. employees are fully engaged in their work** at any time. On the other end of the spectrum, **19% of employees are actively disengaged**, meaning they intentionally act in ways that negatively impact their organizations. The annual cost nationwide to employ this actively disengaged group exceeds **$300 billion**.

Are disengaged employees a problem in your organization? Do your employees complete only what is asked of them and nothing more? Did you know that actively **disengaged employees miss an average of 3.5 more days of work per year** than engaged employees? Consider some other effects of disengagement:

- increased turnover
- missed deadlines

- low morale
- complacency
- finger-pointing
- lack of accountability and responsibility

Do you recognize any of these? If you answered "Yes," that's an indication you have an engagement challenge.

Disengagement is simply the result of unfulfilled needs. Nothing fancy here; these are basic human needs that leaders either forget, choose not to remember, or simply don't know how to fulfill. When people's needs are fulfilled, they can become engaged and perform at their peak ability. When their needs are met, they are motivated to help those who meet their needs. When their needs are not met, they become frustrated, out of control, unfocused, and disconnected - in a word, disengaged.

To meet these needs, leaders must first see them and acknowledge them. In order to see them, leaders must view their employees as people and not just workers. If you look at your employees as people, you can identify six basic needs, three intellectual and three emotional. Listed with those needs are some strategies that can be used to help "Meet those needs."

Needs	Strategies to Meet Those Needs
Intellectual	
Achievement	– Eliminate barriers to achievement. – Define crystal clear goals.
Autonomy	– Involve employees in improving their work processes. – Set broad yet clear boundaries.

Mastery	_ Fit person to position for highest and best use. _ Seize teachable moments to coach employees.
Emotional	
Purpose	_ Connect roles to a compelling purpose. _ Stay focused on activities that support your purpose.
Social (part of a team)	_ Maintain small teams. _ Create and reinforce team rituals.
Appreciation	_ Find opportunities to appreciate employees' contributions. _ Demonstrate a sincere interest in your employees as people. Learn what makes them tick.

These strategies are simple and cost little or no money. Take a moment and assess your company and employees. Do you think it would be possible for you to engage more employees if you applied one or several of these strategies? If yes, set a goal and take action. Change is a wonderful thing and only through change can you engage more of your employees.

- Adapted from the pamphlet, *Passionate Performance: Engaging Minds and Hearts to Conquer the Competition* by Lee J. Colan

Survivor Productivity & Morale

In my classes at the University of Phoenix, I teach students to identify problems by clearly describing the "**As Is**" condition and then identifying and stating what the "**Should Be**" results are that they want to achieve. Using this format, a chronic problem facing many businesses today and a powerful solution is described in the following article.

284

As Is – Most industries and their businesses have suffered severe economic declines that have negatively impacted their business results. Many people have had their jobs disappear because there isn't enough value-added work to support their position. The survivors of downsizing and layoffs are feeling the pressures of doing the same work that, previously, two or three people did. Remaining employees are not sure if their job will be the next to be cut. The negative psychological impact of seeing coworkers downsized, uncertainty of having a job in the future and heavy workloads can lead to a **real decline in individual motivation and personal productivity**. People often respond to this challenge by working harder instead of smarter. "If I spend more time at the office, the boss will think that I am contributing more than others and therefore I will keep my job." **NOT SO!** This behavior only leads to decreased effectiveness and productivity, eventual burnout, and loss of a valued employee (added cost of recruiting and training a replacement: often estimated at tens of thousands of dollars $$,$$$).

SHOULD BE – Winning businesses are concerned with getting results. Leaders focus on establishing and achieving goals that strengthen business results, profit model, and ensure short and long-term success. People are constantly improving the effectiveness and efficiency of their business systems. **Leaders are constantly coaching and working at improving the effectiveness and efficiency of their people**. Why their people? The reason is that leaders realize that the most valuable business asset in any company is the people who work there. They realize that without highly effective people working on and in the business, they are doomed to becoming second-rate, mediocre, or even worse, **noncompetitive**. This means that everyone loses. Leaders take action to

285

create a productive work environment where employee morale is high and people are effective and productive in their work.

A POWERFUL SOLUTION – The question is, "How can you help surviving employees work smarter and boost their morale and productivity?" The answer is, create a development program where participants evaluate all aspects of their work looking for and applying ideas to get improved results. It's a back to basics development program where over a period of twenty weeks people actually break through old conditioning, and establish new more productive and effective work habits and attitudes (meeting only two hours bi-weekly). They learn to work smarter, not harder. Being selected to participate sends a strong positive message to each of your participants about his or her worth and longevity in your organization. Our life changing development program always increases participant morale and delivers tangible, measurable results to your business. Return-On-Investment of between three and five is consistently achieved by participants.

Accountability

My employees seldom deliver the results I expect. They waste time, miss deadlines, don't do a complete job, and in general just don't seem to care. Why, when I was a worker, I worked hard and did a great job for my boss. Why can't they do that for me now?

What I can do to help my employees deliver the results I want is to establish clear work expectations, specifically define goals, measure and report results, teach them how to "own their monkey," and finally celebrate results. Let's briefly look at each of these items.

CLEAR WORK EXPECTATIONS – When you hire an employee, do you just show them their work and give them their tools, or do you take time to orient them to your company. Do you teach them what your vision, mission, values and purpose of work are? Do you spend time to explain what your expectations for their work are? Do they clearly understand what it takes to move up in your workplace? Do you teach them what success is for the company and for its employees? Do you teach them what results you need to get? Do you make a specific point to clearly communicate what responsibilities they have and what they are accountable for? If not, then they won't know how to work for you, will they?

SPECIFIC GOALS – If there are no goals for employees to achieve, then how can they be held responsible? If it's just installing this skylight, tile this floor, or install these cabinets, what really is the goal? Goals should establish work targets. Targets like reducing labor hours, conserving materials, satisfying customers, keeping to schedules, arriving at the work site on time, doing a quality job the first time, or any specific goal that strengthens your business and produces positive results. Communicate them in a way that all employees know exactly what you expect.

MEASUREMENT & REPORTING OF RESULTS – Goals must be measured! *What gets measured gets done.* Track actual labor hours versus what you estimated, wasted materials, cost of mistakes, costs to satisfy a customer service failure, cost of arriving at the work site late (return trips), and anything that impacts business results in a negative way. Measure and report the results (keep score) or you will not know where you are in the game of business.

OWN THE MONKEY – Problems always come up during work. Some managers and supervisors readily make all the decisions. That's not good! How can people learn to take ownership of problems and solve them? How can they grow personally if they never make the decisions and

287

experience the consequences? Think of problems as **monkeys**. When an employee brings a problem to you (**monkey**), ask yourself if the employee can solve the problem. If he or she can, then lead them through a problem solving process. Help them discover the solution. Don't take responsibility and accountability from them by taking ownership of their problem. Empower them to implement the solution and report back to you the results. Keep them responsible and accountable for owning their monkey. You solve the problems that only you can solve. Take the time to train your employees. The long-term benefits of this approach will stun you.

CELEBRATION OF RESULTS – Recognize the employees who deliver the results you want. Too often the squeaky wheel gets the grease (your attention). As a rule of thumb, provide three times more recognition for the good results than you give to mistakes and negative actions. Always recognize the results your employees deliver especially when they contribute to achieving the results and goals you establish for them. Celebrate positive results every day.

Accountability in the work place can be directly attributed to the attitude of the supervisors and managers of your company. The attitude you want to possess is one that believes that all employees want to be responsible and accountable for the work that they do. Employees don't usually wake up in the morning thinking they will dodge responsibility for their work. With the right belief and attitude, it is much easier and effective to set clear work expectations, specific goals, measure and report the results, encourage employees to solve work related problems (own the monkey), and celebrate results. As supervisors and managers you need to be responsible and accountable for establishing the right work environment where employees can and want to be held accountable and responsible for their work.

The OZ Principle

According to the book *The Oz Principle*, "**People hold inside themselves the power to rise above their circumstances and get the results they want**." In my opinion, this book is by far one of the best books on accountability in existence.

The Oz Principle introduces the concept of "**The Line**." **Above the Line** and you are being responsible for your actions and getting the results you want. **Below the Line** and you become the victim by blaming others, acting confused, and using an attitude of helplessness. Below the line and you become a responsibility "ducker." You get trapped in the victim cycle. Stages of the victim cycle include:

1. Ignore/deny
2. It's not my job
3. Finger pointing
4. Confusion / tell me what to do
5. Cover your tail
6. Wait and see

If you recognize any of these six stages in your organization or life, then, you ought to read further. According to the Oz Principle, the "**Steps to Accountability**" or to getting "**Above the Line**" include:

1. See It (courage to see the reality of a difficult situation)

2. Own It (accepting full ownership of all past and present behaviors contributing to the situation)

3. Solve It (asking, "What else can I do to achieve the results I want?")

4. Do It (expending the effort and action needed to make it happen and get it done)

289

For most of us, becoming more accountable will involve a break with past actions / habits and thoughts / attitudes. In other words, we need to change. And "Change of any kind is a struggle with fear, anger, and uncertainty, a war against old habits, hide-bound thinking, and entrenched interests." However, "The greatest power we have is the ability to envision our own fate - and to change ourselves."

If you connect with any part of this article, then you will benefit from reading The Oz Principle. Being accountable for getting the results you want is the only way to "Build on Your Success." When you ask the question, **"What else can I do to achieve the results I want**?" and take action, you will progress in the direction of realizing your goals and dreams.

P.S. The Oz Principle is written by Roger Connors, Tom Smith, and Craig Hickman.

Personal Investment

Personal investment may be hard to describe, but seeing it in the actions of others is easy. We heard of one military official who used to measure how far the members of his platoon could run after he pulled the pin of a practice grenade. He had all of the distances recorded for each man. After practicing for a week he told the men that this drill would be done with live ammunition. He told the men to get ready to run after he pulled the pin. He was not the least surprised to find record distances for every member of the platoon with most the men nearly doubling their past personal best. When people in the organization are invested in the work they are doing they put more of themselves into their individual efforts to achieve results.

■ CHAPTER TWENTY-FIVE ■
COACHING

When you were born, your mother was your first coach. You learned words through coaching. You played your first games and sports with the aid of someone who was a coach. If you consented, your parents coached you through your teens and they are probably there to coach you now if you seek it. At work, it's probable that someone has informally coached you in achieving some goal or outcome. So, **unless you reject all help or don't want to grow as a person, coaching is for you**!

FOREVER GROWING: Fine-tuning your knowledge, skills, and competencies is a sure way of keeping up with changes in the world. Keeping up with changes in the world will keep you engaged in life, growing in competency, and actively thinking – all necessary for longevity and a challenging happy life. Failing to do this, you will atrophy, decline, and fall into mediocrity, or worse, failure. Developing your knowledge, skills, and competencies takes insight, deliberate planning, and effort. It takes a self-directed, goal seeking, positively motivated individual. It takes the tenaciousness and the self-discipline of a determined person. But what if you don't seem to possess all these characteristics? Then what do you do? The answer is, "**Get a Coach**" to help you.

What is a Coach? A coach is a consultant who establishes a formal helping relationship to assist you in working on stubborn issues, developing new competencies, improving your performance, achieving new goals, or becoming a better personal and organizational leader. The coach uses a variety of behavioral techniques and methods to help you achieve new results.

Typical recipients of coaching include:

- **High Potential Performers** who are targeted for advancement / succession within the organization,

- **Solid Performers** whose current behaviors are interfering with their performance and putting the company at risk,

- **Developing Leaders** who know that to advance and lead their organizations more effectively, they must accelerate their learning / development and model new leadership behaviors, and

- **Aspiring People** not content with where they are in life and willing to explore, take action to change, and grow. They engage a coach's help to live life more fully & abundantly.

PURPOSE: Coaches provide a confidential, comfortable, and safe environment in which to talk about, explore, learn, and develop new knowledge, skills, and competencies. Coaching gives a person valuable third party feedback. They help people look at problems and life in different ways and all points of view. Coaches provide the opportunity to dialogue about ideas, discuss current issues without judgment, and discuss strengths and opportunities for improvement. Coaches help you to more rapidly advance to new levels of achievement in the direction of your desires, goals, and dreams.

BENEFITS: Benefits from coaching include improvements in:
- development,
- performance & outcomes,
- different perspectives,
- being an objective person,
- feedback and support,
- self-esteem, and
- relationship.

There is modest evidence that coaching positively impacts the following areas: job performance, productivity, learning, and leadership effectiveness. One recent study of forty-three executives has reported an average value of $100,000 for each executive establishing a Return-On-Investment of 5.7 times their investment made in coaching. This investment and return makes sense!

DECISION & TAKING ACTION: So, there you have it. Coaching is for everyone. It is appropriate for High Potential Performers, Solid Performers, Developing Leaders, and Aspiring People. The benefits can be rewarding and profitable. Only you can choose to accelerate your growth and development through coaching. Make that choice now.

Why Coach?

Why coach? Two executives (or leaders, managers, supervisors, etc.), one is effective, a solid worker, and delivers good quality results on time. The other does the same but delegates, empowers, and masterfully coaches his or her subordinates to use more of their potential. What will be the eventual outcome of this comparison? The one who coaches will undoubtedly deliver more results because his or her people will be delivering more and better work. Which executive will you want to advance in his or her career first?

What is coaching? The book *Masterful Coaching* by Robert Hargrove wonderfully describes coaching in great and useful detail. "Masterful coaching involves impacting people's visions and values as well as helping them reshape their way of being, thinking, and actions. It involves challenging and supporting people to achieve higher levels of performance while allowing them to bring out the best in themselves and those around them. It means going through a deep learning process that results in embodying new skills and capabilities. In the simplest, day-in day-out terms, masterful coaching involves expanding people's capacity to take effective action. It often comes down to making it possible for people to succeed in areas where they are most stuck or ineffective."

LEARNING TO COACH. – To learn how to coach, a person must "know him or herself" and "be actively engaged in personal growth and development." Part of that personal development needs to be the subject of coaching. The benefits of learning to coach people are quite positive and will have great impact on your company. What might not be obvious is the personal satisfaction, joy, and happiness you will experience during that journey. Being able to help others achieve greater success in your organization can be a huge win-win-win (you, the company, and the coached). Your journey starts with your choice. I'd be happy to chat with you to discuss what that journey might be like for you. By the way, I have a coach!

P.S. A coach is someone who tells you what you don't want to hear, who has you see what you don't want to see, so you can be who you have always known you could be.

– Tom Landry

294

Who Needs a Coach?

Who needs a coach? Only those courageous souls who want to **achieve extraordinary life results**! Why is it that in athletics every team has a coach or several coaches? Is it to push paperwork? Is it to keep the grounds or buildings in good shape? Is it to act as liaison with the fans? Nooooo! Coaches observe and provide specific performance feedback to individual players and the team, they recognize strengths, provide improvement pointers, and help their players to develop and use more of their unlimited potential. Great coaches want to win, but their idea of winning is to see their players become more skilled, confident, and performing at a more advanced level. They want to see their players win not only in the game but in life.

You can accelerate your personal growth and develop more of your unlimited potential with a coach. However, you will need a variety of coaches for you to develop in all aspects of your life. You could seek coaches in financial matters, your work, physical conditioning, family relationships, educational goals, health initiatives, spiritual development, and many other life development areas. With the help of these guides, you can make rapid progress and realize more of your potential. You can realize more of your wants and dreams. You can enjoy the achievements that you once thought were impossible in this lifetime. So, what's holding you back? There is no better investment than in yourself. **You need a coach! You need to coach others!**

What are the steps to becoming a coach? You must first choose to become all that you can be. You must choose to change, grow, and develop more of your human potential. You must choose to become a better personal leader of yourself. You must choose to shake-up the status-quo, challenge the way you do things, and move in the direction of your dreams. It's all up to you! After you have made these choices and started to develop yourself, then you can begin to effectively coach others. Here are ten tips that will help you:

1. Always develop yourself first. Become the example of personal growth.

2. Develop and display an attitude of love, care, respect, and life-long learning with others.

3. Listen, listen, and listen deeply to the person and what their soul is sharing with you.

4. Ask questions to learn more and truly understand.

5. Lead by questions to develop insights. Let the person you are coaching discover what needs changing.

6. Solicit a commitment for action where change is desired.

7. Follow-up on commitments. Hold yourself and other people accountable.

8. Positively acknowledge every small victory. Celebrate growth, both the person's and your own.

9. Enroll in a coaching development program to become an even better coach.

10. Understand that this process cannot end until the end.

12 Personal Growth Tips

1. You are unique and unlike anyone else. Compare yourself with NO ONE!

2. Risk and choose to change and grow. Stagnation is the kiss of death!

3. Set one "To Become" goal and develop more of your potential. Act on the goal daily.

4. Read thirty minutes daily (business or self-development). In one year you will have 182 hours, at least eighteen books, and you will become an expert in at least two new subjects.

5. Setbacks are the world's way of telling you what you need to learn to get ahead.

6. Seek to learn the habits and attitudes of successful people. Do what they do.

7. Teach others what you learn. They will then free you for more valuable work.

8. Ask for feedback about "YOU" at every opportunity. Be grateful and thank the people who give you feedback. They are giving you a precious gift.

9. Always look for and recognize the best in YOURSELF and others.

10. Work for results, not perfection.

11. Happiness and joy results from pursuing goals in all areas of your life.

12. Get a coach. Successful people (and athletes) seek help to sharpen their skills, improve their performance and develop faster than their peers.

■ PART FOUR ■
BARRIERS TO SUCCESS

"There was a very cautious man who never laughed or cried.
He never risked, he never lost, he never won nor tried.
And when one day he passed away and his insurance was denied,
for he never really lived, they claimed he never died."

■ CHAPTER TWENTY-SIX ■
FEAR

*Our deepest fear is that we are powerful beyond measure.
It is our light, not our darkness that most frightens us. We
ask ourselves, who am I to be brilliant, gorgeous, talented,
and fabulous? Actually, who are you not to be? You are a
child of love and light. Your playing small doesn't serve the
world. There's nothing enlightened about shrinking so that
other people won't feel insecure around you. We were born
to make manifest the glory of love that is within us. It's not
just in some of us; it's in everyone. And as we let our own
light shine, we unconsciously give other people permission
to do the same. As we are liberated from our own fear,
our presence automatically liberates others.*

- Nelson Mandela

PROLOGUE: Is there fear in your business environment? Or do people feel free to learn, grow, and develop more of their potential. Are you creating the environment that liberates people from their fears and enables them to do and become the great persons that they are? Are you liberated from fear? Are you pursuing a path to greatness? If not, why not? Greatness begins with you and is called personal leadership. Isn't that kind of leadership important to your business success? And since personal leadership precedes effective organizational leadership, isn't it important to grow in your own leadership now? Call us for coaching in developing personal leadership.

■ ■ ■

Shortly after 9-11, I flew from Phoenix to Chicago. The flight out was half full, the off-airport parking lots were half full, there were no waiting lines, and check-in was quick and easy. Everything was operating smoothly. Flying back Saturday, the plane had twenty passengers. When I arrived back at Sky Harbor Airport, I realized that the parking lot was almost empty. What a change from the last time I flew. What accounts for the difference?

Fear! Fear makes the difference. People are afraid and it's affecting everything that they have normally done in the past. You and I know that this kind of fear will be overcome with time. Things will get back to normal. So why am I sharing this? Fear keeps us from adapting to the changing world around us. We get comfortable and happy with our current situation. Doing things differently is uncomfortable and risks the status quo. Change threatens the comfort that we have created around us. We fear change. The problem with this fear of change is that if we do the things we have always done, we will continue to get the things in our life that we have always gotten. I don't know about you, but I choose to "Add to My Success." We all have this choice. In this great land of freedom and opportunity, don't let fear defeat you.

It takes courage to step out and do something different, to try new things. To take seriously and apply an improvement idea that involves changing your attitude (habit of thought) or behavior (habit of action) is difficult.

The payoff of exercising this type of courage is astronomical. Those who exercise it will enjoy great benefits. You can trust me on this one.

Today, make a note in your Personal Planning System and make a change that you have wanted to make. Exercise courage and try something new and feel the exhilaration of risk and added success. Conquer fear. Develop more of your potential. You are a thoroughbred, not a donkey!

Fear of Failure

Fear of failure is the major contributor to poor goal achievement. The logic follows, "If I don't set goals, I won't fail. If I fail, I will have to face a loss of self-confidence." We've all heard that setting high goals and miss is better, than to fail to set them at all. But this simple philosophy doesn't work. You can't listen to a motivational speaker pump you up and suddenly expect to be an achiever. It's a little like the salesman who walked into his manager's office and said, "I can't make my goals this month." The manager said, "What do you mean you can't make your goals this month? I paid a motivational speaker $7,500 to pump you up. Do you remember what he said? Be positive. What do you have to say for yourself now?" The salesman said, "I'm positive I can't make my goals this month."

Fear destroys all that it touches. If you don't believe me, then analyze why people are prospering or why they are failing and languishing in mediocrity. When you analyze these people, you will find that they fear the unknown and get stuck in life. Success is created by the exercise of courage, change, caring (love), and service to others. Set big goals, march forth with courage, risk failing, work intensely for the success of others, conquer fear with love, and watch your success multiply many times over. Fear of failure or the courage to act on your goals is always a free-will choice. Be responsible for your choice and don't make fear an excuse for stagnation. Choose to act and press the limits. Go after those goals, wants, and dreams. Make them happen for **if you think you can, you can**!

Creating Safety!

Safety is Mr. Maslow's second level of hierarchy of needs, just above Physiological, or the need for biological maintenance (food, water, and sustenance). Safety includes the need for security, protection, and stability in the physical and interpersonal events of day-to-day life. Safety means knowing where you will sleep and where your next paycheck is coming from. It means knowing that wherever you find yourself, you can regularly provide for your physical life. Steady work is usually one of the items that enables a person to create stability and provide for their daily needs. What happens when work vanishes? That's been happening a lot lately!

For the person who does not prepare for this eventuality, **panic, fear, doubt, depression, and a sense of loss and victimization** runs rampant, sometimes for a very long time. For the person who has prepared for this event, **confidence, opportunity, hope, challenge, belief, and faith** become the commanding emotions. OK, so how can I create this last state of mind in my life?

A person becomes confident, has faith, embraces hope, sees things as worthy challenges, knows that (s)he will be ok, and sees opportunities in everything they experience if they **set goals to learn and develop continuously more of their potential**. For instance, spending thirty minutes a day reading a book will result in 182 hours of reading a year. If you can read a normal book in ten hours that means you read eighteen books a year. Reading eighteen books a year will make you an expert in any subject you choose to study. Heck, it might even make you an expert in several areas. A few years of this activity and your confidence will soar! You will gain perceived and actual expertise that makes you instantly employable wherever you go, and can lead to a possible pay raise or promotion in your present job. If you don't take action to increase your employability though, your safety will be at the mercy of changing business systems that one day will not need your outdated knowledge and services. The choice is rather obvious, isn't it?

Take a subject that you have a **passion to learn about** and **set a learning and development goal**. Complete the whole goal planning sheet to include affirmations and visualizations. Get your action steps into your Personal Planning System or Outlook. Prioritize your action steps high enough that they get done regularly if not daily. Track your progress. Look back and **celebrate your success and the confidence and safety you have created for yourself**.

Breaking Free of the Victim Cycle

When you encounter a difficult situation, ask yourself whether you want to remain mired in the difficulty or attempt some sort of breakthrough to extract yourself from the situation. Even the most habitual victim would rather be leading a better life. However, achieving a "break through" usually requires a "break with" past actions and attitudes. That means that any person feeling victimized must replace his or her victim story with a willingness to see things as they really are, and not as they appear to be from the tenuous safety of the victim cycle. To create a better future, you must often break with the past. Failing this, you will, sooner or later, suffer serious consequences for your inaction."

- Extracted from *The OZ Principle: Getting Results Through Individual and Organizational Accountability* by Roger Connors, Tom Smith, and Craig Hickman

■ CHAPTER TWENTY-SEVEN ■
AVOIDING DERAILMENT

"It's a recession when your neighbor loses his job;
it's a depression when you lose your own."

- Harry S. Truman

When a leader's career derails, there's a good chance that problems with interpersonal relationships are a major contributing factor to the wreck. That's according to research done by the Center for Creative Leadership (CCL), which defines derailed executives as "individuals who are initially quite successful but later in their careers are fired, demoted, or repeatedly passed over for promotion."

Such people typically aren't aware of the interpersonal deficiencies that could lead to their derailment, a recent CCL e-newsletter states. For example, these leaders are often described by coworkers as insensitive and competitive. They isolate themselves, they're dictatorial and they get angry easily. They're overly critical and overly demanding, as well as arrogant, manipulative, and emotionally explosive.

On the other hand, executives for whom the risk of derailment is lessened due to their superior relational skills are described as being good listeners, teamwork oriented, not an authoritarian, collaborative, and honest. They're also accessible and supportive of others' ideas. So how can a leader determine whether he or she is heading for trouble in this area? "By taking an honest and open look at your own strengths and weaknesses," the CCL says, "you can identify the areas where you might be at risk for career derailment and address them before you run off track."

But, if you aren't aware of the deficiencies, then how can you take an honest and open look at your own strengths and weaknesses? Let's just say that it is difficult. The most effective and efficient way is to engage the services of a coach! An experienced coach can help you uncover and see the world views and attitudes that may be traps in your own career development. Your coach can identify and gently lead you through the minefields of personal growth and advancement in work and life. Who better to invest in than yourself? You are worth it, aren't you?

We Build Our Own Jails

What is a jail? Each of us has a picture of a jail in our minds and it's not pretty. Stark walls on three sides, toilet, sink, hard bunk, bars, and locked cell door. A jail cell prevents the occupant(s) from mingling with others. They isolate you and limit your actions and interactions. They confine, punish, and severely limit what you can and cannot do.

What do I mean when I say, "We Build Our Own Jails?" Think of a newborn baby. How much potential does he or she have, and what are the possibilities for this new person? *Unlimited*, right? Did you fit this description when you were born (ask your parents)? As you grow up, you learn the dos and don'ts around the house, especially the don'ts. In school, again, there is a new set of rules you must learn and follow. Just about when you are feeling like an adult, the parents put further restrictions on your driving, dating, and all sorts of other activities. After fighting this, you finally break free only to find that there are credit cards to pay, car payments, house payments, kids to raise, etc. To make all these things work, you establish your own rules and thinking processes around the life you lead. All this past conditioning of thoughts, attitudes, behaviors, and habits that has occurred throughout your life can become your own jail. Your jail can be preventing you from using all of your potential and realizing all your possibilities and dreams.

Here are some steps to "**Break Out of Jail:**"

1. Identify Your Jail Walls: Reflect and recall conditions that are preventing you from using all of your potential. These are your jail walls. They consist of limiting thoughts, attitudes, behaviors, and habits that limit the progress you make in your life.

2. Decide to Break Out: Make a decision to break out of jail. Choose to change the limiting thoughts, attitudes, behaviors, or habits you possess.

3. Get Outside Help: If you don't know how or you've had trouble in the past, get help! You can get help from places like your church, counselors, psychologist, coach, or friends. Leadership Advantage is also a resource with programs and coaching designed to help you break free.

4. Plan Your Escape Route & Go For It: Set goals and develop a plan of action. Take action on your plan every day. Make the necessary changes and escape.

5. Enjoy Your Freedom: Chart your progress and celebrate each jail cell wall falling from your goals, planning, and actions. Replacing old thoughts, attitudes, behaviors, and habits with new more positive and productive ones that will serve to create a better future for you.

Slavery

Are you a slave to your past? That is, past conditioning, past habits, past attitudes? How can you tell if you are a slave? If you are comfortable and engage in the same activities the same way over and over again, then you are a slave to your old habits and attitudes. If you don't engage in new activities where you feel uncomfortable or try new ways of doing your work or living, then you aren't stretching, risking, growing, or developing your potential. You must venture outside your comfort zone to learn new and powerful skills that will help you become all that you can be.

Trying new productivity techniques that can add to your present effectiveness and efficiency will feel uncomfortable. Initially it may take more effort and an additional few minutes to try new ways of working, but in the end you will gain significant benefits. You will not be hurt, injured, killed, or persecuted because you try new ways of working or living. It may even be fun, exciting, and energizing. You can expect to become more goal directed, motivated, and gain a more positive mental attitude because of risking to try new ways of working and living. Without this risking, you are doomed to **mediocrity** or worse, **failure**.

So get with it. Try the productivity ideas you have not tried before. Get uncomfortable. Become more successful! Grow, stretch, and develop more or your unlimited potential.

Eliminate Your Toleration

A toleration is anything in your life that you're, well, tolerating! Professional Business Coach Leah Vanpoelvoorde says, "Toleration cost you time, money and energy that would otherwise be used to grow your business or do the things you love. Are you using toleration as an excuse for not taking action?"

Last weekend, I spent about four hours purging my office of stuff that had accumulated, as stuff is known to do. I cleared out files, my bookcases and drawers (it wasn't too bad as I really do practice what I preach). Now, I have a new level of energy and enjoyment being in my office. It's more efficient, and it feels good to walk in there. Naturally, I'm getting more done. I hadn't realized how my energy was gradually being depleted the more that stuff was accumulating.

Begin a list of tolerations in your life that are costing you time, money and / or energy. Schedule time to get those things crossed off your list. Add to it as needed. Set a goal of the number of items you are going to take off your list each week. Don't let the list become another toleration! And enjoy the added energy and freedom that comes with eliminating toleration.

Insanity

A Chinese proverb defines insanity as doing the same thing over and over again and expecting a different result. We say that when you do the things you have always done, you will get what you have always gotten. At least 90% to 95% of what we do is habit. The repetition of actions to form habits is essential to simplifying our lives (repetition of thoughts form attitudes). However, ineffective or inefficient habits will become barriers to your success.

Take a moment right now and think about your work habits. Are you using the productivity ideas, tools, or techniques you learned from your program to their best advantage? Which idea, tool, or technique do you need to re-apply to your work that will bring you the greatest gain? Fill out a Goal Planning Sheet and plan that change (make it a twenty-one plus day goal). Schedule your planned action steps and take action on your goal. Change your habit so that new results may come into your life. Remember that time is your only resource.

> *"Yesterday is a cancelled Check.*
> *Tomorrow is a promissory note.*
> *Today is ready cash . . . spend it wisely."*

Reacting to Work

Are you reacting to your work? In other words, is your work managing you instead of you managing your work? I could also ask the same questions about your life. The answers you give to these two questions could add great quality to your life. Or, your life could stay the same as it has always been! It is your choice.

A recent manager I shadowed experienced ten interruptions during the hour I observed her work (she thought there were about six). She made telephone calls the moment she thought of them. People passing her office reminded her of items needing communication, and so she instantly communicated. There was no written plan for the hour and she did not follow the mental plan communicated to me. One period of three or four minutes was entirely wasted waiting for an employee to arrive. She made many trips between offices to get forms, talk to people, give instructions, and there was one trip to the bathroom where a colleague interrupted her before arriving. **Psychologically, the manager probably felt that she was getting a lot done**. In reality, if the time had been planned properly and productive work habits established and exercised, much greater productivity could have been achieved. Here are some techniques the manager should have been practicing to increase his/her productivity:

312

• Plan and schedule your day. Communicate your plan with the people who work for you. Block times to work on important items. List action items and set priorities. Create an ideal day to act as a template for your work day. Schedule time to do the miscellaneous non-urgent HPAs and LPAs that must be handled. Use the conference planner to record mind traffic to communicate with others at one time. Maybe walk the floor each hour (or twice a day) to communicate the items you note.

• Clear the desk of post-it notes and write all notes and commitments in your personal planning system (Outlook or PDA).

• Organize work items in your desk in folders according to "quick finish" or more "involved work tasks." Then when a few minutes become available, work on the quick finish items. Alternately, clear out your e-mail inbox and check and handle voice-mail.

• Organize telephone calls to accomplish them at one time. Schedule two or three times to make them each day.

Control your work. Don't let the work control you. Take time to observe your habits and the results they are producing. Change and try some new techniques that will add to your productivity and success. If you do the things you have always done, you will get what you have always gotten! That's not what you want, is it?

Procrastination

Procrastination is often the choice that gets us nowhere in life and work! Often procrastination nags us and fills our mind with counterproductive thoughts and a lack of productive action. We all have procrastinated in our work and lives. How do you feel when you procrastinate? I know that I feel a new heavy weight on my shoulders, pulled down by something I should do and haven't done yet. I feel that there is something eating away at my self-esteem and I'm just a little sad at myself because I know I should just do it! Often people procrastinate because they fear some outcome, they are just allowing themselves to be lazy, or they are just not deciding to do something and acting on that decision.

PROCRASTINATION BUSTING: Just deciding to do something, and then taking action on that decision can beat procrastination. It's actually very simple but for some people it will take courage. If you should do something, don't waste any more time. Choose to do it now. Immediately start action to accomplish the task, and follow through to finish the project. Then, take a moment and pat yourself on your shoulder because you accomplished the task. Celebrate the fact that you are one step closer to your goals and dreams. Celebrating your success at procrastination busting is important to establishing the new habit of just "Doing It NOW!" Why go thought all the mental torture procrastination can bring, limit its harmful effect on you by Doing It NOW!

p.s. If there are many tasks you are procrastinating on doing, make a list, prioritize each item, and begin work on the highest priority. Before you know it, you will regain more control and feel much better about yourself and your progress in work and life.

Seven Things that will Destroy us All

I would like to pass on a few inspiring thoughts from the Teachings of Gandhi. "Seven things that will destroy us all."

1. Wealth without work.
2. Pleasure without conscience.

3. Knowledge without character.

4. Commerce without humanity.

5. Worship without sacrifice.

6. Politics without principle.

7. Science without humanity.

Think on these statements. How can you ensure that you don't fall into these destruction traps? Then take action to bolster your guard.

Extreme Thinking Styles

In the book *Enlightened Leadership: Getting to the Heart of Change* by Ed Oakley and Doug Krug, one of the most important chapters is entitled, "**The Mind-set Issue**." Ed and Doug go on to apply the Pareto Principle and state that about 20% of the people will be open to change, or change-friendly. These are the same 20% that are providing 80% of the effective work. They will naturally operate from the *mind-set that sees the value of whatever change is introduced*, and they will be open to it. The other 80% can usually be counted on to resist change to some degree, no matter how much sense it makes.

Ed and Doug state that the difference between 20% - ers and the 80% - ers comes down to one simple overriding element: **attitude**. An eighteen-year study of outstanding performance scores of teams have validated that attitude is by far the dominant factor separating high performance **Creative Thinkers** from their less productive **Reactive Thinker** counterparts. They identify Creative Thinkers and Reactive Thinkers by identifying the attitudes that dominate the separate Thinking Styles. Which attitudes or thinking style do you use most often?

REACTIVE THINKERS

- Are resistant to change.
- See reasons they cannot do things.
- Focus on finding problems to fix.
- Are blinded by problems in a situation
- Avoid blame or responsibility.
- Are limited by what worked in the past.
- Are poor listeners.
- Run out of energy quickly.
- Find it difficult to choose & decide.
- Feel they have no control of environment.
- Often work very hard.
- Are afraid of risks or major challenges.
- Suffer excessive inner stress.
- Cannot let go of the past.
- Are devastated by failure.
- Have low self-esteem.
- Focus on what they want to avoid.
- Do things right.

CREATIVE THINKERS

- Are open to change.
- Are "can do" oriented.
- Build on success and strengths.
- Seek the opportunity in situations.
- Take responsibility for their actions.
- Think in terms of new possibilities.
- Are good listeners.
- Have a continuous supply of energy.

- Make choices and decisions easily.
- Feel in control of their environment.
- Get results without trying hard.
- Are driven to excel by challenge / risk.
- Enjoy an inner calmness.
- Are current & future oriented.
- Learn and grow from their mistakes.
- Have high self-esteem.
- Focus on results they want.
- Do the right things.

After comparing yourself to the two different attitudes, you may find a couple of ways of thinking (attitudes) you may want to change. Set a goal and change your way of thinking. Through repetition of new ways of thinking, you may find that change of attitudes can be made. Using affirmations is an excellent tool in helping you change your way of thinking.

The 12 Bad Habits That Hold Good People Back

1. Never feeling good enough
2. Seeing the world in black & white
3. Doing too much, pushing too hard
4. Avoiding conflict at any cost
5. Running roughshod over the opposition
6. Rebel looking for a cause
7. Always swinging for the fence
8. When fear is in the drivers seat
9. Emotional tone deaf
10. When no job is good enough

11. Lacking a sense of boundaries
12. Losing the path

- James Wardroom, Ph.D.

I'm Too Busy!

I'm too busy! Our first meeting. Self-limiting attitude. The lessons and assignments seem very basic and they are. I had the initial reaction that there would not be much to be gained from such basic stuff. Then my attitude changed to one of, "**looking for ways to improve myself.**" The basics, assignments, and insights took on a new meaning. I started to get ideas and take actions to improve. It started to work. It's an ongoing process with me. It reflects an attitude of learning and growing as a person, an attitude of developing more of my potential. The process we are using has been developed over more than thirty-five years with more than 1,000,000 participants. It works if you follow it!

When people fail, it is because they lose sight of the fundamentals. Ask any athletic coach and they will agree that returning to the basics and executing them flawlessly is foundational to future wins. It's the simple mistakes on the field that defeats the person and then the team. What we are doing is brushing up on the fundamentals. If you don't have the time to stop for a short time and ask yourself how effective and productive you are, then you won't find ways to become more effective and productive. Not stopping to sharpen the saw will results in working harder not smarter. It's something to think about.

A. A. A. D. D.

They have finally found a diagnosis for my condition.

Hooray! I have recently been diagnosed with A.A.A.D.D. = Age Activated Attention Deficit Disorder.

This is how it goes: I decide to wash the car; I start toward the car. But first I'm going to go through the mail. I lay the car keys down on the desk, discard the junk mail and I notice the trash can is full.

Ok, I'll just put the bills on my desk and take the trash can out, but since I'm going to be near the mailbox anyway, I'll pay these few bills first.

Now, where is my checkbook? Oops, there's only one check left. My extra checks are in my desk. Oh, there's the coke I was drinking. I'm going to look for those checks.

But first I need to put my coke farther away from the computer, oh maybe I'll pop it into the fridge to keep it cold for a while.

I head toward the kitchen and my flowers catch my eye, they need some water. I set the coke on the counter and uh oh!

There are my glasses. I was looking for them all morning! I'd better put them away.

I fill a container with water and head for the flower pots - Aaaaaagh!

Someone left the TV remote in the kitchen. We'll never think to look there tonight when we want to watch television so I'd better put it back in the family room where it belongs.

I splash some water into the pots and onto the floor, I throw the remote onto a soft cushion on the sofa and I head back down the hall trying to figure out what it was I was going to do? End of Day: The car isn't washed, the bills are unpaid, the coke is sitting on the kitchen counter, the flowers are half watered, the checkbook still only has one check in it and I can't seem to find my car keys! When I try to figure out how come nothing got done today, I'm baffled because I KNOW I WAS BUSY ALL DAY LONG!!!

I realize this is a serious condition and I'll get help, BUT FIRST I think I'll check my e-mail ...

River & Rut Stories

River stories are generally those of personal growth, self-renewal, and transformation. When people tell a river story, they speak with clarity, power, authenticity, and vulnerability regarding their growth edges, learning places, and breakdown spots. River stories are those where people reflect on and inquire into their way of looking at things, their deep beliefs, and their assumptions. This allows people to penetrate individual and collective illusions and to see things in a new way. It also leads to a new way of being, and an expanded capacity to take effective action. River stories are always laced with wisdom, compassion, and humor and often contain a revelation of people's foolishness. River stories are born out of a commitment to learn and grow as a person.

Rut stories develop when people use defensive reasoning to protect themselves. For example, people distort reality in order to save face, collude to avoid talking about any topic that could cause upset, and cover up errors by blaming others. These defensive stories and actions become so ingrained that people are hardly aware of them. They lead to unintended results, limited learning, escalating errors, and individual and collective illusions.

Here are a few Rut Stories:

- The "I need other people's approval" story - people's intention to look good replaces intention to be good.
- The "I'm afraid to lose what I have" story - People play it safe, take no risks.
- The "Artful victim" story - People give away their power and can't create what they want.
- The "Tranquilizing" story - People cover up incompetence; no learning occurs.

- The "Why bother" story – People get stuck in resignation and do not create the future.

What stories are you telling?

> – River and Rut stories are extracted from the book *Masterful Coaching* by Robert Hargrove.

■ CHAPTER TWENTY-EIGHT ■
RESISTANCE

"We must have strong minds, ready to accept facts as they are."

- Harry S. Truman

RESISTING CHANGE: The one behavior I can count on during my leadership development programs is people's resistance to change. Between 90 percent and 95 percent of a person's actions and thoughts are habits and so they are functioning on autopilot most of the time. That means that most of their work and thinking are relatively unconscious. Imagine that! It's no wonder that people slip into unproductive habits of working and thinking. And since it is habit, consciously changing actions and thoughts can become very uncomfortable. **To become more productive and effective, you must change.**

RESISTANCE: **Emotional or Rational?** I have an insightful exercise that my program participants complete. I ask participants to list four or five insightful change ideas they discover from the reading material that if applied in their work, would help them become more effective or productive. Then, I ask them to list all the reasons they would resist applying these ideas to their work. Next, I ask them to categorize the reasons for resisting the changes as either rational or emotional. And what do you think they find? The majority of reasons for resisting the application of new ways of working are **EMOTIONAL**! We resist changing what we do because of emotional responses, not because of rational reasons. **RATIONALLY**, we have compelling logical reasons to embrace the changes that help us become more effective and productive.

CHANGE: Think about the reasons why you might be resisting change. If your reasons are emotional, maybe it's time to embrace the rational reasons for changing your habits and thoughts. Changing to become more effective and productive in your work can cause great financial rewards and increased work satisfaction. Try embracing change!

Resistance, a Great Teacher

Resistance is nature's way of telling you that you have a new life lesson to learn. Often in your work and interactions with people, you may feel the hair stand up on the back of your neck and the defenses start to rise. Recognize this situation, pause and tell yourself that there might just be something to learn in this situation. Stay cool and calm and actively look for the gift that the person is trying to give you. Fighting the situation will only cause negative consequences that you don't want. Staying open and looking for the positive contribution being offered can unlock renewed personal growth.

■ CHAPTER TWENTY-NINE ■
YOUR VIEW

*"Keep your face to the sunshine
and you cannot see the shadows."*

- Helen Keller

WORLD VIEW – HELP OR INHIBITOR: Your world view can help you succeed or it can inhibit the added success you seek in your work and life. The good news is that you can develop your world view to help you achieve greater results.

WORLD VIEW: You grow up experiencing the world with your senses. Your brain must process the billions of bits of data you receive to create meaning from the data you collect (your perception). To simplify the mind's processing, you form patterns of data and assign standardized meanings to those patterns. Those patterns enable you to receive a smaller amount of data that you instantly associate with a standard meaning. Over your life, those patterns form your "**World View.**" Today, as you sense the world, patterns and meanings instantly jump into your mind before the brain receives and processes all available data. The brain just ignores

325

and jettisons excess sensual data as unnecessary. In other words, you may have an inaccurate perception of the world. Some people call it a narrow world view. Then, you act on the inaccurate perceptions. Now you know the problem. You may not perceive the world as it really is and thus create huge problems for yourself. Complicating this inaccurate world view is your own unique personality and its development. Your personality may keep you channeled in narrow mental processes and attitude preferences that can become ineffective and unproductive, even disastrous in your work and life. So, how do you expand your world view so that you don't experience the adverse effects of inaccurate perceptions?

Know yourself! Learn all about yourself. Take every opportunity to participate in assessments, pro-actively solicit feedback, slow up and take time to gather more data, stop yourself and truly experience each moment. Savor the rich abundant information that surrounds you, with gratitude. When I work with a person, I like to share Myers-Briggs Personality Type information. Recipients get new insights about themselves and others. Their world opens up to new perspectives and perceptions of themselves and other people. When you see your world differently and more accurately, then you can take the effective actions that will result in more successful outcomes. Often, **you are blind to your own inaccurate world view**. Engaging the help of others to transcend the perceptual barriers that form in everyone's lives is essential. Your supervisor, friend, mate, colleague, **coach**, or other acquaintance may play this helping role. I've learned one thing that may help you in your life journey. If I'm having challenges or problems in my own life, I always ask myself, "What must I change to get the results I want?" I look at myself and identify my own limitations because that is what I must change to get the results I want.

Blindness

Once I was blind and now I see. Well, I see much more than before. Blindness is a condition that we develop through experiencing the world as we grow-up. The world being the environment that we explore, experience, learn from, develop in, and in which we mature.

At birth we are bombarded with overwhelming data input from all of our senses. We can easily recognize this abrupt overload when a newborn baby cries and screams. When the baby is placed on its mother's chest and it hears the heartbeat and feels the warmth (familiar data), it settles down, becomes calmer, and starts to organize and process the new information it is sensing. Throughout life we receive data through our senses, process it, and assign meaning to it. No two people develop the same meaning for the same set of data. We store meanings in the brain. In a lifetime, millions of data sets are processed, assigned meanings, and stored. To process the ever increasing data we sense, the mind samples and detects patterns of data and assigns an automatic meaning and response to the pattern. We develop thousands of these automatic responses to data sets. These automatic responses can be recognized as attitudes (automatic thought responses) and habits (automatic action responses). Therefore the filtering of data and automatic processing and responses come to be called a person's world view. It's how they automatically see the world they sense. Each person's world view helps him or her automatically sort through the thousands of data sets that they collect. It helps them filter through the overwhelming data that bombard us, and select only data that appears useful. It enables the person to handle more of the complexity of life by drawing upon their automatic meaning and response library.

The **problem with our world view** is that it automatically rejects, ignores, or screens out information that could change the meaning. The person is blinded by their world view, to the reality that exists considering all the sensory data available. This blindness can be observed when a person reacts or makes a decision based on an incomplete or partial data set that results in an ineffective outcome or destructive result. The automatic meaning and response system can severely limit a person's success if they are unaware that it exists. In other words, blind spots caused by world views can negatively affect performance in both work and life. How do you increase your awareness and remove any blind spots?

Shared Vision

You may remember the movie Spartacus, an adaptation of the story of a Roman gladiator / slave who led an army of slaves in an uprising in 71 B.C. They defeated the Roman legions twice, but were finally conquered by the general Marcus Crassus after a long siege and battle. In the movie, Crassus tells six thousand survivors of Spartacus' army, "You have been slaves. All you will be slaves again. But you will be spared your rightful punishment of crucifixion by the mercy of the Roman legions. All you need to do is turn over to me the slave Spartacus, because we do not know him by sight."

After a long pause, Spartacus (played by Kirk Douglas) stands up and says, "I am Spartacus." Then the man next to him stands up and say's, "I am Spartacus." Then the man next to him stands up and also says, "No, I am Spartacus." Within a minute, everyone in the army is on his feet.

It does not matter whether this story is apocryphal or not; it demonstrates a deep truth. Each man, by standing up, chose death. But the loyalty of Spartacus' army was not to Spartacus the man. Their **loyalty was to a shared vision** that Spartacus had inspired – the idea that they could be free men. This vision was so compelling that no man could bear to give it up and return to slavery.

Do you have a powerful vision that motivates you? Does your company have a shared vision that commands your loyalty? Whether it is you alone, or the leader of a business, if you don't have a motivating vision, then take time to develop one. It can make the difference between success and ultimate failure.

The World, a Reflection of You

If you are positive, the world will be a great place to live. If you expect good things to happen, then good things will happen. If you care (even love) all people, they will care (love) you back. If you expect the best in every circumstance, then the best will occur. If you think of your job as a great opportunity to learn and grow, then you will find joy and happiness in your job. If you are grateful for every minute you live, life will be filled with happiness and satisfaction.

Do I need to list the opposites? I've found that happiness comes from having a positive attitude about work and life. How a person habitually thinks about work and life is the most important determinant of their well-being (if not the only thing). So, when things aren't going so well with the troops in the office or plant, check your own attitude (habit of thought). It might be that you need an attitude adjustment.

Affirmations are one tool you can use to make that adjustment. Affirmations work! If you are not using some now, then take action to incorporate them into your normal daily routine as a "manifestation tool."

Your Happiness

HAPPINESS: The pursuit of happiness is useless for it can never be caught. Just like a cat chasing its tail, you will be running in circles wondering why you never caught it. Happiness follows serving and growing as a person.

SERVING: By serving, I mean engaging in activities in pursuit of a higher cause than yourself. It may also mean worthwhile work. Viktor Frankl in his book, ***Man's Search for Meaning*** said, "life is the attaining of some aim through the active creation of something of value." He also said that, "striving to find meaning in one's life is the primary motivational force in man." Frankl identified these three main avenues on which one arrives at meaning in their lives:

1. Creating a work or by doing a deed.
2. Experiencing something or encountering someone (meaning can be found not only in work but also in **love**)
3. Grow beyond himself, and by so doing change himself.

GROWING: You **grow** beyond yourself by engaging in the pursuit of knowledge, wisdom, and new positive skills. Learning and developing yourself so that you evolve and use more of your potential as a human being, are what makes a difference. It doesn't matter how much potential you are using now, but what does matter is that you are engaged in developing more of your potential. Little by little, huge life changes will occur leaving you feeling happy, fulfilled, and purposeful.

LIFE SECURITY: If you are not serving and growing, you are just treading water and going nowhere. Swimming to new shores should be your guiding vision. Life security in today's world is gained through becoming more employable (more valuable), establishing freedom for yourself, and exercising choice in everything you do (choice has associated with it the responsibility for outcome). Developing life security involves the risk of doing new and different things. It means growing and serving as a human being.

The big question is, "Are you growing and serving as you should?"

GOALS: If you want to grow more than you are now, set a few goals in one or more of the six areas of your life. Then fill out a goal sheet. Plan how to achieve your goals. Communicate your goals, measure your progress, and lastly, pause to celebrate your growth, success, and life.

■ CHAPTER THIRTY ■
NEVER GIVE UP

"I firmly believe that any man's finest hour - his greatest fulfillment to all he holds dear - is that moment when he has worked his heart out in a good cause and lies exhausted on the field of battle - victorious."

- Vince Lombardi

One of the lessons embodied in Norman Vincent Peale's life is that even he struggled with discouragement. More than that, he gave up before reaching an important goal. When he was in his fifties, he wrote a book and sent it to a host of publishers. Regarding the stack of rejection notices in frustration one day, he threw the manuscript in the wastebasket.

Ruth Peale reached in to try to salvage it. "No" he said sternly. "We've wasted enough time on that. I forbid you to take that thing out of the wastebasket." The following day, she personally visited yet another publisher. Shown into his office, she handed him an oddly shaped parcel - much too big and bulky to be a manuscript. Unwrapping it, the publisher was startled to see a wastebasket. It contained the manuscript of **The Power of Positive Thinking**, one of the most influential books of the 20th century.

- Story found in Empires of the Mind by Denis Waitley

The Seven Universal Conditions of Success

Tom Morris, Ph. D., has spent a lifetime studying the greatest practical thinkers in history. During his studies, he discovered that there were seven universal conditions of success, and that if they were applied to what you were doing they would guarantee your success. These seven conditions are:

1. A clear **CONCEPTION** of what you want, a vivid vision, a goal clearly imagined.

2. A strong **CONFIDENCE** that you can attain that goal.

3. A focused **CONCENTRATION** on what it takes to reach the goal.

4. A stubborn **CONSISTENCY** in pursuing your vision.

5. An emotional **COMMITMENT** to the importance of what you're doing.

6. A good **CHARACTER** to guide you and keep you on a proper course.

7. A **CAPACITY TO ENJOY** the process along the way.

Take one of your important endeavors (work, project, goal, or dream) and measure how well you are committed to that endeavor using the seven conditions of success. Then plan and take the necessary actions to bolster each deficient condition. If you fully commit, as described in the seven conditions of success, there is no way you cannot achieve the success you desire.

Take Time

There is a book that I highly recommend, entitled, ***Even Eagles Need a Push*** by David McNally, that is one of those keepers that you go back to because it is filled with great thinking and nuggets of wisdom. It fills me with inspiration every time I review it.

In that book on page 140, David quotes this anonymous poem saying that it "demonstrates an enlightened attitude toward the ***scheduling of our daily lives.***" Enjoy!

> **Take time to work - It is the price of success.**
> **Take time to think - It is the source of power.**
> **Take time to play - It is the secret of perpetual youth.**
> **Take time to read - It is the fountain of wisdom.**
> **Take time to be friendly - It is the road to happiness.**
> **Take time to love and to be loved - It is nourishment for the soul.**
> **Take time to share - It is too short a life to be selfish.**
> **Take time to laugh - It is the music of the heart.**
> **Take time to dream - It is hitching your wagon to a star.**

Making Things Happen

Making things happen effectively is a function of four simple ingredients.

1. A vivid, positive vision of what you want. Visualize your success as a "done deal." Create harmonious, multidimensional images of your vision already realized. See it, feel it, smell it, touch it, taste it, be it.

2. An accurate perception of what you have. Question your assumptions and mental sets. Seek objective feedback. Assess the resistance, competition, and other obstacles you must overcome or transform.

3. A plan. Plan backwards - start with the realization of your goal and work your way to the present, then, set time lines. Think strategically and tactically. Line up allies, resources, sponsors, and supporters. Make a thoughtful plan and be prepared to improvise.

4. Commitment and accountability. Throw the full force of your being into achieving your aims. Act as though you are 100 percent responsible for the results.

Successful people know that it is easier to ask forgiveness than for permission. Many good ideas rot on the vine, "waiting for permission and approval." Other common strategies for non-achievement include:

- Subject your idea to exhaustive analysis
- Wait for certainty
- Ignore other's interests
- Waffle on your commitment
- Make excuses
- Claim all the credit
- Assume that nothing will change
- Don't anticipate obstacles and resistance

Think of some thing that you want to make happen. It could be anything that you hope for, have ignored, or want to get but have not acted on to make happen. Follow the four steps outlined above and see what happens. Then repeat those steps forever in your work and life.

Three Feet from the Gold

Napoleon Hill tells this memorable story in his classic, *Think and Grow Rich.*

A certain Mr. Darby had a gold mine in Colorado during the Gold Rush days. It served him well for a short while and then apparently dried up. He drilled a little farther, dug a little deeper, but nothing. So he gave up and sold the mining tools and the land to a prospector for a few hundred dollars. Within three feet of the place where Darby stopped drilling, the new owner tapped into a gold vein worth millions.

The incident changed Darby's life. He never forgot his mistake in stopping only three feet from the gold. Years later, he said, "That experience was a blessing in disguise. It taught me to keep on keeping on, no matter how hard the going may be. It's a lesson I needed to learn before I could succeed in anything."

"One of the most common causes of failure," concluded Hill, "is the habit of quitting when one is overtaken by temporary defeat."

Don't stop three feet from success. Go back and dig some more.

■ INDEX ■

339

D

Ford, Debbie, 153
Ford, Henry, 181
Frankl, Viktor, 150, 164, 178, 330
Franklin, Ben, 145
frustration, 173, 193, 247, 261
Fundamentals, 318
Future, Who Creates Your, 196

G

Gandhi, 314
Garden Lesson, 25
Gates, Bill, 223
Get-Along Tools, 261
Getting Started, 14
gift, 127
Gift of feedback, 74
Gift, Today is a, 115
Giving 100% Today, 115
Giving Feedback, 74
Goal Achievement, 335
Goal Plan, 20, 200
Goal Planning, 224
Goal Setting, 14
Goal Tracking, 27
Goal, To Become, 111, 296
Goal, Write a, 184
Goals, 17, 331
Goals, Chunking Down, 23
Goals, Communicating, 24
Goals, Garden Lesson, 25
Goals, Life, 215
Goals, Monthly, 36
Goals, Organizational, 50
Goals, Personal, 50

Goals, S.M.A.R.T., 28
Goals, Set Big, 303
Goals, Sharing, 24
Goals, Specific, 287
Goals, To Become, 19, 26, 152, 182, 261
Goals, To Get, 20, 26, 152
Goals, Value of Written, 50
Goals, Why?, 26
Gold, Three Feet from, 337
Gratitude, 76, 106, 130, 210
Gratitude & Love, 210
Gratitude, Attitude of, 173
Growing, Forever, 291
Growth, 188, 197, 264, 330
Growth vs. Stagnation, 183
Growth, Accelerate Personal, 295
Growth, Road to, 193

H

Habit, 160, 193, 311
habit of thought, 164, 169
Habits, 12 Bad, 317
Habits, Success, 166
Handling E-mail, 71
Handling Problems, 77
Happiness, 204, 329, 330
Hardest Work, 159
Hargrove, Robert, 294, 321
Heart, Follow Your, 223
Helpful People, 95
Heroes, Firefighting, 87
Herzberg, Frederick, 24
Hickman, Craig, 290

347

Y

■ Ready for the Next Level? ■

Now that you have learned these powerful tactics on building leadership, are you ready to take your leadership to the next level. We're ready to help you do that. We have four valuable bonuses that have a retail value of $347, which will continue to help you implement the strategies you have learned, plus give you even more tools and techniques to help your business soar to success.

These bonuses include:

1. A one-year subscription to Leadership Advantage's **Weekly E-Articles** on inspirational subjects affecting your leadership, effectiveness, and productivity.

2. Access to an archive of over **65 new Tool & Techniques** that can help you in Building Personal Leadership.

3. Access to a downloadable **Building Personal Leadership Assessment Tool**, which you can use to see where you are in your work & life.

4. A **30-minute Coaching Telephone Call** with the Coach. Your call may cover any leadership challenge or subject that you wish.

Logon to www.building-leadership.com/bonus and subscribe for the Weekly E-Articles. After subscribing, you will receive access to the Tools and Techniques archive and the downloadable Personal Leadership Assessment. Please keep a record of the Coaching Code displayed on that page. You will need to use that code when you call to schedule your 30-minute coaching appointment.

Don't wait to subscribe, as this bonus will be offered for a limited time only. Visit www.building-leadership.com/bonus and subscribe NOW!

▪ ABOUT THE AUTHOR ▪

Joe Farcht is the President of Leadership Advantage, Inc. located in Phoenix, Arizona, a performance improvement company. His company specializes in conducting Leadership Development Programs and Executive Coaching that lead management level individuals into dramatically improving their effectiveness and productivity. The distinguishing feature is attitude and behavioral development centered on delivering measured tangible bottom line results in critical business areas. Joe is a certified Master Personal and Executive Coach (MPEC) and is qualified in Myers-Briggs Personality Type Step II. He is a twelve-year continuously active faculty member of the University of Phoenix teaching business and leadership subjects. He served on the 1995 and 1998 Board of Examiners in the Arizona State Quality Award process focusing on leadership development. Previously he worked in a fortune 50 company leading a successful Leadership Development initiative. He has successfully completed a career in the United States Air Force as an Instructor Fighter Pilot with extensive experience in leadership and training. Joe earned a BSEE from the University of Kentucky, a MBA

ABOUT THE AUTHOR

from the University of Utah, and numerous academic achievements and decorations from the USAF. He possesses an innovative and positive can-do attitude and superb integrity who is totally committed to helping his clients develop more of their potential and achieve their leadership, business, organizational, and personal goals.

356